Around the World by Train

Also by Ian Sutherland:

From Pericles to Cleophon (joint editor, Rivington 1954)
Health Education: Perspectives and Choices (editor and contributor, Allen and Unwin 1979)
Health Education: Half a Policy (NEC 1987)

AROUND THE WORLD BY TRAIN

Ian Sutherland

BG

The Book Guild Ltd.
Sussex, England

This book is sold subject to the condition that it shall not, by way of trade or otherwise, be lent, re-sold, hired out, photocopied or held in any retrieval system, or otherwise circulated without the publisher's prior consent in any form of binding or cover other than that in which this is published and without a similar condition including this condition being imposed on the subsequent purchaser.

The Book Guild Ltd.
25 High Street,
Lewes, Sussex.

First published 1991
© Ian Sutherland 1991
Set in Baskerville
Typesetting by Ashford Setting and Design,
Ashford, Middlesex.
Printed in Great Britain by
Antony Rowe Ltd.,
Chippenham, Wiltshire.

British Library Cataloguing in Publication Data
Sutherland, Ian 1926-
  Around the world by train.
  1. Journeys around the world.
  I. Title
  910.41

ISBN 0 86332 622 6

CONTENTS

Acknowledgements		7
Maps of Journey		8
Chapter One	*Beginnings*	11
Chapter Two	*Frontiers*	29
Chapter Three	*Railways*	62
Chapter Four	*Journeying*	110
Chapter Five	*Crowds*	145
Chapter Six	*Deserts and the Moon*	180
Chapter Seven	*Water and the Weather*	216
Chapter Eight	*The Awesome Demon*	249
Chapter Nine	*Endings*	304
List of Illustrations		325
Index		328

ACKNOWLEDGEMENTS

I am grateful to my son, Glenn, for reading all my manuscript and for stringent criticism, and to my granddaughter, Hannah, aged six, for help with numbers at the beginning of Chapter Three, on page 62. Neither of course is responsible for any of the errors which survive.

I am grateful, too, to the publishers of *Marco Polo: The Travels*, translated by Ronald Latham (Penguin Books), and *The Gobi Desert*, by Mildred Cable and Francesca French (Virago Press), for permission to use extracts from these books on pages 76-79.

I am also conscious of a special debt to the *Encyclopaedia Britannica* and to Irving Stone's *Men to Match my Mountains* (New York, 1982: Berkley Books) for valuable background information on desert exploration in Chapter Six.

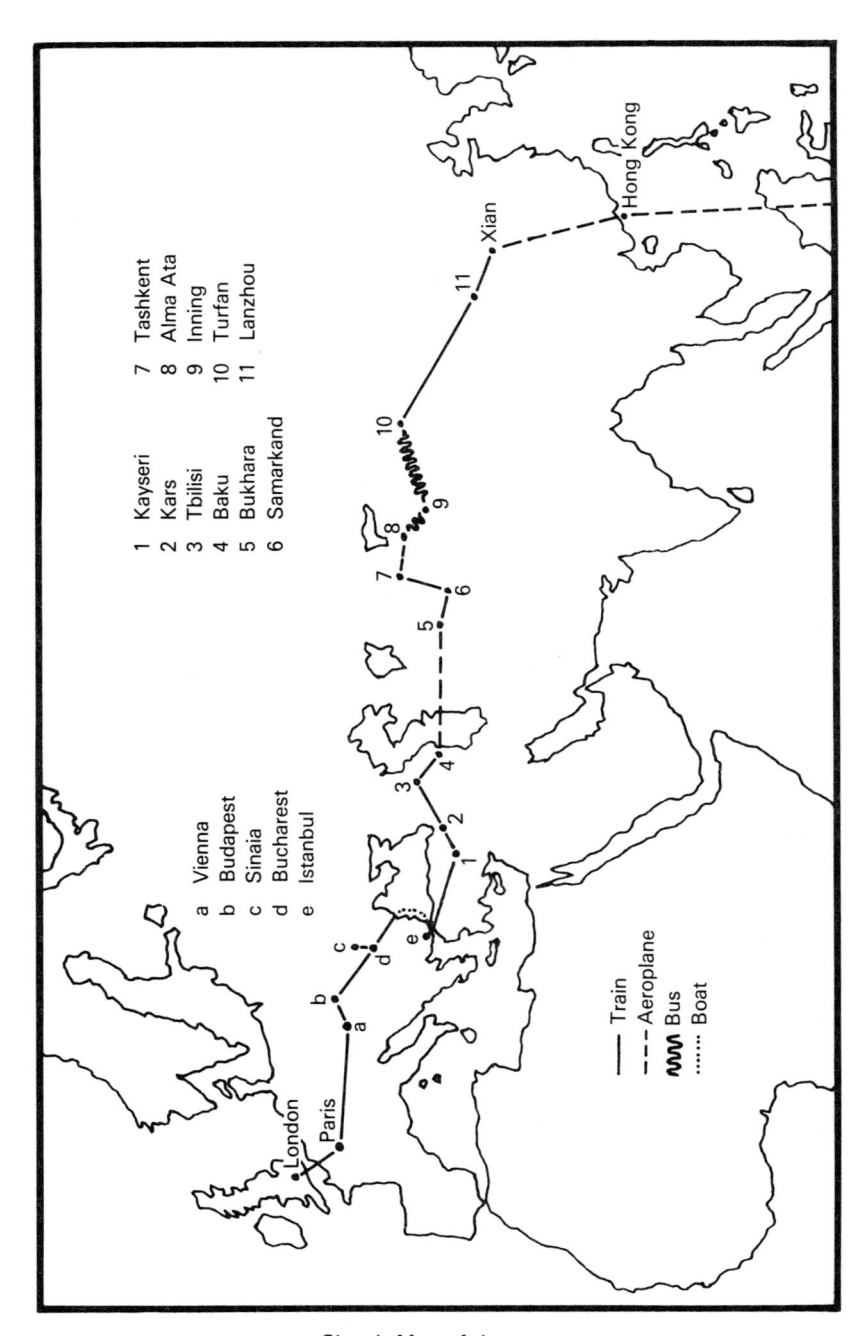

Sketch Map of Journey

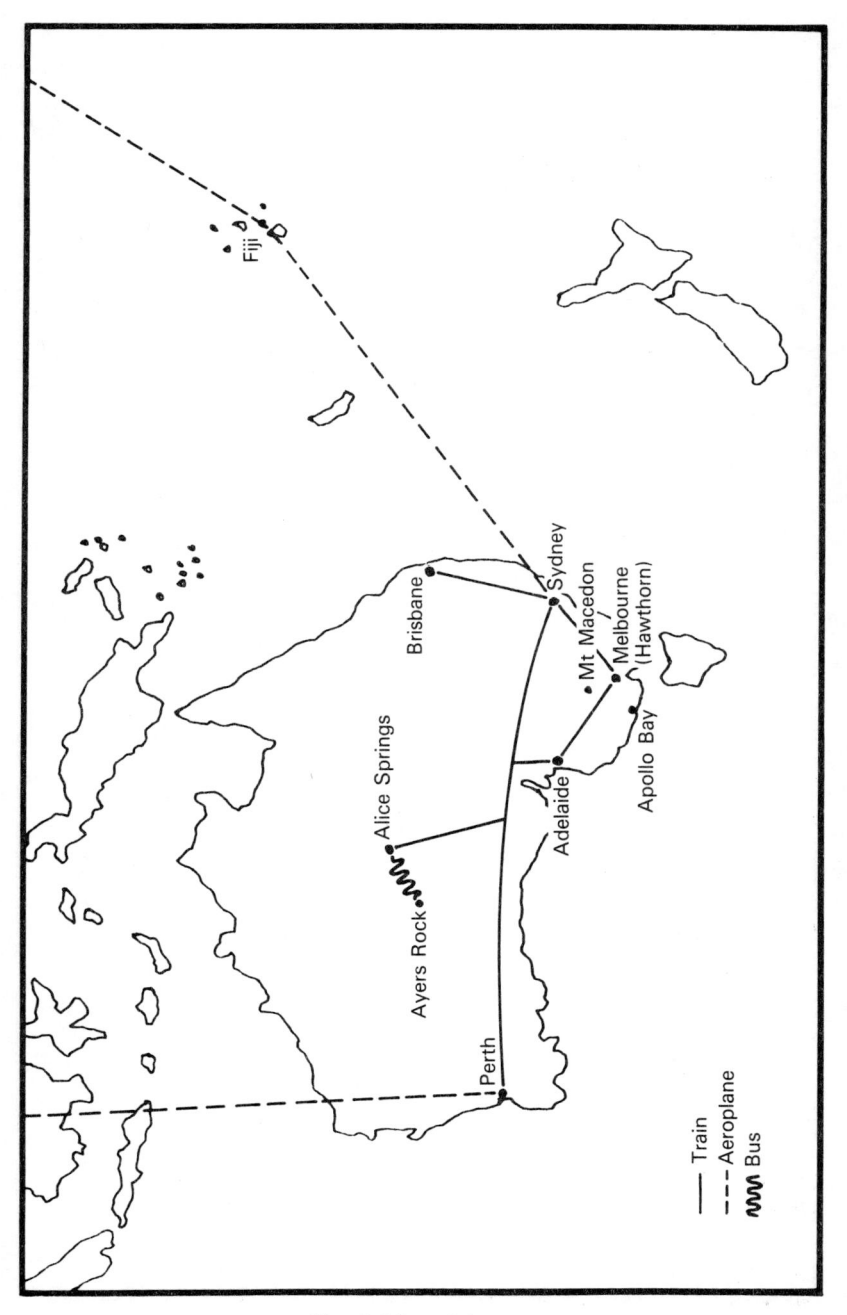

Sketch Map of Journey

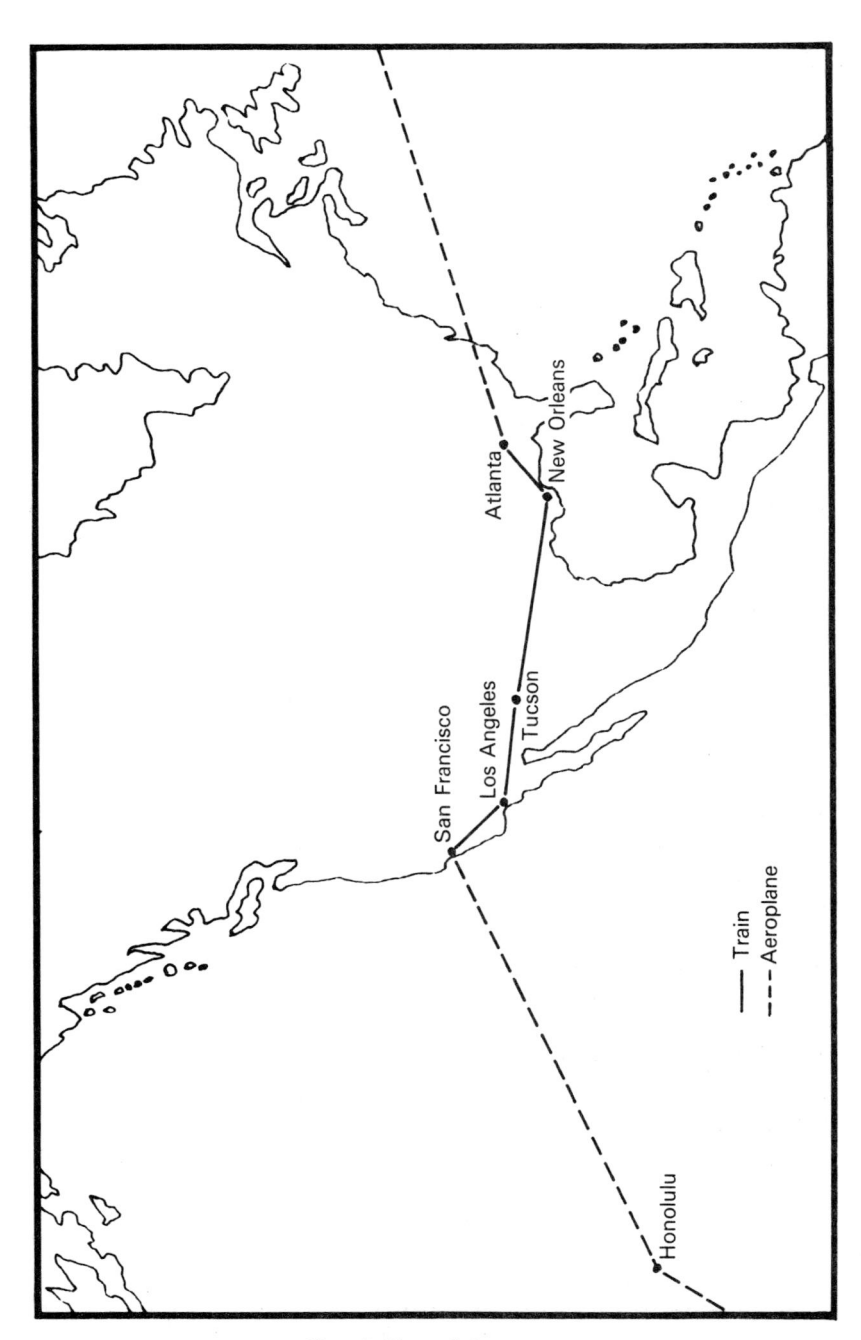

Sketch Map of Journey

1

Beginnings

It was Mr Moore who for me started it all. Mr Moore was eighty years old. While we were waiting for the others to come back from exploring an underground tomb in north-west China on the edge of the Gobi desert, he appeared from behind a bus, and said to me, 'Mr Sutherland, they tell me you are the one who would know. They've brought us here by train and bus to the back of beyond, safe and sound in all sorts of ways. In heaven's name, how did Herodotus manage it in his day?'

I gave him some kind of answer, on the spur of the moment. He travelled on foot mostly, riding sometimes; he crossed the sea in engineless, wooden boats. He was however like us in two important ways: as we speak English, he spoke Greek, a language widely understood throughout most of the known world in his day; and, as we have the American dollar, he had the Athenian drachma, which, in the fifth century BC, was the hardest currency you could expect to have in your possession: utterly reliable, made of silver.

Like Mr Moore and me, he travelled for the sheer interest of it all. Born in 484 BC in Halicarnassus, modern Bodrum, in the south-west corner of Turkey, he had the Aegean Sea as his homeland, and, in exile from Halicarnassus at the age of twenty, he settled in Athens as a place of residence. He travelled widely round the Black Sea and the Balkans, in Egypt, Syria, Turkey and Iran, as far as Babylon. He died at the age of fifty-four.

Travelling was his abiding interest. In later life he regarded it as his duty to spread abroad his traveller's tales. He used the word history to describe his writings; by 'history' he meant 'investigations'. Investigating the world had become his business. As something of a sideline, he also set down how it came about that the Greeks and the barbarians came to quarrel, and fought a war.

All travellers have something in common with Herodotus. Mr Moore and I, in our way, had embarked upon a series of investigations of a personal kind into the world we lived in. Like Herodotus, we had travelled a long way, having already crossed his route ourselves several times. Indeed, by the time of our conversation behind the bus, we had progressed well beyond it. Like him, we owed much to the inventive nature of the times in which we lived. There was a sense in which, like him, we were repaying some kind of debt to life itself, by investigating the world of our day as extensively as we could.

As far as I was concerned, before setting out I had three purposes in mind: to go round the world with as much deliberation as possible, just to make sure for myself that it really was round, as they said it was; to compare, as far as I could, in all too brief a time, the ways of living in East and West, which was Greek and which was barbarian, you might say; and to watch Test cricket in Australia, a Babylonian type of activity which I had enjoyed watching since my earliest times in England. If I could accomplish the first two of these purposes, at least in part, I said to myself, I would be in some sense repaying a debt to the times in which I had had the good fortune to spend my working life. They had been interesting times.

I had retired from work in February 1986, and I was to have a sensible insurance mature on my sixtieth birthday in the following July. I was in fact to be even more than fortunate. I would have in the near future both the time and the money with which to put my travel hypotheses to the test. I felt I had learnt something in the course of my working life, but I was sure that it was not enough. What kind of knowledge was it, I asked myself; how much was it worth, and how would the world look when tested by the kind of English parochialism which living had taught me? Herodotus had asked himself similar questions; was the world really like what they said it was, and what did it mean to be a Greek? As for watching Test cricket in Australia, Oh! my Bradman and my Hammond long ago! And the mystery of it all! It would all be wonderful.

In writing a book about what happened to me on my travels,

in telling some of my stories again, I must at all costs avoid giving the reader the impression that I set out in any way to imitate or rival one of the greatest story tellers of all time. That would be an absurd thing to attempt. All I really have in common with Herodotus is my liking for travel. As a result of this, I share with him a kind of arrogance, born — so I think — of unique experiences. We both think our stories are worth the telling, for their own sakes. They exist, and must exist, in their own right. We try to tell them with a keen eye on the truth, above and below the surface, but, just as important to us, we have to tell them as we ourselves are, and as we found ourselves in relation to the things that happened to us. We concentrate on being no-one else. If you leave personality out of consideration, you cannot be telling all the truth. If you leave it in, you take the risk of bias and subjectivity, especially where personal enthusiasms are concerned. Herodotus's contemporaries often thought of him as being economical with the truth. I have tried not to lie, but, like Herodotus, I leave it to the reader to decide how often and by how much I stretch a point, for I would never wish to be taken seriously at every corner. Occasionally, however, I do wish to be taken seriously; like Herodotus, I draw lessons, make unconventional judgements on contemporary matters, and moralize. At such points I imagine the reader watching out for the effect of my English parochialism; Herodotus wrote, 'If anybody at all is given the chance to choose for the rest of human kind the best laws, customs and beliefs from those that exist, after due consideration he would be bound to choose his own. Everybody thinks their own laws, customs and beliefs are the best. He would surely be a madman who would pour scorn on that choice.'(111.38) I set out believing something like that, and I expected also to find out what kind of parish England was.

Mr Moore's question about Herodotus was not his only distinction. Like me, he liked wholemeal bread, and we found little of that in China. More important, he and his wife, who was travelling too, were both eighty years old. They were the ones who finally proved to me that the belief that extended travelling was the prerogative of the young and agile was no longer correct. Longevity, the freedom offered by early retirement and a worldwide network of practical travel facilities have meant that the ardours previously faced so assiduously by the 'haversack brigade' have to be endured no longer, if you have no wish to endure them. Nor is that impractical requirement of the immediate post-war years, an unlimited bank balance, the only alternative to a haversack. These days there is a third choice, the middle road. This is the road which the Moores and people like them choose to follow. They are not without resource, but by no means rich. These days they may see as much of the world as they wish, and return home in comfort and without bankruptcy. I followed the middle road too. I travelled simply, in reasonable comfort and without extravagance.

There was therefore an important factor underpinning the three purposes which I described earlier. I had somehow to achieve what I wanted to achieve without undue strain on my limited resources. In my home, I was comfortable, and wished to remain so. I had to be able to finance my travelling as part of the pleasure, not as a burden, either physically or financially.

Time too was a second factor underpinning everything. When I was working, as a matter of practicality no holiday could be longer than four weeks, or five, if taken over the Christmas break. In that time I could have, and did have, pleasant holidays in the sun, exploring this and that at some leisure. The choice was vast, but realistic comparison difficult. The time available would be insufficient for comparing anywhere with anywhere else. I was suspicious of the so-called 'two-centre' holidays. Limited locality limits perspective when time is short. Time, however, is not a serious consideration for those of us who are retired and without full-time commitments.

How I managed to deal with the time available, money matters and the journey itself, seemed to me to be of special interest to people of my own age and older. The problems I encountered were potentially theirs, and the pleasures. I decided to write a book about how I managed, particularly with them in mind.

I also write with them in mind for a more personal reason. Not infrequently I feel neglected by publishers of non-fiction books. No-one seems to publish specifically for people of my age these days. Those of sixty years or more may well be, statistically speaking, increasing as a proportion of the country's population as a whole, but you would not think so from the number of books that are published with them in mind. We are living longer, and we are staying healthy and energetic longer and deserve some attention for that. I would not expect an artist, a playwright, a composer or a novelist to think of providing specifically for the interests and tastes of the older generation. That generation already has the pictures, plays, music and novels of its own day to remember and to experience again and again, if it wishes. The modern age provides more and more mechanical help for those who wish to remember and experience again. Pictures, plays, music and novels are not for us a problem or a matter of neglect. We have our books from the past, too. What is peculiar is that new books have the ability to be specifically relevant to types, tastes and, in this argument, age groups. Just as there are books specifically written for children, why are there so few books specifically written for those with a life-time of work and experience behind them? You would have thought that that leisured ready-made market would have appealed to all but the least financially motivated of publishers. I can think of no answer to my question on this matter.

Perhaps it is pretended that our tastes are everybody else's tastes, or should be. Hath not the older person eyes? Such a pretence is only half an argument. Naturally we are no less a part of the times we live in than younger people are. We too can learn from the changes which ultra-modernism inflicts upon us, and we do. We even like some of it. What is special about us is merely that we are older than the others. What separates us? We have seen more, we have heard more, we have felt more, and we have more to remember. We can look down the telescope of the years and focus with some clarity on events, tastes and feelings well beyond the visual reach of younger folk. Perhaps even more significant, we can remember what our grandparents could remember, and that, in my case, takes me back well beyond the year of their marriage in 1888. I realize that I am neither alone nor unusual in this, and the number of those with such extended memories is increasing steadily. As a result, we are a varied lot. Experiencing war was to blame for most of that. Then we went on to have differing views about, for example, the Attlee government and the Suez affair. Our disagreements have nevertheless left us mildly optimistic, and we mingle varying opinions with degrees of tolerance and kinds of courtesy. A small incident on a bus in Adelaide may serve in a simple way to illustrate my point. We had just set out from the bus station on our way to the wineries of the Barossa valley, and our driver, having introduced himself, was describing our way out across the city. As we moved in to Victoria Square, he said, 'Over there you can see a big statue. That's a statue of Queen Victoria, one of Australia's most famous queens. She was married to King William the Fourth, you know, and the street we are crossing now is named after him.' I could not guess what Prince Albert's reaction might have been, had he known the whole truth about his wife, and whether the driver in earlier days could expect to be imprisoned in the Tower on a charge of high treason. I was at once surprised at the muted, unconcerned response of my fellow passengers. They gave no smile of recognition at the mistake or its implications, and uttered no word of comment to any neighbour. Two South Africans apart, I was by far the oldest person on the bus, and the only one to be innocently entertained at our driver's expense. To tell the truth, I hold his memory in great regard; he was to regale us with many other extraordinary facts before our day with him was over. His error, on its own, was of no importance at all; it could have been made just as easily in London as in Adelaide. The point was that, having heard my grandparents speak of Queen Victoria's sorrow at the death of her Prince Consort, and having remembered some details from my own schooling, I was the only person on the bus in a position to derive any amusement at all from an ordinary mistake's mundane absurdity. From that moment on, I felt somehow special on the bus; I felt isolated. I had a thoroughly good day, nevertheless.

I write then for people of my own age, thereabouts and older, in the hope that any amusement they find in the story I have to tell may combine with another agreeable feeling, that of being understood.

In outline, the journey got put together like this. First of all, I wanted to miss as much of the English winter as possible. That was no problem, because, in order to be able to watch as much Test cricket as I could in Australia I needed to be in that country for three months, from the beginning of November until the end of January. Those three months in Australia were for me and my journey immutable. Everything else had to happen either before November or after January.

I had already decided to travel by train as much as I could. Why? The answer is simple; I like travelling by train. Sometimes

I think being on a train is like being in the womb. Certainly, being on a train reminds me of childhood: the smell, the sliding doors, the comfortable seats, the windows and their sturdy leather straps. First, I feel safe on a train. Next, I can move about and perform my natural functions on a train. Third, I can sleep on a train, whenever I want to (that usually saves money at night time, in place of a hotel bill). Fourth, I can eat and drink on a train; I like eating and drinking and travelling all at the same time. Fifth, I can gaze out of the window on a train, and see things which I would not otherwise see; trains go where roads do not. Sixth, trains depart and arrive, and often on time too. Seventh, and very important, I can have conversations on trains; I made four new good friends on this journey, all of them on a train.

The next decision I took I am quite unable to explain in rational terms. From the beginning, I had imagined travelling eastwards round the world. It was an assumption I made, and I never questioned it. Possibly it had something to do with an older person's subconscious wish to be as adventurous as possible. After setting out from London, to arrive on the eastern seaboard of Canada or the United States would certainly have been unadventurous; I had done it before. I had even travelled across Canada by train before. To do that again, or something like it, was for me not attractive. To set out eastwards, on the other hand, would be quite a different matter; Berlin, Warsaw, Leningrad, maybe Moscow, and across Siberia to China; to go that way smelled both astringent and romantic. I did not rationalize at all; I planned to set out eastwards in any event. I started to plan in the autumn of 1985.

My first idea was to begin my journey by using the orthodox route eastwards, on the Central Kingdom Express from London to Hong Kong, a train journey of 9,331 miles to Moscow via Paris, Berlin and Warsaw, and then onwards across Siberia to Irkutsk, thence into Mongolia and China, via Ulan Bator, Beijing, Shanghai and Canton. I was to be beguiled however, by the romance of another plan, which the organizing agent, P & O Air Holidays, was advertising with the name '2,100 Years on the Silk Road'. This journey from London to Hong Kong took a more southerly route, through Europe, Turkey, the southern USSR and north-west China, via Paris, Vienna, Budapest, Bucharest, Istanbul, Ankara, Kayseri, Erzurum,

Kars, Tbilisi, Baku, Bukhara, Samarkand, Tashkent, Alma Ata, Urumchi, Turfan, Lanzhou and Xi'an. What names! What a prospect! Chartered trains from six different national railway systems, with first class accommodation, were to be used throughout. Plans included stops for one or two nights at each of the places mentioned, and appropriate sight-seeing arrangements were included in the total cost, as well as all travel, accommodation and food. Cost was a formidable factor, but I calculated that, if all the arrangements took place as advertised — and these also included complicated visa and travel permits — then, for an inclusive period of forty-four days, £88 a day was probably a bargain. The Central Kingdom Express would be slightly cheaper. I was beguiled. I decided on '2,100 Years on the Silk Road', booked my place in December, and joined the group, setting out from London Victoria on 14 September 1986. I never regretted that decision in any way. Arrangements were, to my mind, superb. I shall take the Central Kingdom Express another day.

In my plan, then, I would reach Hong Kong on Sunday, 26 October. At that point, ideally, I wanted to do a Joseph Conrad, and take ship for Darwin, Northern Territory, Australia, but, try as I would, I found no shipping line willing to take me. Not merely that; I found not even a shipping line out of Hong Kong bound for Darwin under any circumstances. Perhaps I did not ask in the right place. At all events, I was forced to abandon my ideal position, and to resort to an aeroplane. The England cricketers were due to begin playing Western Australia in Perth on Thursday, 6 November. I decided to fly from Hong Kong to Perth overnight, arriving on Saturday morning, 1 November. The cost of the flight by Cathay Pacific was the most expensive piece of travelling in the course of all my journey, £730 for six hours' flying. I could find nothing cheaper. I wanted, as second choice, to land in Perth not only to watch some cricket but also to have the chance of crossing Australia as soon as possible by train, on the 'Indian-Pacific', all the way to Sydney. The First Test Match in Brisbane was due to begin on Friday, 14 November.

I decided to leave my three months' stay in Australia to take care of itself. All I did about that before leaving London was to make sure that my Australian visa was in order, and to purchase a first class Australian Railcard, covering my stay.

That cost £500, and was another bargain.

I planned to leave Australia at the end of January, and to fly to San Francisco by way of Fiji. I checked, first, that my US visa was in order. The only other travel detail I wanted to settle before setting out was my crossing of the Pacific Ocean. The Atlantic was for me a less uncertain brook. I would have to fly. As luck would have it, for some reason, Continental Airlines were offering cheap fares for one-way flights out of Nandi in Fiji to San Francisco. I picked one of these, flying out of Nandi, by way of Honolulu on the evening of Thursday, 29 January 1987. The price of the ticket was £400, for twice the distance from Hong Kong to Perth, at four sevenths of the cost. I also booked to fly out of Brisbane to Nandi by Air Pacific on Monday, 26 January, so that I could have three nights on some secluded island paradise. I would arrange for this later, in Melbourne probably. The flight from Brisbane to Nandi cost £50.

I made no plans at all for my journey across the United Sates from San Francisco. I was sure, when I thought about it at the planning stage in July 1986, that, if I reached San Francisco in good order on 29 January 1987, having just crossed the international date-line, I would certainly be capable at that time of making satisfactory arrangements for a stopping itinerary across the United States by Amtrak (US railways), so that I would be able to arrive in London by air before the end of February, the approximate time of my return, already agreed with friends who were to be living in my house.

Such, then, were the travel plans I made before leaving London. My arrival in Hong Kong was in the hands of P & O Air Holidays, and I had made arrangements to reach San Francisco by air, having crossed and travelled Australia by train and having stopped over for a brief respite in Fiji. For the rest, I would rely on my own devising on the spot.

I visited my GP, and made sure that my inoculation record was in order. It was. I took out full insurance cover for the whole period of my absence from home. I was already a member of Centurion Assistance, provided by American Express. For an annual fee of £70, this provided worldwide cover for three months while abroad. In addition, any loss of bankers' cards or keys, by accident or theft, a persistent anxiety as far as I am concerned, could be remedied by a telephone call in an instant.

I had full insurance cover, therefore, until 14 December. As Centurion Assistance would not extend their time limit, I turned to the 'haversack brigade' for help. Sensible travel insurance for students and others is provided by the International Student Insurance Service (ISIS). I took out another ninety days' cover with them from 14 December, at a cost of £61. I felt secure after that. In the event, I had need to call on neither Centurion Assistance or ISIS. 'In heaven's name, how *did* Herodotus manage it in his day?'

I have already mentioned that friends of mine, wishing to move house themselves, found it convenient to borrow my home while I was away. This was convenient also for me, because they were able to deal with all financial outgoings in my absence, and that was a big saving. Their presence also allayed any anxiety I might have had about my home's welfare.

Other friends provided sanctuary as I wandered about. I was especially grateful to Ken and Bill Mappin, and their two children, Margaret and Pete. Whenever I was in or near Melbourne, they offered hospitality at one of their two homes, in town or in the country. I had known them for a very long time, and their continuing friendship in Australia was not only a delight but also meant that I had safe refuge whenever I had need of company or cosseting. I was always popping in and out. Two others, who were just as kind were Keith and Kym Taylor, whose home was in Palo Alto, California. Keith, a former colleague, introduced me also to a new kind of academic vitality, the University of Stanford. What an exciting place, and what a collection of Rodin! One reason for my being happy to delay taking decisions about how and when I would cross the United States was the knowledge that the Taylors were willing to provide me with hospitality while I made my plans.

Then, as I have said, I made friends on the train. Soon after the start of the outward journey, there was a most astonishing coincidence. On our first evening out of Paris, over some celebratory champagne, someone suddenly said to me, 'Come on, let's have dinner together. I know of two others whom I know you would enjoy meeting.' So it was that I met up with Don and Sally Brayton, from Los Angeles, and the nice person taking the initiative was Sally Blaine, also from Los Angeles. She had only met the Braytons that day. We had the most splendid dinner, in old-fashioned SNCF style, in a compartment

The first dinner party aboard the train with Sally Also and Sally Too

Don and Sally Brayton on Danube river trip near Budapest

to ourselves. As a quartet thereafter, we became largely inseparable, and entirely notorious, all the way to Hong Kong. It was delightful. To identify the two Sallys, Sally Brayton became known as Sally Too, and Sally Blaine as Sally Also. They are thus identified as necessary in the story that follows. Also on the train, I met Nan Warren from Sydney. She kindly offered me hospitality which I accepted with alacrity, when I was in Sydney for the Fifth Test Match. We also saw a performance at the Opera House, and had dinner at Doyles.

Travelling alone has its compensations; you alone are responsible for decisions; you alone make the choices you choose; and you alone pay the bills. However, I doubt that I could have survived being alone for six months continuously. At the time, my gratitude to the friends I have mentioned above was immense, especially for the pleasure of being with them. Now, my gratitude at the memory of having been present at such friendly oases leads me to suppose that the adventurous older traveller, however adventurous, should not undertake any lengthy journey without arranging to meet up with friends from time to time. I found that I relied upon my friends a great deal, and I hope they know it. Yes, that part of it, having friends to see, was especially good.

One other person mentioned in the text is Christopher Knowles. He was our courier, friend and counsellor, from London to Hong Kong. His was a tiresome job, but throughout he was unvaryingly skilful, patient and good-humoured. I for one would always be happy to travel in his company.

Before setting out, I had also to do some financial planning. As it turned out, I was unnecessarily cautious in this regard. As far as Hong Kong, all expenses were to be covered, except for laundry and other incidentals. I took £100 in cash with me, that is, £2 a day to cover these. This amount proved to be more than adequate; after travelling for forty-four days, I arrived in Hong Kong with some £20 to spare. I spent little in the USSR and China. In addition, I had £500 worth of US dollars in travellers cheques, and had £500 deposited in a bank in Melbourne for emergencies. I did not need either. I found that cash could easily be obtained in Hong Kong, Australia, Fiji and the United States with my Visa or American Express card, and I frequently paid hotel and restaurant bills with one or other of these. I used up my travellers cheques, but found that I had no special use for them. I arranged with my bank at home to pay all Visa and American Express accounts while I was away.

Overall, my financial plan was as follows. I considered that I would assign £10,000 of the insurance which matured on my sixtieth birthday to the cost of travelling, which would also include the full charge for the journey to Hong Kong. Since travel by train later on from San Francisco to Atlanta, stopping over in Los Angeles, Tucson, and New Orleans, with first class accommodation while on board, was to cost £325, and the flight home from Atlanta to London Gatwick by Delta Airlines £430, my travelling expenses from London and back to London turned out to be £6,406, including travel insurance. Not negligible by any means, but well within my budget. I bought a new car on return to London, having sold my old one before departure, on the proceeds of the sale and the excess balance. I hoped that my day-to-day expenses in hotels and on food, would be covered by the monthly income from my pension, remembering that there would be no outgoings from my house to take account of. Roughly speaking, there would be five months' income to cover four months' day-to-day expenses. The hospitality of friends of course was a very important subsidising factor, and also the cheapness of an overnight bed on the railways, £13 a night in Australia and within the total fare in the United States. I calculated that I would have about £40 a day to spend as an average; I managed quite well within the limit which I set myself, presents for my hosts and for my return home included. It happened that I made a good guess at what my requirements would be. Given that, if I had stayed at home, I would have been spending from income at my customary rate, though at less than £40 a day, I hope, you could say that the cost of my whole journey was £6,406 — found from savings accruing over the past twenty-five years.

There were other coincident factors which helped my budgeting considerably, though I did not know about them before setting out. In Australia, arranging for accommodation was blissfully easy. I can think of no way of bettering it. In each of the big cities and tourist centres, the various States, including the Northern Territory, have tourist offices. You can walk into any one of these and receive the same efficient service, each office dealing with its own State's affairs. You can choose from computer listings the location and nature of the accommodation of your choice, book it for the period you want and pay for it. The booking and payment are both secure, and your welcome on arrival most hospitable. I soon decided that staying in hotels was too expensive for my budget, and not much to my taste; eating out became too much of a monotonous routine. I chose instead to seek self-catering accommodation, and so provide for myself more cheaply. Usually this kind of accommodation, whether in a motel or somewhere more private, never cost more than £15 a night, and consisted of a bedroom, bathroom, kitchen and dining space, and a comfortable TV area for relaxing in. As an example, I walked into the Queensland Tourist Office in Perth, was at once recommended that kind of accommodation within five minutes' walk of the Brisbane Cricket Ground, where the First Test was to be held, booked what was recommended, and paid for a week's stay there. Nothing could have been simpler, less worrisome and more commodious, when the time came — all for £12 a night. Carmel Lodge was an easy taxi ride from the railway station. That kind of experience was to be repeated everywhere I went in Australia, Canberra, Sydney, Adelaide and Alice Springs, and never a complaint. In the United States, it was not possible to plan affairs quite so easily. However, Don Brayton was a member of the American Automobile Association (AAA), and so was able to let me have accurate maps of the places I wanted to visit, together with recommended listings of hotels and places where self-catering would be possible. I would make a choice from the information available, telephone through, and book the accommodation I had chosen, on the security of my American Express card number. I had little difficulty with this process either, though I had some trouble in Tucson, where hotels were heavily booked because of an international congress on precious stones. Even there, I found something to my liking, and was most comfortable. Things were more expensive however than in Australia; you could expect to pay between £30 and £40 a night for similar accommodation; I found nothing cheaper.

I learnt at least one important lesson from experience, without mishap as it turned out. Always check on the viability of your outward flight as soon as you reach a country of temporary residence. I was extremely lucky in wanting to book accommodation in Fiji when I did. As a result of that, I discovered that my Air Pacific flight from Brisbane had been cancelled. It would now be necessary to fly out to Nandi the day before, from Sydney. There were still seats available. If I had found out about the change only seventy-two hours in advance, as the airlines advise, I would have been in trouble. It was the holiday season, and flights would have been heavily booked. As the inquiry I made was six weeks ahead of time, I was able to make a change in arrangements which took account of the airline's change in its timetable. Make sure that airlines know your whereabouts in any country of temporary residence as soon as you can; they are then obliged to tell you about any changes in flight plans. Lucky Herodotus had no such anxieties.

He would have had problems however deciding what luggage to take with him. He travelled over country in which the weather could be both hot and cold, depending on the time of year. Travel for him always transcended seasons. So it would for me. In that regard, I travelled with one eye on the temperature. After reaching Hong Kong, I planned to travel in warm countries only, and so it turned out, except for some bleak spring weather in New Orleans. I took a few precautions: some warm underclothing, and a heavy woollen sweater and jacket. Otherwise, my wardrobe was light in weight, and meant for warm climates. Shoes are heavy items; I took only two pairs, one pair sturdy enough for anything that could happen, and the other comfortable and meant for walking in. Most important, I took a pair of slippers and wore them whenever I could, especially on train journeys, keeping them at the top of one of my bags at all times. I was able to pack everything I needed into two bags of similar size, one of which had to be unpacked only when a change of regime was imminent. In the other, I kept all that I required for sleeping, washing and shaving, all documents (though money was always scattered about), reading and writing material. Keeping luggage separately organized in this way helped my memory wondrously, though not invariably, as we shall see. One consequence of splitting some of my personality in this way was that my two bags were always evenly balanced, with the result that I could carry them both without having to change and change about. They were both quite heavy of course, but it is always much easier to handle evenly balanced bags. Again, laundry was a problem on only one occasion, even in furthest Asia. I like to think that I managed my luggage problems well, although I was sometimes forced to pay less than proper attention to many of the social niceties. I was to be improperly dressed at several social gatherings, without embarrassment, however. To avoid embarrassment in other circumstances, I took two rolls of spare lavatory paper, and two adaptable plugs for plugless hand basins.

So it was that, having packed my bags, I considered myself ready to set out.

* * *

I must however delay the reader from doing the same for a short space yet.

To set out round the world and to return five-and-a-half months later, makes a long journey, but does not make a good story. If I had tried to tell it sequentially, I would have suffered in the same way as Herodotus did, for ever being obliged either to anticipate what would happen in due course, or to turn backwards so as to pin-point similarities or their opposite between what was happening in the present and what had happened in the past. A journey round the world is in fact a higgledy-piggledy affair, always a matter of fact, hardly ever a matter of logic and, if left to its own devices, inevitably tortuous reading. Telling how you return whence you set out makes for not much of a climax.

Being certain of all this, I planned a book about my journey so that it may reflect what interested me most about it, and still retain some kind of logical, reflective progression. I have written a book about a progress of a mind rather than a progress of a body, though at no stage able to neglect what happened to a body. In writing for myself in this way, I find I have also written for those of my age and older. Experience, values, opinions and prejudices always precede what is done or written.

For instance, frontiers have been in the forefront of the times in which we have lived. Alsace-Lorraine, the reorganization of Europe in 1919, the Rhineland, Poland in 1939, the Yalta Conference in 1945, Korea, Hungary, Czechoslovakia, Vietnam: take the name or the event, frontiers and frontier changes have dominated world history since we and our parents were born. We belong to their times. I was to cross fifteen frontiers in all. I grew to be rather fond of them, and now, much against the fashion, believe in them. After all, they made the shape of my world.

Second, I write about my main means of transport, the railway. In another sense, railways have also dominated history in our times. Railways supplied the warring armies, crossed frontiers and invaded countries, and allowed deportations. Better by far, they allowed us to travel great distances in our youth. Taken together, railways and frontiers divide up our world into smaller pieces, rather as the sea does. Taken together, they make a man-made matrix of the land. 'Matrix', the Latin for 'womb'. What an intriguing idea! Taken together, railways and frontiers have been a kind of womb for our world.

Next, I write about myself on my travels, how I managed, what went right and what went wrong, as I explored my route around the world.

Fourth, I write of other people. I was able to make a vivid discovery that it really was their world too. Our views about it did not always coincide, but sometimes they did. For me, other people represented no kind of hell, but they could be wondrously strange.

Fifth, I try to forget about man and woman, boy and girl, and the varied mischief they make. Instead, I find myself unworthily joining that long train of distinguished predecessors who have been fascinated by the desert. First, it fascinated me; now, it holds me in thrall.

Sixth, the sun shone, and it rained, and I was always seeing the sea, a lake and a river or two. The world is in large part just weather and water, continually being threatened these days by human machinations. I like it as it is.

I keep special occasions to the last, occasions which I have described as being blessed by the presence of awesome demons. Awesome demons really serve to define matters of taste. I could never pretend that mine is anything else but my own. The world was a wonderful place for me, full of demons.

A return to London was the purpose of my progress. What happened there is best left until my story reaches that point.

* * *

So it was then that I set out, above all cautiously aware of Herodotus' assurance that, much as I might consider the merits of the places and customs I witnessed, I would be mad not to think England and English ways best of all in the end.

The date was 14 September, 1986. I was taken to Victoria Station in the rain, by the friends who were to be staying in my house. Spirits were high. We arrived on the dot. I registered my presence. My bags were collected. Two hundred of us took breakfast, packed into a hot hotel room. Spirits lowered. I did not enjoy my breakfast. It was noisy and far too hot. Having eaten, we emerged to more noise, to the shrill and strident shrieking of pipe music. A trio, in full tartan dress, were telling us about 'Scotland the Brave', and how it would be sensible to go 'Over the Sea to Skye'. By now ill at ease and scowling, I joined the others in a bizarre procession behind the pipers towards Platform One. Those responsible for the management of the station were in the process of hiding away the elegantly shabby ghost of the station's neo-classical architecture behind a veneer of red, white and blue paint and plastic. The incongruous music of the pipes was by now echoing off discordant paint and plastic. I decided that England, and Victoria Station in particular, that rainy Sunday morning, were not attractive places to be in. We climbed aboard our train, and were soon racing past Bromley South and all drenched suburbs east. The Garden of England was hidden in mist, and Folkestone was gloomy beyond all measure. Herodotus's assurance was by now unpromisingly insecure. Could I with any honesty commend to myself this sodden, tawdry place, addicted to the pretence of being Scottish? Had it any charm at all with which to keep me loyal? Would not the long journey ahead soon dissipate any loyalty I might still have? I was certainly glad to be leaving. I would just have to make sure that I would see all that I could see in the weeks ahead, just in case there was no better place than England.

2

Frontiers

Those of us who like to travel but live most of the time on an island, whether it be a large one like Australia or a small one like Great Britain, have an uncommon perception of what constitutes a frontier. Either we see it as an inconsequential and insubstantial line like that we cross as we pass from England into Scotland, and from New South Wales into Victoria, and vice versa, or we think of seaside places like Dover, Folkestone, Newhaven, Fremantle and the Sydney Heads, scarcely ever of Heathrow, Gatwick, Luton, Prestwick and Tullamarine. The sea, not the land or the air, is our horizon; the coast is our frontier. Neither for us nor our ancestors were the Solent, the Mersey, the cliffs of Dover and the Bass Strait put there for nothing.

We descended from our train at Folkestone, were obstructed by the usual collection of obtuse behaviour on the part of people and things who got in our way, and took ship in the continuing drizzle and familiar clatter and clutter. The sea journey was our islander's no-man's-land.

Good fortune on a Channel crossing is a rarity, but one can stumble across happy auguries in the course of it from time to time. Indeed, while I was stumbling over my baggage in search of a seat on our Townsend Thoresen ferry, a former colleague and friend steadied my path by smiling a greeting from across the gangway. Jointly we blessed our respective journeys with conversation and a drink. I would say for myself that my particular journey began in the course of our happy conversation, and not at rainy, inauspicious Victoria Station with its pipe band two-and-a-half hours earlier. Our conversation and drink not only renewed a friendship, but also brought about the pouring of a libation in support of continuing good fortune. A courier jolted my arm in haste and so spilled red wine on the sleeve of my jacket, newly purchased from a charity shop in Canterbury a few weeks earlier. The courier, a delightful person, known to us all presently as Sue, apologized apoplectically, snatched the jacket away and washed the offending sleeve religiously clean in the shelter of the ladies' lavatory, drying it successfully under the hair-drier and returning all to me duly restored and accompanied by a replacement drink. As a result of the pouring out of this libation and its ensuing good omen, I became sure that my journey had started, and would continue well, as would my friend's. There was to be evidence, if not proof, of this three months later. She was pregnant at the time of our encounter. Her son, his sex forecast by me with unerring accuracy in September, was born in December in Leeds as I was watching cricket in Adelaide.

What then when we reach Calais, Boulogne, Singapore or Hong Kong after crossing the sea? Subconsciously reminded of the old joke about the continent, and all continents, being cut off, consciously and just a trifle warily we step ashore, new travellers and adventurers again. This land is not ours and so ever new; even though altered little and with a tawdriness not unlike our own, an obstacle race like that on the other side but with obstacles looking different, and where habits and customs are changed but have similar meanings, France is never England, and Singapore never Australia. Yet, treading warily, we become safe in the journey we had intended. Our assurance is the differences we see and feel, and the differences we see and feel become the substance of what we wanted.

Between embarkation and disembarkation extends a no-man's-land in time and space. The truth as always is simple but difficult to express; those of us who travel, but live most of our lives on islands, have two frontiers to cross before our travels can begin, not one. The islander is a separate kind of traveller.

One thing the Channel Tunnel will do when it is completed is to alter us in Great Britain at our roots. The Channel will become, for those who use the tunnel, land, not sea. In this way, Australians, and others like them, may add one more idiosyncratic blessing to their already extensive list. Personally

I shall continue to cross the Channel by sea as long as I can, continuing to count that as a blessing still.

I like the clatter and the clutter, even the obtuse behaviour of queues and their protagonists, and all the signs and signatures (long live *Tenez la droite* and *Aux bateaux*). I enjoy, too, delay because I enjoy persuading myself that what happens next is bound to be eventful and amusing. I do not really like excitement, I must admit. The customs shed and the passport control desk are assuredly not exciting places, and to be avoided if they become so. It should not be thought, however, that I am ungrateful for what has been done in recent years to enable those areas of concern, especially within the Common Market, to treat travellers more expeditiously and without the chalk, stampings and rigmarole of former years, but I am sure nevertheless that I should feel unclean and uncleared if one day I were to climb aboard a train in Boulogne without the benediction of a critical stare and uniformed authority on the sidelines. As it is, stares and authority, if placid and detached, give me time to ponder where I am and to anticipate where I am soon to be. Landing in France, experiencing due formality, climbing aboard a train and uttering a word of two of rusty French, in search of a *baguette jambon* for instance, are to me harmless, desirable and unexciting pleasures. May the new tunnel not inhibit such things, and may it certainly not prevent them!

About to depart from the Gare de l'Est for Salzburg and Vienna

After two nights in Paris, we spent the third crossing the frontiers between France and Germany, and between Germany and Austria. That was a silent night, without arousal except for the routine noise of the train and trains. No real frontiers these, without event, without sudden jolts and without stress. It would also have been churlish of us to complain about an uninterrupted night of fitful dozing. None of us regretted the omission of jolting stops at the European frontiers of former years, the hissing and banging while the train, or other trains, were at rest or shunting, the approaching noise of opening sliding doors, the lights switched on and off again, the decisive bangs of sliding doors being closed again, the soft shoe shuffle of the train moving warily along the line a bit, stopping once more with a shuddering jolt, accompanied perhaps by the tapping of wheels faintly now, growing louder as far as deafening intensity, and then faintly again. Again the door, again the light. A polite but peremptory, 'Passport, *bitte*', a hasty, anxious search among crumpled trousers, shirts and pillows, a quick offering answered by a cursory glance at a page or two. One more stamp and one more date added to all the others, evidence of one more frontier crossing. '*Haben sie einfass declaren?*', translated into crumpled English perhaps, as a bonus. '*Nein.*' '*Danke schön.*' Light off, door shut with a bang once more. An uninterruptable routine.

In earlier days this game with passports, stampings and question and answer would have been played out as frontiers rivalled each other with the intensity of their earnestness. By the time each game had been concluded, you were wide awake and fully aware that you had crossed from France into Germany over the Rhine. All a symbol of achievement, of something left behind, of something done and of something to look forward to, worth every waking second, and evidence into the bargain that would hold up in any court of law that you had been where you said you had been. I used so to enjoy it all.

It would indeed be churlish to complain that we regretted the omission of all this rigmarole, but I missed it nevertheless. As a result, I found myself with the predatory discomfort of feeling guilty about something I had not done but should have done. I was away into Germany and Austria scot free. All I could do was to allay the discomfort and blink unbelievingly beneath the blind of my compartment window at the glare of the stations at Stuttgart, Munich and Rosenheim as they passed.

By then it was growing light. The cold billowing rain of Paris had given way to a misty, autumnal sunrise. We had done it without paying any penalty. At such a time, in such a light, we had Salzburg of all places to look forward to. I shall write about the magic brought about by a change in the weather later on. Meanwhile our next frontier was to be of sterner mettle.

* * *

Our journey between Vienna and Budapest, taken by day, together with our brief experience of those two cities, was to summarize for us much that was so moving and dramatic about the old Hapsburg Empire. Previously all that I had learnt about it had been at the feet of a schoolmaster nearly fifty years before. We heard then, all too briefly again, of its romance and charm, of its subtleties and eminence, and of its division into Austria and Hungary after 1918. Its previous divisions, its reserves of envy, rivalry, and resentment, at the base of all imperial power, were not the subject matter of classroom debate in those pre-war days. We were taught then to have sympathy for Austria, for its smallness and reduced capacity and influence, but to respect the separate identity of Hungary and Hungarians. The drawing of the pre-war frontier between Austria and Hungary, an important part of the peace policy of the victorious allies, to romantically-minded school-children was not merely a piece of political expediency but primarily a spiritual injustice.

In front of Hegyeshalom, the town on the frontier between Austria and Hungary, the meaning of a continental frontier became for us at last articulate. In accordance with precise instructions we had completed and handed in visa forms, supported also by two passport photographs each, between Salzburg and Vienna. On return the passports had Hungarian visas stamped on them, visas using a language of inextricable wizardry, only the word Magyar able to proclaim to us part of the drama. Even more warily this time, our train drew to a stop with a finality reserved only for such occasions. The Austrian officials not surprisingly gave us each but a cursory glance, their colleagues in front of Salzburg having been entirely careless of our existence. Their Hungarian counterparts were however of different temper, uniformed like soldiers, stern, cautious, thorough, unsmiling and silent. The good soldier Svejk was not with us; we were all impressed by a formidable atmosphere. We faced the proper stuff at last, the stuff of unpretending and unrelenting reality. None would pass unless known on paper and by ordeal of photograph. A visa check, a confirmatory glance at faces and corroborating documents, and then a deciding stamp of approval were not mere tokens of finality. As far as I could tell from my passport, no date of entry or due date of departure were recorded, instead just a series of inscrutable numbers. By number we would be known, and by number officials in Hungary and desk clerks at our hotel in Budapest would detain us if they wished. Hegyeshalom was plainly a Magyar word. We did not know its meaning, but it had spoken clearly enough. There was no spiritual injustice any longer and the frontier was certainly no mere piece of policy, in 1986, at least.

* * *

In comparison moving from Hungary to Romania, between Lököshava and Curtici, was a holiday, a laughing, happy occasion. The Hungarians were as expected, formal and detached, as though relieved to be rid of us. The Romanians on the other hand were cheerful and friendly. Possibly the fact that we had transferred from a French train in Budapest to a Romanian one influenced how we felt (not that one ever likes to leave France, but on this occasion the difference in atmosphere was striking). As a symbol at breakfast that morning on the new train we partook of a Romanian national drink, called '*svika*' I think, plum brandy with peppercorns, served hot. I remember having more than one tasting, and was thus enlivened at breakfast well beyond my wont. As soon as we had stopped at Curtici, dining car attendants appeared in the corridor, calling into each compartment, 'Welcome to Romania!' and passing gratis to each of us a bottle of white wine as further liquid evidence of their welcome. My diary records that I was suffering from dehydration by the time I arrived in Bucharest. Everyone has experienced perfunctory attempts to use frontiers to symbolize gateways to paradise, but none so patently genuine as that the Romanians used at Curtici.

* * *

Two happy days in Romania, spoiled by evidence of poverty and the limitations that puts upon the happiness of many, had us return, sadly in fact, for we had enjoyed ourselves, to a Romanian frontier, this time that with Bulgaria at Ruse. We did not know then how shallow our happiness had been, and at what expense, since we were to be only in transit through Bulgaria, being due to take ship that evening from Varna. We had not expected much of a performance, but we were wrong.

Having breakfasted early, once more to the accompaniment of 'svika', by the time we reached the Bulgarian side of Ruse, we were hungry again, for it was lunchtime. Hopes were high; we were sure our Romanian friends would do us proud as part of their farewell, and appetites were growing by the minute, notably mine.

The train stood ominously still for a time. We had been ordered to remain fixed in our compartments. Ruse was no metropolis, and our view of a small marshalling-yard on both sides of us placed a limit on our discussion of what was going on outside and encouraged discussion of what was going on inside. After a time the distant sound of sliding doors heralded an event. Slowly, the event, whatever it was, approached our door. In its own due time, we too experienced it. A small man in uniform, plainly of junior rank and in himself betokening little, treated us each in turn.

On average he spent four minutes with each of us, collecting our completed forms, stowing them away, examining our passports in great detail, stamping each form as he extricated it from its store-place, stamping each passport in consequence and finally gazing at each of us with a superficially fierce but fundamentally youthful stare. The good soldier Svejk would have made a feast of it, lucky man, but, being hungry, we had no wit. A quick calculation revealed that one official, plus one railway coach with about twenty-five passengers in it, all passengers being separated into four minutes each, would consume no less than one-and-a-half hours of lunch time. The misery of other quick calculations followed; if there were to be only one official allotted to the whole train of six coaches, that would mean having to wait for nine hours before we might be allowed to eat. We became gradually and painfully aware that we were facing a crisis, and perhaps lunch was only a small part of it.

Two other factors become increasingly more significant than lunch. First, rumour. Though we were confined to our compartments, rumour somehow spread wildly and without reason. Much of our baggage was being unloaded onto the platform. At once it was cunningly concluded that some ass had packed his passport, and no further progress would be possible along the train, let alone towards Varna, until it had been found and duly perused. Then it was rumoured that others were having lunch, out of turn, for we were due to be served as 'first sitting' that day. Why them, and not us? In fact, no-one was being served lunch; I went along to see as soon as I saw our official descend from the train at our end of it. No lunch for anybody, at least not yet. Second, temperament. Reactions to crisis and emergency are immensely varied. Irrationality takes over at varying paces and about a variety of matters. Some wanted lunch most of all; why can't we have lunch while we are waiting? Some wanted to know why we were waiting in the first place; any reasonable explanation, they assured us, would placate them. Some wanted to protest and cause a stir, no sitting back for them. Some just became anxious and close to tears. Fortunate those who knit. Others like me grew silent, hugely silent; that way from long experience, I for one knew that we had a crisis on our hands. I began to measure the amount of noise that was being made, all the way from silence through whimpering to bawling and shouting. As a matter of fact we all knew that potentially the crisis might have no solution; if the Bulgarians wanted it, we could stay in Ruse, unfed, for ever. Frontiers are not that unimportant. Yes, some concluded, it was plain; the Bulgarians were to blame; what could you expect from a load of 'communists'?

Then, at first without perceiving it, slowly the train began to move forward. Baggage aboard once more, we were finally rid of Ruse and on our way to Varna, five-and-a-half hours late. We had lunch that evening — at the second sitting, blow me down — at six o'clock. Not unreasonably, the Romanians were as disconsolate as we were.

The explanation of it all was simple enough in the end. The Bulgarian officials at Ruse claimed that our group visa had been incorrectly processed, and the only remedy was a further payment in sterling. Chris with courage refused to pay the surrogate fine, and chose to fight the argument on its own ground, that is, bureaucratic procedure. If further payment in sterling is necessary, then proper sanction for that payment had to come from above, that is, from Sofia. Telephone call followed telephone call. In the end for whatever reason, Chris's view was upheld, all was in order in the first place, bureaucratic procedure had been satisfied, no extra charge was payable, and the train was enabled to move forward. You could not with any reason blame 'communism' or 'communists', for there had been 'communism' and 'communists' at Hegyeshalom and Curtici, but you could blame bureaucracy and bureaucrats, or peculation and peculators, if you had a mind to.

Chris worked beyond his stint that day. He continued to perspire profusely as the train moved on its way and we broke bounds to find out from him what had happened. We never did find out however about the baggage; possibly moving our baggage out of the train was a calculated threat to show that we might not be moved on. Our first guess about the matter was wrong for sure.

After Ruse I concluded that henceforward every frontier would be bound to have a lesson of its own to teach. At Ruse I learnt most about my neighbours.

* * *

Another consequence was our late arrival in Varna, where perforce our tour of the city took place in the dark and where the main solace was an excellent English commentary from our Bulgarian guide. Oddly, following our experience at Ruse, our departure from Varna brought gifts (for me a carnation and a piece of local pottery, which, grateful at last, I used as a drinking bowl) and an expeditious passage through passport control and customs. The good ship *Vlagonev* was a cramped, airless affair, and, after a late departure and a late dinner, further suffering ensued. The four of us volunteered to share a cabin, which we might not have done had we known that it was to be near the bilges and stuffy beyond endurance. They forced open a rusty port-hole for us, and in consequence I spent the night clinging to my bunk lest the gale at my head blow me out of my nest. My friends were less stuffy and less at risk.

The Bulgarian crew made a touchingly valiant attempt in the morning at bacon and eggs, and my spirits at least became fully restored since the bread and the coffee were good as well; my spirits were soon to become exhilarated by a sunlit morning's sail down the west coast of the Black Sea, towards the Bosphorus and Istanbul. I make the reader delay reading further about the causes of my exhilaration until chapter seven. I merely record here that I became exhilarated between bacon and eggs and arrival at the Turkish Maritime Terminal before the Galata Bridge across the Golden Horn. I have already described the English Channel as a buffeting, vital place in any British idea of a frontier, but that sun-drenched morning sail on 24 September 1986, taught me as much as I ever want to know about the meaning of the gap between setting out and arriving.

One more thing. Never convenient because of the volume and weight required for long journeys, baggage had impeded us little at Folkestone and Boulogne. Arrangements at both places, mixing trolleys with proximity, were adequate if not easy. At the Turkish Maritime Terminal, old and not so old had at least 400 yards to go, fully encumbered, without any trace of mechanical aid between the ship and passport control, and another 100 yards between customs and our waiting transport. Friendly smiles and bunches of grapes could not erase the effect of the heat, the effort, the dust, the jostling and the crowded street. Contrast and sudden change mingle haphazardly as the traveller makes his way forward.

* * *

We then travelled eastwards through Turkey for a week or more and came face to face with contrast and sudden change at the frontier between Turkey and the Soviet Union. A cold, early start from Sarikamis found us reaching the border by ten-thirty am, a desolate spot but green still despite the frost, with no habitation nearby that one could see. The autumn sun peeped at the day through a thin mist, still, silent, and, some may have thought, ominous. For myself, I was enjoying being deranged by a tense wordlessness.

Turkish guards, cheerful and informal, stood on the platform close to our train, and then, as we drew quietly away, waved us goodbye for ever, for we were going beyond their frontier. We waited for some time after stopping again where nowhere was. The Soviet train would arrive at the platform opposite where we could at once see that the gauge was unusually wide. We continued to wait while our baggage was unloaded. The Soviet train would be late, they told us, perhaps two hours late. Warily we stepped down on to Turkey for the last time, enjoyed the autumn air, and pondered the future and, once more, our stomachs; we were due to lunch in the Soviet Union. I suppose we had conversations, but I have no memory of their content. No doubt they strayed no further than we did, which was not far from our baggage. Previously we had been united with all our baggage only in hotels, apart of course from the Turkish Maritime Terminal. Waiting near our baggage became an occupation; this time I was not anxious but curious.

Trains until now, in Europe and in Turkey, had been dark blue in colour *à la Wagons Lits*, with gold or yellow figuring. Sliding as a log might, close by a bank on sluggish stream, a sombre green train with white figuring and a yellow line stretching below its windows sidled up to the platform and halted. Disciplined and under orders, we did not move until at last a signal was given. A hectic minute or two, helping ourselves and each other, shook us out into some kind of pattern. I was in compartment no. 5. The coach had been made in the German Democratic Republic, I noted subliminally. Chris, following hastily in the wake of a diminutive, brusque, bossy uniformed official, was trying to see that all were settled and comfortable, but the official was steadfast in pursuing his own path, not Chris's nor anybody else's. For instance, he objected roundly to my having a compartment to myself.

Chris told him just as roundly that it had to be, that was the case and it couldn't be helped. It was good to know that as well as firmness he had some Russian on the tip of his tongue. It was a foreign, invigorating moment, chaotically urgent. Then, in a blink, all became quiet.

Again we had been told to stay in our compartments, and not to leave them until released. Because of the tension at the time I have forgotten at what stage we were given our documents for entry to the Soviet Union. Logic suggests that we already had them in our possession when the border guards made their visitations on the train. The documents were of two sorts: first, an identity document in Cyrillic script with a carbon copy beneath it (how interesting to see one's name and nationality written in a different manner!) and, second, a form with a carbon copy attached for completion, concerning financial details and items of value like cameras, precious metals and jewellery (particular it was, and not easy to complete accurately because of the variety of currency one accumulates while travelling). These documents, logical and clear, heralded the manner of our forthcoming examination, painstaking and courteous.

First, two officials carried out passport control, one of whom collected and stored the carbon copy of the identity document. We were to keep the top copy with our passports throughout the visit to the Soviet Union; it served both as a visa and as evidence of entry and anticipated departure. Meanwhile a third individual, young and athletic, and not in uniform, followed the others compartment by compartment. His task was to search everywhere for hidden objects, living or dead, and this he did with acrobatic zeal and skill, above and below, north, south, east and west. Satisfied that no-one was hiding either in the luggage racks or in the coffin-like metal containers beneath the seating, intended for baggage, I was brusquely told, unlike the upper berth where mine was, he passed on to my neighbours. After an interval, another group of three persons, two men and a woman in civilian clothes, inspected our possessions and our money. The woman, the first I recall to be employed at any frontier up to that point, inspected me and mine, the former by interrogation only. She was a nice person and not unamused by the seriousness with which I was treating everything. Satisfied that my record of money was accurate, that my camera was a cheap one and that I had no gold, silver or diamonds in my possession, she took a close interest in my reading matter which I had at hand (at the time, W H Hudson's *Hampshire Days* and Peter Hopkirk's *Foreign Devils on the Silk Road*) and my diary. She handed the latter over to her colleagues for further examination. I guessed that I would not see it again, for in addition to an illegible script it had several drawings of the ground-plans of churches we had visited and a pencil sketch or two, all of which might at once give rise to suspicions about my motives for keeping such a diary. To my surprise, it was handed back with a nod and a 'thank you'. Smiling, almost grinning, my lady inquisitor, to whom I had taken a liking, and who was later revealed as of Armenian extraction, tidied my cases and closed them for me.

I had been impressed by the thoroughness especially, and by

the efficiency of it all, but conceded to myself that six people had every cause to be thorough and efficient. Others were not so impressed, it must be said, and several had books and magazines confiscated. I remember now feeling glad that the ordeal was over; it was like hearing the news that you had passed an examination, which perhaps I had.

As the inspection process moved on to other coaches, we in ours relaxed and compared notes. Opinion was divided; though in the minority, I was not to be dissuaded from a favourable view of Soviet frontier procedures. They had shown us with some emphasis that their frontier with Turkey was an important one to them, and that no-one crossed it without due process of what was reasonable as far as officials were concerned. We all knew it would be like that anyway.

Five hours after our arrival at the frontier platform, our new train slipped away, like a log this time edging towards the ocean and increasing speed — at last in Soviet Armenia moving towards the border town of Leninakan. My passport had no Soviet Union stamp on it, nor was there to be any rubber-stamping in China. How then did I travel between Kars in Turkey, they may ask, and Hong Kong? Officials in the Soviet Union and the People's Republic of China know, and so do I. Isn't that the main thing? I would have liked the stamps, however.

For the first time, between Kars and Leninakan, we gazed at completely different countries and did not need stamps to prove Eastern Turkey, formerly Turkish Armenia, had been a smiling, happy place, but drastically poor. The poverty of the towns Sarikamis and Kars, in the streets and the shops, the quality of the food and clothing for sale, the status of the ordinary people, especially the women and the children, all was not unlike that to be seen in Madras, except that the number of people suffering was incomparably smaller. I remember no restaurants like those in Ankara and Kayseri, only small grubby eating houses, and a few bedraggled coffee shops. The time of year made it muddy and cold. You would not automatically expect much in the way of happiness thereabouts. But at every corner and on every step, there was a smile and a greeting, perhaps proudly in English, poverty but no depression on view. In the country the land was mostly barren, high upland plateau, few trees and only small peasant farms, with sheep mostly, but some chickens, rabbits, geese and ducks. Houses were made mostly of mud, the roofs idiosyncratically protected by small stacks of hay and stubble. Each collection of buildings was surrounded by a low mud wall, token of the farmer's precinct. Most cattle were already inside and but few could be seen beyond the precinct. Cattle dung was the fuel, being dried in neatly ordered piles. Only the main road was decently paved; side roads were muddy and rutted. In any case there was no traffic to speak of. Unlike elsewhere, few watched our train pass by; there were few to watch anyway, an old man perhaps, a dog and two boys with sticks. The dried-out grasses were pale fawn in colour, the rest, the soil, the stones and shallow hills were grey, as grey as the sky where they both met, a placid, lowering unity. Mist hid all clarity except that which was close at hand.

As the train passed beyond the barbed wire eastwards, suddenly we found ourselves in a new land, not merely a new country. There were few smiles, it must be said, but the land was green and closely tended. I remember maize, sunflower, corn, orchards, vines, cattle pastures, and all kinds of vegetables, especially cabbages. Houses were spare but soundly built of red brick. Roads were wide and well constructed. Traffic was sparse but more frequent than in Turkey, even private cars from time to time. Leninakan seemed the same size as Northampton, and as unlikely to suffer earthquake. Its station, with real people on it going about their business, and the shunting yards, with real wagons jostling together, were not dissimilar. Good housing, good streets, paving, traffic lights, traffic, few shops (but I noticed from the train few shops in Birmingham, Alabama); it was going-home time, scarcely a rush hour, but people enough with work to do and homes to go to. It was a most striking contrast and a most sudden change. Because clocks went forward two hours at the frontier, it was now well past five o'clock in the afternoon. We had lunch at six.

The two sides of the frontier had only one thing in common, soldiers, tanks, lorries, guns, military installations and sensor equipment. The Turkish soldiers wore khaki, and the Soviet soldiers wore green.

* * *

There followed frontiers between the separate Soviet Republics of Georgia, Azerbaijan, Turkmenia, Uzbekhistan and Kazakhstan, none receiving more notice than those between England and Scotland, or New South Wales and Victoria, guides invariably making slight comments in terms of personal loyalty and feelings for home. From Leninakan in Armenia to Alma Ata in Kazakhstan was a journey of some 2,500 miles, a journey which took some nine days.

We set out from Alma Ata early on the morning of 14 October by bus, since Alma Ata was the end of the southern railway eastwards. We were to travel some 1,000 miles by bus southeastwards, as far as Turfan in Xinjiang in north-west China. The rail-head was in fact at Shihezi, 300 miles or so closer. There were technical reasons however, beyond my comprehension, why we could not join our Chinese train there. A temperamental cloud of some kind rested over the regional capital of Urumchi, and Urumchi lay between Shihezi and Turfan. Whatever the merits of the case — and Urumchi had certainly had a blood-stained past, if not a blood-stained present — we faced a long journey by bus. During the course of its first day we were to cross into China at one of the most remote frontier posts there are in the world, and where only one other group such as ours had crossed previously a year earlier. It was said that only high-level intervention from Moscow had enabled that crossing to take place; the Soviet Union and the People's Republic had been on sensitive terms thereabouts for years. The chequered history of the frontier's very existence is subject matter for the final section of this chapter. Crossing it might well turn out to be more than individual tenacity would be able to endure. What is more it might offer more excitement than I for one could enjoy.

We had had a lovely journey from Alma Ata, below clear skies and in autumn sunshine throughout, the splendid snow-capped range of the Tian Shan, the Heavenly Mountains, to our right towards the south for most of the early morning, the road traversing an intensely cultivated alluvial plain. I would guess that there could be no richer, or better watered land within a thousand miles. Such plains, and we were to see several others like this one in China, reminded me of the flat richness of our own fenlands, the local water conservancy arrangements being just as adequate everywhere. Lines of poplars measured out the distance in fading regimental autumn colours. The road, straight as an arrow, crossed their short, slanting shadows as in a flickering film long ago. The air was icily fresh but not cold, given that you could persuade your neighbour to have the window open. Mine as it happened did not know what she wanted, and so we had trouble with our adjustments.

Then, suddenly, turning right we found the land more arid, and the road was zig-zagging upwards towards jagged hills, such as the Alps and Europe had never seen, the Kokpek Gorge. Led upstream, upwards, we passed our first sight of lived-in Kazakh yurts, portable shelters using felt made of wool to cover do-it-yourself wooden frameworks, their inhabitants tending cattle and sheep for a living. Having followed the twisting road upwards for some twenty miles amid towering crags that were now black and now red, from the gorge's head we descended quickly to a plain at a greater altitude than that we had crossed an hour before, dry grassland this time with snow-capped mountains on both sides, growing more distant with every mile as we travelled more south than east.

Picnic spot, mid-morning, near the Chinese border with the USSR

A sudden descent to a fresh, green cutting, where a river had worn away rock for some poplars and a pasture or two to flourish, brought us in sight of rows and rows of metal bowls filled with piping hot water, soap and towels at hand, and then, close by, rows and rows of freshly cooked lamb kebabs, fresh bread, milk, red wine and rosy red apples. It was time for elevenses; clean hands here before eating and drinking in the dry sunshine. Rarely have I felt such a personally based exuberance. The smoke, which rose from the herbs and the lamb, fanned over fires by local cooks, beneath a tenuous, temporary awning, can scent my nostrils yet. I ate and drank sitting on a rock, speechless among my mouthfuls. As far as I know, it was a nameless place, already within the border's military zone, where no camera clicks.

Pamphilov, a small border town named after a war-time general, not content with *al fresco* elevenses, went further and entertained us to lunch at tables, with caviar, smoked meat, vodka and champagne, music, songs and a speech from the mayor. Pamphilov was a flourishing little place, basing its wealth in part, I daresay, on the local military. It was there too on the Soviet side that we saw our first Chinese mosque, calm, with low tiled roofs and upturned ridges, an antique school and courtyard nearby. Within, its stately wooden pillars had the structural certainty of early Romanesque and the painted colours of carving belonged to the earth as those of mosaics do. I was reminded of Sant' Apollinare in Classe near Ravenna; a neighbour disagreed.

All that had preceded lunch and all that Pamphilov and its community of mixed Asian blood had done for us became an incomparable, unforgettable farewell. I for one was sad to leave the USSR.

The habits of frontiers change when they are faced with buses. Soviet thoroughness remained constant. We drew up in a desolate spot at some wired gates, and waited while other travellers proceeded in the opposite direction — no two-way traffic here. Then entering a courtyard and faced with a tall brick building littered with frontier guards, we alighted, collected our baggage and queued interminably, as a T-shaped customs bench and a desk at the end of a corridor dealt with each of us, one by one. As the queue progressed, I noticed a lavatory door, and the fact that entrants had to be accompanied by a uniformed officer. In their wisdom many were making use of this facility, and a subsidiary queue was forming with some speed. I made a quick assessment of my own condition, and decided that, having been stalwart thus far on our journey, despite scares and alarms, I would bide my time, thinking idly that similar opportunities would occur before long. Nothing daunted, and unconcerned except about a successful passing of the bench and the desk ahead, I remained where I was, and in due time the desk arrived. Two urgent, busy women were seeing to things on the other side of it. We had collected a number of forms during the course of our stay in the Soviet Union, to do with currency exchange and our purchases there. We had also been required to complete a further form on our own part, describing our present financial state, which of course would have to tally with those we already had in store from elsewhere. Having answered as before questions about gold and silver and jewellery, and having presented once more my cheap camera for inspection, I handed over my forms and my identity visa for review by one of the women. The other, a counterpart I came to think of the Armenian at Leninakan, smiled and, I believe, winked with amusement. I passed muster and passed on, outwards into another open courtyard on the other side of the building. Surviving the queue and accompanied throughout by cumbersome baggage was a triumph which all of us, old and not so old, managed to achieve in the course of time.

Assembled, we waited for other buses, smaller buses we were warned and without separate space for baggage underneath. Smaller buses meant that we were to be distributed differently, and despite the uncomfortable experience of doing likewise on board the good ship *Vlagonev*, I volunteered, for the smallest of the buses as it happened. It turned out to be similarly uncomfortable. Baggage had to have a bus of its own, and those of us who were fit enough, without at least one scrimshanker, man-handled it all on behalf of our companions and ourselves. It was exhausting work; baggage is obstinate, idiosyncratic stuff. Those little trolleys to which the tender attach theirs are the most obstinate and idiosyncratic of all. We perspired but endured. I was in due course to be grateful for that perspiration and that endurance.

Presently we embarked and advanced aboard our Mitsubishis, squeezed and crowded now, on vehicles made for those of smaller stature, and advanced into China, where we halted. Then, we halted, halted and halted. A glance at our watches showed that it was now some five hours since we left Pamphilov. It now appeared that five hours was par for the course.

A slight and smiling young man boarded our bus and introduced himself in almost inaudible English. I will call him John, for his Chinese name was unpronounceable. He was from Beijing University, and had studied English there. This was to be his first experience of being an interpreter and guide, and he hoped that we would understand him, and be sympathetic towards his nervousness.

By now it was dark, lights were few, and as we moved forward once more we could see that we were close to a frontier post, a small one this time, less impressive than that we had passed one-and-a-half hours earlier. New forms for completion were handed out and our passports were collected. The forms were again on financial matters, and had to be authenticated by officials at the frontier post. Then they with our passports were returned to us for retention while we were in China — all this while we sat cramped in our seats.

It was thus, while I was completing my particular form and reviewing my financial circumstances, that I realized that I completed my Soviet version incorrectly, leaving out the fact that I was still in possession of 500 French francs. I winced at the thought of having escaped the charge of forgery at a Soviet border by the skin of my teeth. What, if I had been found out in my negligence? Could I have been detected? Certainly I would have held up the others considerably. But I would be near a lavatory at least, I said to myself. Expelling perspiration had enabled me to survive without stress until that moment, but wincing had reintroduced to my consciousness the physical fact that my bladder was becoming full beyond endurance, very full indeed. Elevenses and then lunch at Pamphilov were still with me, and the Pamphilovians had not yet in fact said their final farewell. Certainly I was not yet able to expel the memory of their generosity from the way I felt.

In the gloom of the bus, I edged my way forward, climbing over all and sundry, and told John of the strait I was in. Mercifully he understood my meaning at once, and said, 'We will be moving shortly. Can you wait?'

'Only for a bit,' I said.

In my extremity I saw nothing wrong with the side of the bus. We did not move shortly, nor did we move in ten minutes either. Or was it ten seconds? Creeping forward again, I said with passion this time, 'I must go now, John, or else.'

'OK.' What idiomatic aplomb!

He went outside, and then beckoned me to follow him. He handed me over into the care of a soldier, who without a word marched me off — away from Russia into China. This activity provided me with some relief, its humorous side becoming apparent. I no longer felt I had to explode water or pass out. My friends, not aware of the state of affairs, thought I had been arrested and became anxious. But why had nobody else but me thought of the side of the bus? Was the ground between the Soviet Union and China somehow sacred and averse to urine? I was further amused by feeling that I ought to keep in step with the soldier, who was small of stature by any standards; I am over six feet tall. His manner however was determined and brisk, and after marching along the road in step for some 100 yards he handed me over to a civilian. At this point I could only hope that the soldier passed on an accurate message. If he had not, then I would have no means of correcting any false impression than by the use of the most explicit and potentially dangerous sign language, dangerous, this is, in terms of being misunderstood. I thought of escaping and using one of the ditches at the side of the road, but I did not care for the thought of returning to the bus without that soldier, who would in any case be expecting me to return in the same company as that in which I set out.

We followed the road as it bent to the right, and ahead was a surprising sight. A large crowd of local people, old and young, 250 strong perhaps, had assembled to greet us as we arrived in China. They were aided and abetted by every conceivable kind of instrument, visual and audible. Dragons, flags, balloons, streamers, fancy dress, smiles, laughter, cheering, drums, tambourines and pipes, like a pageant or tattoo with all its colour and noise. At the sight of me and my companion, as we entered a lighted village square, all burst into a conflagration of noisy jubilation. Greeted now with abandon, I was poked and pointed at in an abstraction of good humour. Scarcely could they know about me and mine. It seems they had been waiting there for some hours, and in my agony I was seen as the promised harbinger of all the good to come. I smiled and waved in return as regally as I could in the circumstances. My companion led me through the crowd, jostling now to catch a glimpse of the round-eyed stranger, and turned right past a lighted, single storeyed public building into a field.

It had been raining. The ground was wet and the grass was long. I could see little but I could sense what my feet thought about it all. I was wearing running shoes, solely for reasons of comfort, having found them best of all when in doubt about what lies ahead when travelling. They were of course by no means waterproof. Mesmerized by now, I followed my leader as a duckling follows its mother. Twenty yards into the field, he spread his legs apart, pointed to a small stream beneath him, which I could just see but mainly hear, and made a gesture in the dimness which I understood unhesitatingly. Following his example, I spread my legs apart and placed one of them in the middle of the stream. Wet at once nigh to the kneecap, I struggled to right myself and became wetter still, indulging both kneecaps at the same time. Undaunted though, I balanced myself with some difficulty astride the banks of the stream, and had my most happy time in China thus far.

Why the stream and not the ditch by the road remains a mystery still. Unworried at last by such questions, and eager once more for the next adventure, I returned with the person I must now call a friend, across the field to the village square, where the crowd was still assembled but silent now. Thinking me gone for good and not expecting my return, they took not one bit of notice of my contented, relaxed stroll back through the square. Why so suddenly sent to Coventry? They merely looked through me, and I admit to being disappointed and disconcerted. They were not searching now for just a harbinger but the real thing, a group of round-eyed strangers.

I found my soldier without difficulty, got myself in step with him again, sloshing a bit the while, and reached the haven of the bus and my friends in due time. Applause and curious questioning now besieged me. The bus had moved forward not an inch.

All was not yet over; one final piece of bathos remained to be enacted. The buses advanced in file eventually, stopping short of the village. Our whole company this time strode into the melée. The exuberant display began a second time, and joy broke out on all sides. Amid the jostling throng we were led towards the public building, as I had been, and there because of an open door we expected something in the way of a reception, as had been the wont elsewhere. But, no; again we were led to the right and into the field of blessed memory, and then, blow me down, on a bit further, to a row of public lavatories. Of such are the Mysteries of the Orient composed. The place was called Korgas.

* * *

Only one more frontier crossing of any significance to me remained, and I crossed that one more than three months later, when I took a trip by bus from Tucson in Arizona to Nogales on the Mexico border. Meanwhile perforce I crossed others by aeroplane, from China to Hong Kong, from Hong Kong to Australia, from Australia to Fiji and from Fiji to the United States. With the exception of two minor escapades on arrival in Perth and in Honolulu, all proved to be ineffably boring, like any airport despatch and receipt anywhere, rigorous, tiring and without event.

Meanwhile I had something to puzzle over. It will have escaped the notice of no reader by now that I am emotionally attached to frontiers, especially, as an islander, when you can cross them on land. My story so far has been concerned with describing that emotion in terms of adventure, discovery and achievement. Nor, it will also have been noticed, do I mind spending time on frontier crossings, tedious though such a way of spending time may appear to others, as long as they have a story to tell which can shed light both upon what happened there and upon who the people were. That far I hope I have been as clear in my intentions as I am clear in myself. What puzzled me, though, was how it came about that some frontiers were patently important, a lot of effort being spent upon sustaining them, and others were not.

Superficially, a frontier's importance can be measured in terms of the time it takes to cross it. It took no time at all to cross from France into Germany, from Germany into Austria and from Hungary into Romania. On the other hand it took some two hours to cross from Austria into Hungary, and more than five hours to cross from Romania into Bulgaria, from

Turkey into the Soviet Union and from the Soviet Union into China. There are those who would argue that time taken is a function of whether you are dealing on the occasion of crossing with a communist regime or not. Accepting this argument to begin with, I came eventually to conclude that it was too simplistic an argument on its own. For again just on the face of it, the effect of communism by itself did not bring about the incident at Ruse, before Leninakan communism was not solely to blame for the fact that it was facing at that border a member of the NATO alliance, and the wait before Korgas one communist regime faced another, albeit where there had been disagreements, sometimes serious disagreements. Perhaps, I said to myself, I should argue that the Soviet Union alone, not communism, was to blame, even though our five hours before Korgas ought in justice to be split fifty-fifty between the Soviet Union and China. Not satisfied by the notion of blaming one side only, when on at least one occasion two sides were to blame, I decided to examine the possibility of the frontier itself being to blame — if in fact it was to be a matter of blame at all.

First, the frontier before Korgas is to all intents and purposes a new frontier. Evidence about the precise date of its establishment has eluded me. Following 'liberation' in 1949, the new Chinese government took some time before taking a firm decision about its north-west frontier. In 1955 it formalized the matter by setting up a provincial government at Urumchi, the traditional capital of Xinjiang (the region's name meaning 'a place where a revolt has been put down'), and gave the region the name, the Xinjiang Uighur Autonomous Region. By this act the region's frontiers with India, Pakistan, Afghanistan and the Soviet Union, if we exclude Outer Mongolia, became fixed, at least in practical terms. The varied nature of the new region's neighbours defines at once for us all how it is that the Chinese are sensitive about its security first and its prosperity second.

As things are, the two sides in front of Korgas face each other with armies. On the Soviet side one suspected, but could not always see, the full paraphernalia of a defensive system in depth, like that we have previously seen in front of Leninakan. The southern Trans-Caspian railway system ceases at Alma Ata, but roads up to the frontier are well-constructed and wide enough for two-way military use. On the Chinese side, it was at once apparent that the military were thereabouts in large numbers, military transport being frequent and by far the most common in the immediate frontier area. The railhead was at least sixteen hours' motoring away, on the other side of a formidable mountain pass at Shihezi, while the roads, particularly near the frontier, were in a very poor condition indeed, muddy, rutted and in many places close to impassable. The administrative capital of Kazakhstan in the Soviet Union, Alma Ata, a new, well-organized and beautiful city, is strategically close to the border; Urumchi, on the other hand, industrial and still beset with communication problems with the rest of China, is further off than Shihezi.

Han Chinese, by a new settlement, near the Soviet border, in Xinjiang

In view of all this, it was odd that the kind of people who entertained us in Pamphilov appeared on the surface to be just like those who welcomed us with such zest in Korgas. The joyful temper of both was identical. The area for many centuries in fact has been a melting pot for Kazakhs, Uighurs, Kirgiz, Tajiks, Uzbeks, Mongolians and many others. The fairly recent arrival of large numbers of Russians and Han Chinese, on their respective sides of the border, makes them for the time being interlopers, not least in the eyes of long-standing residents. (A delightfully made Chinese film, called in English *Yellow Earth*, which I saw in Sydney, makes a special point of this issue.) The influx of these new populations followed mainly as a result of the revolutions of 1917 in the USSR and of the years previous to 1949 in China. Before those dates there was a sense in which a frontier between the two countries did not exist; over the centuries people came and went as they felt inclined. In fact a static frontier could be said to have followed on from the coincidence of the two revolutions, and so to be a revolutionary frontier.

Previously, Xinjiang, because of its isolation and natural boundaries, desert on one side and high mountains on the other three, so similar in many ways to Tibet and Afghanistan, had been over the centuries a buffer between China in the southeast and the other countries on its other borders. Power and trade ebbed and flowed. The Silk Road was only a part of the ebb and flow. The Han dynasty, 206 BC-AD 220, the Tang dynasty, 618-907, the Yuan dynasty, 1271-1368, and finally the Qing dynasty, 1644-1911, all held Xinjiang firmly in their grasp, with long gaps in between when external influences encroached. The Uighur Moslems, for instance, infiltrated the area with some strength, mostly between the Tang and Yuan dynasties. Peter Fleming, in *News from Tartary*, brings the story more up to date by a description of the conflicting pressures in the region before and during his journey there in 1935. Han Chinese fought for and defended Urumchi against Tungan rebels from north-west China, the Chinese being subsidized by the Soviet Union, the Tungans always being able to fall back on Uighur support in the west and sundry White Russian refugees liable to complicate the issue at any time. Trade and the struggle for military dominance were the ugly sisters. But who was Cinderella? The hotel where we stayed during our first night in China at Inning, beyond Korgas, had been once an enclosed Soviet trading post (when I came to think of it, its architecture gave it away). The trade had been for centuries mostly in furs; the skins of unborn lambs were especially prized. With the passage of time the mining of metals and coal took the place of furs.

At base the frontier is a Chinese frontier. The Soviet Union might like to control Xinjiang, but does not really need to; the

Chinese, however, would become extremely vulnerable in their north-west if they were to let Xinjiang go. The largest of its autonomous regions, 11.6 million square miles in area, it is a powerful and highly significant buffer. Its population, thirteen million in 1982, continues to rise as more and more Han immigrants flow into the area, and because no limit is placed upon the size of Uighur families. Through irrigation policies, agriculture flourishes; wheat, corn, cotton, beet, grapes, melons, pears, apples, apricots and pomegranates as well as wool, skins, mutton and pork. Xinjiang's only weakness, given the Han Chinese recent but short-lived desire for racial harmony and cultural tolerance (an Uighur uprising is said to have occurred also in 1980), are its railways and roads. Both are being improved. Given the region's steady growth, anyone may guess what is likely to happen when the time comes for an efficient road and rail link at Korgas with the Soviet Union. If the frontier were to become a friendly one, I would suppose that the balance of world trade would alter drastically within five years of that happening.

Meanwhile the frontier is a strong one. Both sides recognize its strength, and recognize too its potential political importance in the years ahead. For the time being it has brought peace to a large part of the world's surface, a stable and not inflexible peace. There may be reason to doubt the quality of this stability for individuals at the moment; the standard of living on the Chinese side would appear to be low, but not desperately low, although well below that on the Soviet side. Stability, given potential for economic improvement, is however not to be spurned, certainly not by me; I would not have been able to journey there otherwise.

Arguments like these eventually convinced me that, before Korgas at least, the frontier itself was pre-eminently important, important before all else. Labels tourists choose to give as an explanation for what they see as their own inconvenience were, I concluded, at best misleading and at worst treacherous. I felt any discomfiture of my own assuaged by the thought that our five-hour wait in front of Korgas had been in a good cause. Long may the frontier continue, as long as its cause is peace and as long as things may improve for people under its shelter. A modest aim, but not for the present time a modest cause.

* * *

Something similar could be written about the Turkish-Soviet border. The security which that frontier affords to both countries now, faced with armies though they are, must be a profound relief after all the centuries of murder and strife the area has endured. For example, the late Roman Republic in the first century BC was forced to seek protection thereabouts for its new rich provinces further west. Names like Lucullus, of luxurious fame, Pompey the Great, and Mark Antony feature prominently in the military history of the region now held by Turkish and Soviet armies. At that time known in broad terms as Armenia, the area produced local specialities like apricots and sweet plums, which Lucullus introduced to his prolific kitchen back home in Italy. One hundred and fifty years later, the region was still cruelly unsettled, and the emperors Hadrian and Trajan tried once more to pacify it by their presence, much as they did in troubled Britain. Armenia, at crossroads for invaders of many varied nationalities, between the Black and Caspian Seas, mountains and deserts, never found peace and security in this world, whereas after discovering a devout Christian faith of their own in AD 301, Armenians became secure in the promises of the next.

Invasion and counter-invasion were never novelties. When the Ottoman Empire joined the Central Powers and went to war against the Allies in 1914, Imperial Russia invaded Eastern Anatolia and took the town of Kars and its surrounding area. In 1917, Kemal Mustafa won it back again as Russia weakened. By the Treaty of Brest-Litovsk with Germany in March 1918, Russia regained the area lost to Kemal but relinquished it once more in 1921, when the present frontier was established by the new Turkish President, Kemal Ataturk, and the new Bolshevik government in Moscow, along the line of the River Arpa and its confluence with the Araxes.

Thus did turbulence settle and peace begin. The immediate cost? The disappearance of Armenia as a separate entity and of most Armenians as inhabitants of the area. Modern maps mark neither Armenia nor former Armenian cities and towns, other than the part of it which is the Soviet Republic of Armenia. This tragedy, aided and abetted, it must be said, by the machinations of perfidious Albion, whatever its final details might be, genocide and massacre still being resolutely denied by the Turks, was probably a necessary precursor to the peace now established. As Christians, the Armenians, living in a part of Eastern Anatolia, were inevitably identified by the Turks in imperial times with Christian Georgia and Christian Russia. Religion had been the very stuff of the long-term quarrel between the Ottoman and Russian Empires, focussed mainly in the Balkans certainly, but fatally articulate also in the area where large numbers of Armenians lived and flourished in Eastern Anatolia.

One further point. If there had not been security on the Turkish/Soviet border in these days, what might have been the consequence now for the large area to the south, at the time of writing either mainly at war or partly at war, and so for the world at large? I for one do not begrudge the five-and-a-half hours we spent in front of Leninakan, for they were both a tribute to peace, at least on that frontier, and a remembrance of others long dead.

* * *

What happened in Perth and Honolulu need delay us little. Both arrivals were by air. In Perth, at six o'clock in the morning, I was away from all controls early on. Because I had decided in Hong Kong that the exchange rate there, especially at the airport, was exorbitant, I had no Australian dollars with me. Perth International Airport, some fifteen kilometres from the city centre, was fully open for the first time that morning, and, unexpectedly, no bank was on hand for the exchange of money. I was thus forced to search for a taxi with only Hong Kong dollars in my pocket to pay the fare. My explanation of the plight I was in received brusque rebuke from a husky Western Australian taxi-driver; 'No, I can't do that, mite; Hong Kong dollars are not hard currency, and it's the weekend.' Which it was. Hard cheese, I thought.

At once a man of slighter stature, from India as it turned out, approached and said, with a smile and a world of confidence in me and my money, that he would take me. His taxi was just there.

A splendid drive up to and over the Swan River was enlivened by our conversation. I had told him that one of my main reasons for visiting Perth was to watch England play cricket. He said we would be passing the 'WACA' (Western

The City of Perth, Western Australia, from the river front

Australian Cricket Association) where they would be playing, and he would point it out. He himself had played for the State of Karnataka in his youth long ago, and was still devoted to the game. We had no trouble finding topics to discuss during the rest of our drive; we moaned together about the same sort of things. And so it was that I came to count my good fortune in having only Hong Kong dollars on hand with which to pay my fare; he took them, it must be said, with every apparent confidence in their hardness. It is true; you never know your luck.

The moral for strangers in Honolulu is, 'Take it slowly, if you can.' If you do not, something is sure to swallow you up; if not that, you will be bound to depart earlier than you arrived. First, your plane lands some distance from all the rest of it, and without your baggage, you have to queue for and board a strange thing called a wiki-wiki bus, which races round and about for ever (ten minutes, that is), and then compulsorily disgorges you at a spot you know not where, presently to find the airy barn where your visa documents and your passport are to be checked. Inevitably there are long queues of others ahead of you, and because they are made up entirely of Japanese who know no English, your progress towards the desk seems painfully slow. At six thirty in the morning, with a plane to catch for San Francisco at eight twenty-five, you wonder what your chances are; they do not at first appear to be at all good, but they are much better than you think.

Eventually released, your next task is to search for your baggage. You have two worries; for not only has it not yet arrived on the specified carousel (some roundabout, this one!) but also you do not know by what means you can get possession of one of those trolleys, all chained in their hundreds to a special taxi-rank of their own. The second worry is resolved first. You are instructed in plain English to place a single dollar bill (lucky you have one) face upwards in the required space. You view the instructions suspiciously. Incredibly, the dollar bill is accepted by the machine with a mechanical readiness which to you is uncanny (an important lesson, this, for all first time travellers to the United States), and a trolley is duly released from its bonds, for your own special, personal use. Lo and behold, your baggage is on hand too.

Impressed but not yet at ease, you are thirsty, still lost and in a whirl. Passengers plainly go that way, and you meander after them, unsure and with a new kind of wariness. Rightly so. Within an ace, your baggage is seized from your trolley (was it worth that dollar?) and pushed down a chute and so gone for ever. You ask wanly where it is going to, and they say casually and cheerfully, with the utmost confidence, 'San Francisco'. You wonder how they knew that was where you wanted it to go. Might not this be how people and baggage get separated so commonly, you ask yourself. What if I had been going to Los Angeles, or even Detroit? Never mind, not now anyway.

You have your flight number, and it features on the signposts. It is not easy however to penetrate the maze ahead of you; 'inextricable' scarcely goes far enough. I can't remember now with certainty, for it was all so hectic and traumatic at the time, but I regard it as almost certain that we caught the wiki-wiki again, and so must have been similarly disgorged once more. For sure there was ordeal by escalator and travelator. For some reason unknown to me I reached the correct departure lounge, with a lavatory and a drugstore close by. Breathless but relieved and no longer thirsty, I checked the time on my watch and on the departure lounge clock. They both agreed. It was only ten minutes past seven.

My baggage duly arrived in San Francisco, frightening me greatly by managing to be gouged out last from the entrails which had failed to digest it. You can get twenty-five cents back by consigning your trolley to any neighbouring trolley taxi-rank.

* * *

The frontier between Nogales in Arizona and the town of the same name in Mexico was to teach me a final lesson. Arriving in Nogales by bus from Tucson, after a splendid drive through desert and between dry, rocky hills, not far in desert terms at one point from Tombstone, I was briefly at a loss to find my way out of the dusty bus station towards the crossing point. The herd-like movement however of a Sunday morning crowd, in private cars and on foot, led me quickly southwards towards the sun — by now climbing just beneath its high noon. Several lines of cars were passing through barriers like those erected ahead of toll-bridges on French and Italian *autostrade*. A single line of pedestrians filed snake-like past groups of guards, the first dressed as Americans and the second as Mexicans, without let or hindrance, or even a stare. Suspicious of this degree of licence and anxious about being able to return the same way before the day was out, I volunteered myself for my own passport inspection, Her Britannic Majesty's edition being something of a rarity thereabouts. The United States guard to whom I offered myself gave me and my passport a cursory glance, and with a smile said, 'All OK, buddy. Return any time.' I gave my shoulders a mental shrug and with the others followed the sun's glare into an immensely busy street, squeezed now into Mexico without ceremony.

The change, in terms of noise, bustle, goods for sale, housing, family life, numbers of children, and, above all else colour, was immediate, and as sudden as a blink of an eye. In addition, on a Sunday morning many go to church but most Americans in Arizona, it seemed, cross the border into Mexico to enjoy themselves, to spend money, to bask beneath a different sun, and to have no trouble at all in doing it. It was like Brighton, Southend or Manly, on any sunny, summer Sunday, and like Brighton, Southend and Manly, free, undiscriminating, and immensely popular. Except it was Mexico.

I enjoyed it; Tucson would be rather a dull pond after this. I confess however to my customary disappointment. The frontier, like that between France and Germany, was not a frontier at all, except in form. I had heard and read quite a bit about the Mexican border, its sensitivities and how its policing by the United States was akin to a tiresome chore. In Nogales neither policing nor tiresome chores were at all in evidence. Other than at the official crossing point only a wire barrier separated the two countries; even I could have scaled it, electricity apart, had I wanted to.

On leaving Nogales that evening, our bus, crowded this time with all and sundry, proceeded on the return trip without hindrance until some fifteen miles out, when it stopped and a US control officer boarded it and inspected our passports. All were in order, and the delay lasted no longer than ten minutes.

It was clear to me from my day in Nogales that the US border with Mexico is not strictly policed, in that area at least, and also that, if I personally wanted to enter one day the US on my British passport without fuss or delay, I would be well advised to consider Nogales as my point of entry. Honolulu after all had been more than a bit stressful.

* * *

What lesson then do I draw from this frontier, which is not a frontier except in form, and from all frontiers, like or unlike? Merely this: if the US, or any other country, does not wish to have illegal immigrants crossing a border, then it needs to enforce the policing of its frontiers with a vigour and strictness like that which I witnessed elsewhere. I imagine the local arguments in favour and against both propositions are many and complex, and I am in no kind of position to make any judgement about the respective merits of such arguments. Nevertheless, each frontier has an argument of its own, and its essential substance is patently clear; where there is an imbalance, one way or the other, of whatever kind, the frontier acts like a membrane, by osmosis attracting the weak into the territory of the strong. Osmotic pressure is wont to be relentless without the imposition of an artificial blocking device, separating the weak from the strong.

When the early settlers in the outback of Australia put up fences, they kept their cattle in. At the same time, by doing this, they also kept aborigines out, aborigine Australians who were bound in terms of their cultural inheritance to wander wheresoever they wished. From such procedures do frontiers derive their origin; from such procedures may the rights of possession become dangerous. The philosophy of the fence is the philosophy of the frontier. Islanders like me are merely lucky to have the sea, and not a fence as their frontier. But, my word, fences have their uses in our present, old-fashioned world, even though I remain unsure about their old-fashioned morality. I for one would not do without them; their neglect may be perilous, until such time as we become a great deal wiser than we have been.

3

Railways

In all I crossed fourteen international frontiers. Five of them involved crossing a sea, on each side of which there were naturally control points. Except for the English Channel, I crossed all these seas by aeroplane. A sixth frontier, that between China and Hong Kong, albeit over land, was also crossed by aeroplane. Between the Soviet Union and China we used a bus. All the others, that is, eight of them, were crossed by train. I estimate the mileage covered by aeroplane was in the region of 14,000 miles, and that covered by train in the region of 11,000 miles. The travelling time by aeroplane was thirty-two hours; that by train was close to fifteen days (I do not include in this total the time taken and distance covered by my many side trips in the course of my main journey west to east; I have counted direct journeys only). We travelled thirty-six hours by bus.

I have enumerated miles travelled and time taken in this potentially tiresome way, because I wish to associate what I have to say in this chapter directly with what I had to say in its predecessor. Just as in the case of frontiers the time taken to cross them was for me the basic criterion for enabling me to decide on their significance and their interest, so with my travelling. In going round the world as I did by the means which I chose to employ, I spent far more time travelling on a train than I did in any other way. On my particular journey, in terms of time taken, travelling by train was for me far more significant and far more interesting than any other means of travel I made use of, except perhaps for walking, and I did little of that apart from walking to and from train stations as a direct part of my journey.

I do not know for certain, but I daresay that a journey round the world by air alone could be done in less than forty-eight hours travelling time. As a consequence, as a means of travel, since it is the quickest available, by my criteria, air travel must always be less significant and less interesting than any other method for the traveller in the course of travelling.

By arguing in this way it does not mean that I cannot see the advantages of air travel for those doing business, for those wishing to see relatives and friends, for those eager to visit strange and exotic places and if, in addition to speed, you also wish to travel economically. Air travel is pre-eminent under such conditions. Your reasons for travelling decide for you whether you are a traveller or not. Chris once said to me, 'The journey is the main thing.' If for you the journey is not the main thing, and you have other main reasons for travelling, you are no traveller other than in a superficial sense. If however the journey is the main thing, and all visits you make alongside your journey merely added bonuses, however valuable, then, like me, you can at least begin to claim the title of traveller. The rest of your entitlement is made up of enjoying what you do.

Buses have a strong case, as my statistics show. Other than bicycles and pedestrians they are the slowest of the lot, and would have cause to feel offended if left out of any consideration. However, though willing to grant them their due and rightful place, they fail to satisfy my tastes. If I enjoy travelling by train more than I do by bus, then by train I will go, the difference between the two, statistically speaking, in any event being in favour of the bus but not decisively so.

So it is that railways above all else become the concern of this chapter. I enjoy using them much as I do crossing frontiers; both give me time to contemplate where I am, what I am doing, what kind of companions I have and what I may be doing next. In this respect an opponent might argue that railways are no different from frontiers, and I do not need both a frontier and a train; one or other would do.

Not so. The best way to cross a frontier is by train, and in order to cross a frontier by train you need both a frontier and a train. Indeed, at the point of crossing, both make the whole, each for the enjoyment of the other, the train fitting the border crossing as a hand fits a well cut glove.

A glimpse of this interrelated enjoyment was given in the last chapter. I shall always remember the speechless pleasure I experienced as our Turkish train drew away from Kars that early morning and aimed eastwards towards Leninakan and no less our gentle, slithering departure from the Soviet frontier platform in a new train into a new land. However well or badly I told it, that to me was the perfect story, setting out, enduring and experiencing, and in the end arriving. By no means is it better to travel than to arrive, because a traveller is continually being renewed by a new arrival, is always on the edge of drawing close to a destination.

As an example of this process of continual renewal, I take what happened to us after we left Leninakan. Already we were alive with the freshness of it all, our compartments, our more sturdy, harder bunks, the clean but abbreviated linen and, perhaps most specially, Nadia, our conductress, a lively, smiling person of slight, comely stature, welcoming us aboard her domain as though we were already one of her own special possessions.

We soon discovered an unpromising defect; she was not good at lighting fires. Russian trains, at least those we became acquainted with, were heated by coal/coke stoves in a small closet at the end of each coach, the conductor or conductress being responsible for its efficiency as a heating device. Soon after we left Leninakan, smoke began to filter along the corridor and into our compartments. It did not take long for it to be billowing everywhere, grey and smelling like coke. We coughed, and some became anxious about their enfeebled bronchial tubes. Nadia was not only called Nadia for a space. We were all forced to engage ourselves in dangerous combat with the sliding windows in our compartments. They were stubborn about sliding, as you might expect sliding windows to be when constructed in the German Democratic Republic: stubborn, that is, to open and then stubborn again to close. To wrestle or not to wrestle was the question. Outside as it grew darker, the air acquired an autumnal nip to it, and the train, now travelling at a decent speed north-east towards Tbilisi, blew the nip inside into our faces if the window was open, and Nadia for her part billowed smoke everywhere if the window was closed. Not for the first time, or the last, did windows bring us to the horns of a dilemma, and quite sharp they were for a time. Like most crises on a train this crisis abated. We managed to close the windows, and began to enjoy the snug warmth of our compartments as the smoke died down. Nadia came along to ask if we were all right. We were, we said. She knew no English and we no Russian, but *Khorosho* always proved very useful, as far as Nadia was concerned. It was so much better than being on a bus. You could not have Nadia or her doings on a bus.

Nor could we have had the next bit either.

We had been assigned 'third sitting' for lunch. As the time for dinner approached — we were over five hours late, it will be remembered — expectations grew great and became greater still, as we noted the expressions on the faces of those returning from 'first' and 'second sittings'. Optimism and appetites soared. What was in store?

Jogging and bumping along the corridors and across the jagged metal gaps between coaches soon became for us part of our expectations. Our appetites grew larger still, as balloons might, blown nigh to bursting for a party.

It was dusk and the lights in the dining car were startling and bright. The silver plate cutlery shone, the white tablecloths reflected the glare. Fresh, autumn flowers in tiny vases winked at us, pretty tokens on top of tables laid for four, laden now with caviar, smoked fish, bread, butter and bottles of vodka and champagne — and glasses, many of them. The dining car attendants, already with two sittings behind them, smiled, welcomed us and then laughed with gaiety and pretended surprise as they saw our eyes sparkling in anticipation — and the sudden pleasure we had. Our welcome to Romania was delightful and enjoyable — and I feel nothing but gratitude to our Romanian friends — but our welcome aboard our first Soviet train on the way to Tbilisi was astonishing. We were taken by storm and by surprise, and the response to our surprise was a glittering enjoyment, which counterbalanced it to perfection. A new country, and now, in the microcosm of a dining car, a new world, created by those who waited at the door of it. Everybody broke down and became themselves, intent on enjoying whatever was to happen. The dining car attendants, by means of hard work and ebullient friendliness in setting the scene, were the springs from which all else sprung. Of that none had any doubt. They were lovely people.

Corks popped, bottles were opened, and bottles were broached. It was then that a form of greed took over. It was not your ordinary, mean, underhand greed, your stridently obvious, gluttonous greed or your gross, self-satisfied, self-centred, bulbous greed, but a joyous greed, a happy greed, a greed you could share, a greed you knew you had in common with others and a greed that did not seem at the time, or has seemed since, to have been a sin; those who ministered to us were in no way subservient or slavish or sullen or grudging. Instead, in an entirely open and extrovert manner, they took part in our enjoyment and did all they could to increase it and improve it. If you combine laughter and happiness with greed, what do you have? Is that pure greed, do you think? If it is not, what is it? What can it be which melts into gratitude as soon as all greed is gone? No ordinary greed, it seems to me. Hospitality and the notion of being a guest have something to do with it. The attractiveness of the room and the people, their responsiveness and their happy carelessness, other than in the interests of their guests, created what was for me a new vice, which I sometimes, now within the promise of my eventual maturity, think of as a new virtue. What is it if you satisfy yourself and know that everybody else is satisfied too? Being a person? Loving? Not a virtue after all. I began to think that I was falling in love with Russia. Why do we call it Russia anyway, when it is so much else besides?

To follow the caviar and the fish, they served us chicken soup, steak and chips and fruit (the grapes were especially good) as well as keeping our glasses full and their cheerfulness brimming. We became rowdy, joyously rowdy. The evening star was a happy, buxom, red-headed lady, dressed in waitress white. She, even above the others, attended us with such abandon and such carefree, incomprehensible, endearing loquacity that we shall remember her for what she was and what she did that evening for ever.

That evening went on a long time. The 'third sitting' for lunch must surely also have been its 'triumphal sitting', we felt so splendidly victorious. And all on a train, you see.

We drew into Tbilisi not quite our former selves, transformed and a little dowdy. It was after midnight, and the station to begin with seemed gloomy and too silent, except that near the opening leading into the place where you buy tickets and wait, there was a group of men, some twenty strong, assembled in three rows, the back rows on benches. As we trooped along with our baggage, curious but no longer sprightly, the group burst out upon their instruments and began to play. At their head was a tall lady, of a studious, even scholarly mien, who was conducting their song with strictness and with immense authority. Her beat stood well above their shoulders, you might have said. The full meaning of the local music they played was quite beyond us, but the meaning of their intent, so late of hour and so inconvenient of arrival, was moving well beyond my capacity to provide words for it. Down the years memories flooded back of Russian music in wartime — there was a small elderly man with two rows of medal ribbons on his chest in the front row of the band — in concert halls and on recordings. Now, on a platform on Tbilisi station, they had waited some five hours for us, just so that they could provide a welcome in sound, rounded, serious, melodic and accurate, as it could be no other beneath the baton then. Their concert ended, our applause concluded, we trooped off again towards our buses, changed and grateful anew, sober now. Yes, I was beginning to fall in love with Russia. Or was it more strictly Georgia?

The next thirty-six hours in Tbilisi were to me a series of revelations, and most of what they revealed to me is described more appropriately later on. However, something was to disturb me towards the end of our stay there, which affected me throughout our stay in the USSR. Strangely it caused me to fall in love even more. It relates to greed, and so to my description of our reception in the dining car on our first evening.

We had had a bus trip on the morning of our second day out into the lower Caucasus, and we were being entertained to lunch most agreeably at an Intourist restaurant among the hills. The rumour spread among us that there was to be no booze on the train we were to catch that evening, and so, if we wished to take precautions against that critical eventuality, we should secrete about our persons and in our hand-luggage such liquid as we might want from the tables in front of us — they were laden much as their predecessors had been on our first night. Herdlike, and unaccountably apprehensive for no reason other than a rumour, many of us, including me, hid away a bottle or two of wine as insurance against our fears. It was nonsensical to imagine that those serving us in the restaurant would not have noticed what we were about. They did, but we supposed otherwise.

Priggishly you may think, in due course I became ashamed. What I and others had done was patently a poor response to all the hospitality we had been shown in Tbilisi and its environs thus far; everyone had been treated with generosity and friendliness throughout, give or take a few tired waiters and waitresses at breakfast time, who had earlier been working well past midnight on our behalf, for little reward, one would guess. My shame then begat a further thought; there being no reason to suppose that we as visitors in their land were other than typical, what opinion could our hosts now be holding about us, and our like? We had enjoyed the food, drink and service since our arrival on as liberal a scale as no ordinary Georgian had ever seen, let alone partaken of. What could they possibly think both at the point of my remorse, and if we include the churlishness and ill-manners which would surely eventuate among us in due course? For some of us assuredly thought from the start that Soviet waiters and waitresses everywhere ought properly to behave exactly in the same way, for all their oddities, as those who wait on us in the West End, Bel Air or Rose Bay. Might they not in return despise us as uncouth barbarians, see us as merely typifying capitalist boorishness and, at the best, just think us discourteous and ill-mannered. I do not know for certain what they actually thought about us. One or two gave us clues, by behaving towards us as we did towards them. I believe I am right; many of them despised us, and for good cause in their eyes.

I am conceited enough to think that I learnt a little from my remorse, and discovered that a 'please' and a 'thank you', however self-consciously uttered in their language, if combined with a smile and some show of consideration, gained a counter-balancing response — just like that we had received on entering the dining car with such pleasure on the first evening. I take the risk in writing as I do here of being charged with hypersensitivity, and even with gratuitous obsequiousness. I reject the charge.

That evening, the band with its conductress had returned to the station, and played their farewells to us in the chilly air, with the same care and zest as when we had first heard them.

At the same time Nadia paraded up and down the platform, smartly accoutred and wearing red, high-heeled boots. We admired her. Her fellow conductresses on the other hand were grouped around, discussing her, as she passed them by with her nose tilted slightly upwards. They disapproved of Nadia. We were to find out why. We had not seen or heard the last of her.

Incidentally, booze abounded in the dining car over dinner that evening.

* * *

Parsee fire temple outside Baku — fire from oil discovered long ago

The following morning, scenery and weather changed radically. Having travelled south-east overnight, through the eastern part of Nagorny Kharabakh, I would guess, we woke to find the sun rising, into a cloudless sky on our right. We were travelling north. There was now no risk of mist or fog. I believe it was my first sight of true desert, though, as it turned out, not a typical one. Amid the sand dunes, in the distance making themselves into hills among the rocks, were long slithers of placid water on both sides of the train. Presently the long, low level of the Caspian Sea crept towards us, smooth, Cambridge blue on the flat shores of the golden desert. Not just a single railway line now nor a double one, but four or five or six amid points and sidings. Then, to begin with, one by one, and later by tens and twenties, oil rigs on the edge of the sea, and inland too, where there were lines of water still. It was glaring and brilliant and bright. I guessed that the sun, though still low in the sky, was warm, and would be hot. We were moving more slowly now. The tracks became complex in their relationships. The oil derricks multiplied. We could see clusters of them out at sea, near the glittering horizon, the sun across the sea. We drew into a habitation, no, a city, no, a large city, no, a huge city with widely scattered housing, built on sand, rocks and oil, and by the sea. The train had brought me at last to a land beyond my cultural inheritance. Here I knew I might get lost. In Baku. In Azerbaijan.

Disembarking was a scramble, and we arrived at our hotel in some confusion. This was soon sorted out, and my room six floors up had a lovely view over the Caspian and a huge municipal square, oil rigs visible on the horizon and a wide bay swinging to the north. Unreasonably but without hesitation, I was reminded of Thessalonica with oil rigs. The Caspian and the Aegean have much in common on a calm, warm day. Unpacking the overnight section of my baggage, I was disconcerted to find that my shaving kit together with my spare wash-basin plug was missing. Allowing myself the customary period of panic, believing indeed that *all* was lost, I remembered what had happened. In my haste while organizing my departure from Compartment 5 and from Nadia — who had been found sound asleep in her cabin that morning, still somewhat the worse for vodka — the bag containing my shaving kit had slipped to the side and fallen under the opposite bunk. I had omitted to pick it up and replace it in my case. And so there it was still, on the train in Coach No 8, Compartment 5, under the left-hand bunk — for sure and nothing clearer. Was it thus that leaving behind my cultural inheritance would become dramatized, I asked myself.

A speedy survey of the hotel shops revealed as a fact what had been thus far a suspicion — no razors, no razor blades and no shaving cream. A beard then, further to dramatize the unavoidable? Quickly discarding the thought as personally repulsive, I approached the reception desk and spoke about my problem, rather easier to explain without giving offence than a full bladder. I was received with charm, delightfully spoken English and a great deal of help. A local guide was at hand. He had no English but had my problem, slight and so silly, explained to him. He offered to go back to the station and to retrieve my belongings, if the train was still where we had left it. I was at once impressed by his willingness, and tried to show how grateful I was to him. Off he went.

Within an hour he had returned with my shaving kit and wash-basin plug intact. Nadia had been just a little obstructive, not feeling too well I would guess, roundly maintaining that she had searched all compartments for items left behind by careless passengers. Nevertheless my new and pertinacious friend went to Compartment 5, looked under the left-hand bunk and found what I had said would be there. He was delighted by his success, and I was immensely grateful not only for his kindness and willingness but also for brooking no nonsense from Nadia, not easily done.

Thus it was that the local guide and I became firm friends. We would have a good laugh together about it all even now, if we were to meet again. I am still grateful to him. Whenever he saw me in the next twenty-four hours — shamefully the full extent of our acquaintance — he would wave and grin, and whenever I saw him, I did the same. The sun shone upon a wholly delightful incident. I was more careful too about my shaving kit thereafter. I was advised to give him no tip, for he would be offended.

Thus, confident in my fate, I made a determined attempt that evening to get lost. We had dined well some distance from the hotel, seated at low tables and scattered around various small rooms, which encircled an ancient Islamic courtyard, which in its turn was part of a caravanserai long ago. The rooms were at two levels, inside and outside, elegant and sturdy, with shallow pointed arches — a vital part of old Baku at the end of a caravan

Caravanserai in Baku like that used as a restaurant by us

trail. Intourist's planning in arranging this event, albeit providing fare quite unlike that in quantity and quality which Marco Polo ever met up with, caused me to reject the idea of driving back to the hotel by bus, and to say that I preferred to walk. No-one else wishing to accompany me as a guide, I set out on my own.

By now it was late, and dark. I thought that all I had to do was to keep the Caspian to my right, and all would be well. I had no idea however how far we had come from our hotel before dinner, and was fully aware that the Caspian would turn out to be a large sea, if for some reason early on I missed the large municipal square. The streets were deserted and the street lighting was to begin with dim. The sea was hidden from me by public gardens and a wide esplanade to the right. Though certain, I became step by step uncertain. The street I was bound to follow was long and straight. There was no sign of light ahead, and all turnings to the left led into further darkness. No, I could no longer be confident about where I was and the direction I should follow. Irrationally stubborn now, I kept on and on and on, pondering the means whereby I might regain my hotel without remembering its name. I did not even have with me one of those little maps they give you at reception when you hand in your key; our hotel still retained the guardian ladies on each floor who kept the key for you there, issuing no maps. As I became miserable at the thought of being lost in Baku without resource or a word of any substance, the road I was on came to an end at an unpromising T-junction, branching left and right. Turn right, I said, which I did. Then I became alert once more, after drooping a bit. The building now on my left looked subliminally familiar, but was not lit up as a hotel would be at home, even at the back. It was however tall and new. I decided to follow the building round its limits to the left, and, lo, a restaurant all aglow, a stop or two more to the next corner, and there, a resplendent, rather magnificent surprise in the floodlights, the municipal square. I had just been round three sides of our hotel, damn it. Now I remembered; its name of course was, not unnaturally, Hotel Azerbaijan. From such forgetfulness do small adventures derive. Baku was so quiet that night that racial and religious violence was unthinkable.

* * *

We flew next morning to Bukhara. I was sorry to have missed crossing the Caspian by boat and the Kara Korum desert by train. It was said that shortage of time, not the proximity of Afghanistan, was the reason. Then, on by train to Samarkand first, and to Tashkent after. Soviet railways made a thoroughly good impression, though we arrived early in Samarkand and late in Tashkent. The service offered was charming throughout. It was a pleasure to travel by train in the Republic of Uzbekhistan.

* * *

As already described, buses took us into China. Our first close glimpse of China railways was on a warm, sunny afternoon at Daheyon. We had driven there by bus from Turfan, an oasis

Our new Chinese train, waiting for us at Daheyon

in northern Xinjiang, through desert hills — except for Grape Valley, where the grapes were sweet but otherwise tasteless. Already waiting for us, our train was a solid, stately affair, externally speaking, dressed in dark blue/green with yellow lines. Conductresses wore trouser suits of a paler shade of blue. Our hosts in China were in fact China Railways in its tourist manifestation, and they made a thoroughly efficient and friendly job of it. Personnel appeared to be entirely Han Chinese, ever agreeable and ever smiling. We were to spend about thirty-six hours aboard, two nights between Daheyon and Lanzhou, with a day off in Dunhuang en route, and a further night and morning between Lanzhou and Xi'an. Unfortunately, we were forced to pass the western end of the Great Wall during the second night, and so were unable to catch a glimpse of it.

My compartment on our Chinese train

Our time on China Railways has for me two memories of differing substance. The first was the unanimity of our surprise at the Victorian elegance of our sleeping arrangements. Those attending the Queen, if not Her Majesty herself, would not have been dissatisfied. On sliding open the compartment door, first to catch the eye was a delicately laid table by the window, a white table-cloth edged with lace, cups and saucers, teapot, hot water jug and tea caddy in white china figured in the same blue as that worn by the conductresses, a bowl of fruit, apples, pomegranates and grapes and a table-lamp with a blue decorated shade. The window had two sets of curtains, the first made of net to shade the sun, and the second of blue velvet. The leading edges of the bunks were trimmed with lace, as were their backs when in use as seats. There were four bunks in all, though only two were to be used by us. On the floor was a large thermos flask of hot water. In the background were a looking-glass and dark wood panelling. If named 'soft', the class was also luxurious. The bunks were wider and longer than any others encountered before or since. The only drawback, at least for me, proved to be a persistent draught at the lower corners of the window, which both sets of curtains failed to staunch. The only solution for me was to place one of my two pillows thereabouts, to keep my head from chill while I slept.

Second, between Daheyon and Lanzhou, we crossed large tracts of the Gobi desert, usually between jagged, tall, remote, desolate mountains. With high cloud around but sunshine illuminating irregular patches of gold, the colours we saw were so tasteful in their matching shades and tones in contrast, never in excess, harmonizing a distant, dun-like classicism. Sights like these led me to count the blessings and detachment of a train. I recalled too Marco Polo's account of a similar stretch of country, and how different our perceptions were.

'The desert, that is, the Gobi, is reported to be so long that it would take a year to go from end to end; and at the narrowest point it takes a month to cross it. It consists entirely of mountains and sand and valleys. There is nothing at all to eat. But I can tell you after travelling a day and a night you find water — not enough water to supply a whole company, but enough for fifty or a hundred men with their beasts. And all the way through the desert you must go for a day and a night before you find water. And I can tell you that in three or four places you find the water bitter and brackish; but at all the other watering places, that is, twenty-eight in all, the water is good. Beasts and birds there are none, because they find nothing to eat. But I assure you one thing is found there, and that a very strange one, which I will relate to you.

'The truth is this. When a man is riding by night through this desert and something happens to make him loiter and lose touch with his companions, by dropping asleep or for some other reason, and afterwards he wants to rejoin them, then he hears spirits talking in such a way that they seem to be his companions. Sometimes, indeed, they even hail him by name. Often these voices make him stray from the path, so that he never finds it again. And in this way many travellers have been lost and have perished. And sometimes in the night they are conscious of a noise like the clatter of a great cavalcade of riders away from the road; and, believing that these are some of their own company, they go where they hear the noise and, when the day breaks, find they are the victims of an illusion and in an awkward plight. And there are some who in crossing this desert have seen a host of men coming towards them and suspecting that they were robbers have taken flight; so, having left the beaten track and not knowing how to return to it, they have gone hopelessly astray. Yes, even by daylight men hear these spirit voices, and often you fancy you are listening to the strains of many instruments, especially drums, and the clash of arms. For this reason bands of travellers make a point of keeping very close together. Before they go to sleep they set up a sign pointing in the direction in which they have to travel. And round the necks of all their beasts they fasten little bells, so that by listening to the sound they may prevent them from straying off the path.

'That is how they cross the desert, with all the discomfort of which you have heard.'

A more modern account, written in English 600 years later by two missionaries, Mildred Cable and Francesca French (*The Gobi Desert*, 1942, Hodder and Stoughton, London), is just as vivid, though in a different vein, and I daresay more to the modern reader's taste. They write: 'The Central Asian trade routes are busy thoroughfares where they link large towns, but narrow to a mere track where oases are few and small. Water can be depended on at each stage, but the size and character of the halt is variable, as is also the amount of water available, and its quality. An inhabited oasis may consist of a few shacks, it may be a fair-sized village or it may even be a large town. Occasionally there is nothing to be seen but the circular mouth of a well near which a landmark is raised lest it be missed by the traveller.

'Man has a passion to conquer the unconquerable, and that great natural defence called Gobi (Wall of Spears) had by some means to be surmounted. Lack of water was the main problem, so ancient diviners brought their skill to bear on the question. The possible daily stage for a man or beast to walk over loose gravel or shifting sand was tested and found to be twenty-five to thirty miles, and it was with this in mind that wells were dug and springs released. Whenever the trek was more difficult than usual, by reason of bad road-surface or rising hills, the stage was shortened and the well dug a little nearer. In a few cases however the divining rod failed to respond, so to this day the traveller still has to negotiate the double stage before he can water his beasts. Centuries come and go but the traffic of the desert path is still the same as when the oasis-makers plied their craft, and whether it be camel, horse, donkey, cart or foot travel, three miles an hour is the accepted pace for the traveller as he crosses the desert.

'It is difficult for the Westerner, accustomed to the tempo of modern life and the conditions of its civilization, to adapt himself to the simplicity of this caravan life which has remained untouched by the pressure of mechanical transport. Yet once he is committed to it he inherits a freedom which he has never known before. His mentality is released from the tyranny of a timepiece with its relentless ticking, and from the dead reproach of its neglect. The flickering needle of a speedometer is not there to urge him to greater effort, and there is no concentration on speed as an objective in itself. He has ample time for observation and nothing of interest need escape his attention. This is the place for talk, and no desert wayfarer is jarred by the annoyance of a hurried companion, nor delayed by the slackness of a fellow-traveller. The human body, having found its natural swing, becomes strangely unconscious of itself and releases the mind to its normal function of transmuting incident into experience. These are conditions in which the wayfarer becomes, according to its own measure, an observer, a philosopher, a thinker, a poet or a seer. He learns to be independent of the calender, for the moon is his time-measurer. He has no road map, but his course is true, for the stars are his guide. The tent which is his dwelling goes where he goes, and compels him to a simple rule of life. In bringing his pace down to desert standard he finds that in all worthwhile things he is the gainer, and that his loss is entirely in the realm of the material, the temporary and the ultimately insignificant. Sometimes the thirty-mile tramp brings him to the centre of a stony plain where there is no vestige of vegetation and no visible means of sustenance for any human being. Such land offers no protection, and the blizzard sweeps over these plains with terrific force but even here there will be a small house built from stones which litter the ground and always just outside the inn is the opening of the well, the water of which, though unpalatable, is life-saving.

'In other places there are sand-mounds and the track among them is wide and ill-defined, but at the end of thirty miles it narrows suddenly to a short street between two rows of houses and for the space of 150 yards the traveller is in a village. Then comes the illimitable plain again, and the widening road spreading itself across it. In that street there is probably one small spring which has been carefully cleared and is kept free of encroaching sand. From its small basin a tiny streamlet runs with a steady trickle to a larger basin, the border of which is trodden by the feet of beasts. This is where the animals are watered while man drinks at the upper pool.

'Overlooking each desert well or spring is a mud shrine which holds a small clay figure wrapped in a little red cotton shawl. This represents the presiding genius of the water-supply, and on either side of the shrine are pasted a few strips of red paper written over with ideographs which ask that the blessing of heaven and earth may rest on the water. In the little mud pot which stands before the figure there is always a pinch of incense ash left from the offerings of passers-by.'

I have read somewhere that the word, Gobi, is Mongolian for 'emptiness' or 'desert'. The missionaries however spoke fluent Chinese, and will have known about the meaning of Gobi in that language. Small unresolved difficulties like this one are as nothing beside the ardours of desert travel in former times which the missionaries and Marco Polo list — uncertain roads and tracks, uncertain supplies of even poor quality water, a lifeless and unaccommodating terrain, habitations widely scattered, spare in terms of their sparse resources, daily treks of thirty miles or so, and extreme discomfort in whatever type of transport you were forced to select. There were always present too the psychological dangers of tiredness, delusion and threat of robber bands.

Pre-eminent however among the advantages of such travel was its slowness, enabling time for contemplation and observation, and the opportunity for self-discovery and for an encounter with a sense of proportion.

Travel of this kind, which can reveal more than can be seen, in the manner in which the missionaries and Marco Polo undertook it, is now almost a thing of the past. A network of roads at the rim of desert terrain had made the old villages and settlements accessible by motor vehicle and by cart, drawn, be it said, at hectic speed by horses and donkeys. These roads, though narrow, are all paved and are becoming of more than passable quality the nearer central China you get; some are being widened and made more direct with the symbolic cutting of corners. There is no longer a need for caravans and camels, and we saw none. Indeed the only camels we saw were in use near Dunhuang as tourist attractions. Those who use roads, as we did when travelling by bus, travel now as fast as they can, often at much more than thirty miles an hour, let alone a day, and are buffeted along roughly with continuous rattling and jolting, racing side by side with others who wish to go as fast as they do. Not unusual was an overloaded van upturned at the road-side. The paved road which has replaced the caravan trail is no place for contemplation or self-discovery, only self-survival, and that precarious, we were sure from time to time.

The train alone, with its sense of isolated detachment from the real world beyond itself, can provide the traveller with any chance at all of pondering upon his journey, its nature, its history and the quality of what is seen and felt inside and outside himself. For sure, we saw donkeys drawing heavily loaded carts at full tilt across deserts on roads beside our track; for sure, we saw the ancient settlements where the caravans used to halt, and where there is now in addition a petrol station; for sure, we saw caves scattered on the side of tufa-like escarpments, where villagers and hermits used to dwell and still do; and, as our train drew itself like a snake onwards, for sure, we sensed the distances and the immensity of it all, which mechanical change has altered for ever. I suspect it is only on a train, albeit unlike those of old, in comparative comfort, that a traveller can any more sense the magnitude of the past achievements of other travellers, and in addition, unlike them, delight in the colours of the stable, classical, desert scenery and the ultimate dryness, bounded only by distant hills and jagged, snow-capped mountains. I was grateful to the train, which like a camel enabled me to live within myself, and I was grateful too that I could still draw upon the truths which the desert and the camels used to teach with greater certainty than they do now, but which otherwise we would be losing in their totality. My gratitude was my second memory.

* * *

I had to leave the train for air travel in Xi'an in Central China, and did not pick it up again until I reached Perth in Western Australia.

Arriving in Australia I had perforce to relinquish the special privileges of travelling by chartered train, where the train waited for you, and not you for it, where you always had a seat or berth, and where meals were prepared and served regularly and without stress, except among those who prepared and served them. In Australia I would be prey to all perils of travelling by train which flesh is heir to. No longer among the privileged in the level world of communist utopias, now I would be the equal of my brothers and sisters: like them I would have to fight my own corner or be left behind. I had been lucky, or wise if you like, in the essence of it all, and purchased an Australian Rail Pass before I left England. This pass entitled me to first class travel on all lines managed for Railways of Australia within a three-month period. In addition to the main national system, my pass also allowed me to use all state railways and local transport in all major cities, except, for a reason I shall presently explain, Adelaide, where I had to pay on public transport as ordinary mortals do — on the spot. Similar passes can be obtained at similarly advantageous terms for both bus and air travel in Australia, but my own preference for travelling by rail made the possession of an Austrailpass, as the Aussie obsession with abbreviation prefers to put it, was sheer delight. Only the cost of meals and a sleeping berth were charged in addition.

One of my prize souvenirs of my journey is the surviving remnant of my rail ticket from Perth to Sydney on the *Indian-Pacific*, a journey in itself of some 2,500 miles. We set off from Perth at nine o'clock on a Sunday evening, and were to arrive in Sydney, after three nights on the train, at four o'clock on the following Wednesday afternoon. My plan had been to catch the six o'clock out of Sydney for Brisbane in order to be there by Thursday, where the first Test Match was due to begin at the 'Gabba' on Friday. Having watched the Englishmen play abysmally against Western Australia at the 'WACA' the previous week, I was anxious to reach Brisbane in time so that I might make proper propitiation there for the six days ahead. If that could be done, an improvement might eventuate for the Englishmen during the Test Match. I continually wished to play my part, you see, as one of their supporting protagonists, pouring libations in due proportion with proper ceremony as each struggle for the Ashes began.

Prophecies of doom among those Australians who had been my companions on the train journey to Xi'an, and who like most of their compatriots had their own peculiarly idiosyncratic view of society and its reality, foretold that my belief in rail travel would be shattered for good and all soon after I put my beliefs to the test aboard Railways of Australia. Industrial action was the main danger; you could be halted by a strike in the middle of the Nullabor Plain for days on end for instance, and the only compensation for such an event was that local inhabitants from all around, not many of them to be sure, would all assemble at the train in sympathy, and at once call into being the most enormous party, which would last for as long as the strike did. The other danger was unpunctuality; if you wanted to reach a destination by such and such a time, do not, for heaven's sake, go by train. Why they said either of these things, I don't know. The truth is, in three months experience of Australian railways, no strike occurred anywhere, and all trains left on the dot and arrived similarly — except once, that time on the 'Indian-Pacific', when punctuality would put my religious observances at risk.

Early on the Tuesday morning, out of Perth and by now well beyond the Nullabor, and close to infamous Woomera, the intercom burst in upon my drowsiness and said, in that flat, amused Aussie way, 'Good morning to you all, ladies and gentlemen, on this dull and gloomy morning at Pimba (pause), South Australia (pause). You will have noticed that we have been at Pimba for some time, two hours in fact. We have just a little problem. Ahead of us, a freight train has been derailed, and we can't get by it until they've moved it somewhere else,

The *Indian-Pacific* stopping at Cook, half-way across the Nullabor Plain

and that I am afraid will take quite a while. We on Railways of Australia are sorry about this delay, and we are sorry too that it's such a dull morning. But no problem; enjoy your breakfast, which is now ready for the 'first sitting'.' By habit, I was 'third sitting', and I always did enjoy it: fruit, eggs and bacon, toast, marmalade, desperately sweet, and coffee. But he was wrong, you know; there was a problem. On present form, two hours late already on Tuesday, we would surely miss our train out of Sydney for Brisbane on Wednesday. There were forty of us who wanted to catch that train out of Sydney, and none for better reason than I did.

Those who plan these things had put together a well-constructed plot of growing tension. To save time, we did not pop down to Adelaide and back from Port Pirie, but waited there at the junction for the Adelaide section to join us, passengers for Adelaide having special arrangements made for them, a laudable device on the part of the administrators. In due course the *Indian-Pacific* was made whole again and we set out across the corn fields of South Australia for Broken Hill in New South Wales, where we should have arrived at dinner time, 'third sitting', but did not reach until I was well asleep, at midnight. We were still seriously late and well behind schedule. All the following morning and afternoon anxiety among those bound for Brisbane flourished. The *Indian-Pacific* had no further delays however, making good time mile by mile, and I spent much of it dreaming beyond my window frame, among some delicious countryside, predominantly farm land, gentle hills and flooding streams, for by now it was raining hard following our cloudy wait at Pimba. The Australia of my schoolboy geography books became alive again, sturdy cattle and sheep, wheat, barley and oats, and, most glorious of all, gum trees and gum trees, in groups, in woods and in forests, rugged gum trees with their tinkling leaves and their patterned trunks, dead gum trees, fallen gum trees, stretches of purple-flowering Salvation Jane amid yellow grass and yellow flowers, homesteads in elegant, traditional 'colonial' style with gracious verandas, and no longer aboriginal names like Rawlinna and Tarcoola but, to a stranger, reassuring, homely English and Scottish sounding names like Ivanhoe, Parkes, Orange, Bathurst, and Lithgow, towns that were lived in, you could see. Just one thing; the rain was not in the geography books.

The *Indian-Pacific* reaches Parkes in New South Wales

At Lithgow, it was announced by our friendly intercom, news could be given about our prospects of catching the Brisbane train. All were agog at Lithgow. No news at Lithgow, but reassuringly contact had been made with Sydney, and the position would be clarified presently. No problem. The position was in fact clarified at Katoomba, in aboriginal nomenclature again, amid the Blue Mountains. The Brisbane train would be held for us at Strathfield, out of Sydney Central, at the junction where the lines split north and west. Relief and abundant smiles all round. Baggage was made ready for a hurried exit. And then, for the last time, out of the Blue Mountains 'We are sorry, ladies and gentlemen, the Brisbane train will not now wait for us at Strathfield. Railways of Australia will accommodate passengers bound for Brisbane tonight, free of charge, at the Southern Cross Hotel, close to Sydney Central Station. Arrangements will be made for all passengers in Sydney; ask at your friendly service desk at the station. No problems.'

As a matter of fact, we passed through Strathfield twenty minutes after the *Brisbane Limited Express* had left it. The Southern Cross Hotel, in rain such that only geography books could fail to give account of, proved to be a desolate affair. I left for Brisbane next morning by air. Otherwise I would have been late for the performance of the rites I had in mind. I still however retained my belief in travel by train, and had no further cause to have it shaken in any way at all.

* * *

The line from Perth to Sydney, and then on to Brisbane, was completed in 1917. Before that, Western Australia, for good reason, had always felt cut off from the newly-founded Commonwealth. The threat to secede from that Commonwealth before 1917 persuaded politicians that a land transport link between Perth and the rest of the country would help to diminish that threat — which it did. Instead of the unattractive alternatives of either having to cross a vast and formidable desert or taking a still dangerous and lengthy voyage across the Great Australian Bight, Western Australians should have made available to them a further choice of a train journey, romantically taking no more than six days to complete, from coast to coast — a choice which quickly proved to be not only the most convenient but also the most profitable; goods as well as people could be cheaply transported by train. The full breadth of Australia was to be opened up.

There was one handicap, or rather five of them. The States of the Commonwealth had for long developed in their own way, preserving their separate freedoms to do as they chose without let or hindrance, the ultimate base of the 'fair go' philosophy. Part of this freedom was to choose, according to their own lights and economic needs, their own kind of railway system, and, worse for Australia as a whole, their own railway gauge. The growth of the railway systems in the late nineteenth century was of necessity, in view of the so-called tyranny of distance, haphazard. Victoria, resplendent in the wealth derived from mining especially gold, chose 5'3", the most expensive of all at £12,500 a mile. New South Wales chose what has since become known as standard gauge, that is, 4'8½", at cost in 1910 strangely in excess of that paid by Victorians, £13,500 a mile. Pay and difficulty of terrain were no doubt important factors. The states which were not so well-off economically trailed behind. South Australia, for instance, wishing to establish as close a link as possible with neighbours in Victoria, built the inter-state line on a 5'3" gauge, but internal lines on a 3'6" gauge, at the reduced cost of £5,800 a mile. Similarly, Western Australia, Queensland and Tasmania also chose the cheapest gauge. Thus, judgements about local economic needs led in due course to a radical and potentially disastrous handicap for any national system which a politician might wish to advocate.

Narrow and standard gauge tracks in Western Australia

As a result, the first trans-continental line had as its base, 3'6" gauge from Perth to Kalgoorlie, standard gauge on the new line opened in 1917 from Kalgoorlie to Port Augusta, 3'6" from Port Augusta to Adelaide, 5'3" from Adelaide through

87

Melbourne in Victoria to the New South Wales border at Albury, standard gauge again from there through Sydney to the Queensland border, and 3'6" again as far as Brisbane and beyond. Frontiers between States in 1917 were no joke either. I have to concede that I would have enjoyed them.

There were thus five handicaps, five breaks in gauge, between Perth and Brisbane, impeding the passage of goods, delaying and seriously inconveniencing passengers. For a time it was taken as all part of the fun, and as in the United States, it was a romantic thing to do, to cross a continent from ocean to ocean.

It was not long however before wiser, more practical and more expensive counsels prevailed. A new line on standard gauge was built from Port Augusta, by-passing Victoria's 5'3" gauge, through Broken Hill in New South Wales to Sydney, eliminating at one stroke the breaks caused by different gauges in South Australia and Victoria. The standard gauge was then extended from Kalgoorlie to Perth, and from Sydney to Brisbane, leading in this way, for people like me, to what is the present heaven — all the way from Perth to Brisbane on the same gauge, having to change trains only once, in Sydney. If you like, you can extend your journey by waiting a couple of hours for a freight train to get back on the rails again at Pimba. Most of all this endeavour had of course to be limited to a single track. Standard gauge has more recently been extended from Port Pirie to Adelaide, so that the *Indian-Pacific* may now also call in at another State capital on its way.

It is at this point that I can briefly explain why my Austrailpass did not suffice on public transport in Adelaide, when it did everywhere else. Australian National Railways, the organization responsible for the inter-state system, manage all railways in South Australia, and have special arrangements in other States with State railway companies, by which they may have access to State-run railways for inter-state trains. All States other than South Australia manage local transport, as well as railways, under a single transport authority. Australian National Railways run railways in South Australia as far as Kalgoorlie and Broken Hill, and a separate transport authority manages local transport in local communities. And so it was that I had to pay my own fare on the lovely old tram from Adelaide to Glenelg, and back. What a delight to pay it was! The slatted wooden seats, the old-fashioned wooden-framed windows, raised and lowered by old-

The Glenelg Tram

A corner of old Adelaide

The *Australind*, the small-gauge train for Bunbury from Perth

fashioned leather straps, caught upon a metal stud by a notch, according to taste — such as not seen in the UK for some thirty years or more, the background delight being the background Edwardian atmosphere — like much else in Adelaide, a lingering and deeply-set atmosphere, carefully nurtured by those who live there.

From Perth a line leads south for some hundred miles, to the small, scarcely flourishing, country port of Bunbury. Austrailpass enabled me to make the journey, on the old 3'6" gauge and in a train which was in its smallness like a toy, except for its diesel engine, which was vast, angular and orange. *Australind*, for that was the name of the train, was cream and green with tiny arched doorways. To begin with, I thought *Australind* was a girl's name, but, since the line ran southwards parallel to the Indian Ocean, I decided the name had to be yet one more abbreviation. Pastoral scenery, on gentle slopes as the land declined towards the west, was overshadowed in the east by the dark green hills of the Darling Ranges, disfigured from time to time by quarry scars, first inflicted long ago but extended still.

The Rose Hotel, Bunbury

Bunbury, scattered now with prosperous bungalows well beyond the patch selected for the first settlement, must once have been a small struggling place, dependent on mining and agriculture for such prosperity as its harbour could garner in. Now, it flourishes like many an Australian township, having become a comfortable place to retire to, and one in which to make wide roads and to build houses appeared to be the main industry. For me, on my day visit, its main attraction was its *Rose Hotel*, on the corner at the crossing of two main streets, and its elegant iron-work veranda on its two main sides, a gracious shelter from the sun overhead for pedestrians beneath and for those above who had rooms on the first floor. Behind the veranda was the angled architecture of a London Victorian pub, on any street corner in Wandsworth or Hackney. Behind the swing-door was to be found a splendid counter lunch, grilled flounder, potatoes, salad and white wine. No worries at all in Bunbury for me.

The Freemason's at Toodjay

Nor either in Toodjay. On another day, I took Westrail's *Prospector* on the line towards Kalgoorlie as far as Toodjay, sixty miles inland from Perth. I loved Toodjay, as I came to love many a small Australian agricultural town; two pubs in Toodjay, the *Freemason's* and the *Swan*, and in truth the lunch at the *Swan* proved less appetizing than that at the *Rose*. But the sun, the light and the air outside were vintage stuff. The breadth, the freedom, the grass, the gums and the flowers, the quiet, the people pottering slowly about and a presidential peace were for me in another time. Settled sparsely in the early 1850s, groups of families built farms and prosperity in a wide, rolling countryside, beside a rocky stream at the origins of the River Swan, I began to learn in Toodjay that my affection for Australia would lie mainly beyond the cities, in the gentle, hot countryside, so succulently enjoyed and lovingly painted by those great Australians, Roberts, Streeton, Conder and McGubbin at a time when its beauty finally dawned on the white man's eye. The

Prospector travelled on the standard gauge, but a third line made 3'6" still available.

Tranby House, up river from Perth, built in 1839, remaining as furnished by the original family, the Hardeys from England

At the end of October I took the train from Adelaide to Alice Springs on a relatively new line fitted to the standard gauge. Formerly on a 3'6" gauge, the *Ghan*, as the train is still called, travelled due north from Port Augusta beneath the Flinders Ranges by way of Maree, and then north-west across rivers and beside lakes, on a more direct route than that which the new line follows from Tarcoola west of Port Augusta, tracing the line taken in pioneer days on the backs of camels, as the centre and north of the country were opened up on the way to Darwin. The camels were imported in large numbers from Afghanistan, as also were Afghan camel-drivers to drive them. The camel-drivers are no more, but the memory of their caravans survives in three ways: Afghan date palms can still be seen flourishing beside desert streams; herds of camels range wild over the desert countryside, put out to graze long ago when machines supplanted them; and the train to Alice Springs is called the *Ghan* after the Afghan camel-drivers.

I never saw or walked the length of a longer train than the *Ghan* — sixteen full-sized SNCF-type passenger coaches, two or three coaches for mail and packages, and a number of trailers at the rear for private cars and other vehicles. Rounding curves, the train was ponderous and made progress scarcely above a walking pace; on the straight however, once clear of Tarcoola, it rattled along at a good speed, swallowing flat land as though it were a thin soup. The journey from Adelaide to Alice Springs takes twenty-three hours nearly to the dot.

The old *Ghan* took three days, winding its way north-north-west. If there was rain and flooding, bridges would be broken and lines cut, and the journey could take much longer, the train isolated from all outside contact for extended periods. Australians loved the feelings of adventure, romance and comradeship of the old *Ghan*, and the new one is for them a poor thing in comparison. The new *Ghan* runs but once a week, a second train being put on during the winter months in order that holidaymakers may escape winter mildness in the south for the heat of the centre. Nevertheless, for economic reasons, even the new *Ghan* is under threat and may be abandoned for good in the name of speed and tarmac, cheaper alternatives.

Accommodation on the *Ghan* was similar in every respect to that provided on the *Indian-Pacific*, sleeping berths and food being an additional charge upon bearers of an Austrailpass. £25 seemed to me to have been more than a reasonable price to pay for a single first-class sleeper, together with lunch, dinner and breakfast (*Indian-Pacific* charges were comparable). The food, be it said, was not exciting; plainly cooked, adequate in quantity, and with the kind of choices that are available on any sensible table d'hote menu, meals had for me only one handicap — insufficient roughage given the needs of the human lower intestine and the inactivity consequent upon lengthy journeys by train.

Service was prompt and cheerful, and early in the morning over the intercom, too cheerful. For those of us who come from the backwoods of the Old World, to be served by somebody, man or woman, whose self-image is unchallengeable, and who believes that Jack and Jill are as good as their masters and mistresses, is as refreshing as drawing clear, cool water from a deep well. If your standards in respect of things like dress, speech and education are as good as any body else's, then you see no need to be grudging or churlish in what you do, to say 'sir' or 'madam', or to accept tips. One reliable way of being able to judge the underlying rules of any society, I would say, is to observe first of all the ways and means of those who serve you on a train. I found this to be particularly valuable in Australia, where in addition, I suspect, those who served us were well paid. And why not, mite? The service we received on trains in Romania, the Soviet Union and China, for instance, was similar in standard to that received in Australia but of a different quality; above all else, the underlying rules of social relationships are of prime importance in assessing quality, which is not always a matter of good and bad, and, in particular, those who served us in those other countries were not well paid. Examine the service on British Rail, and see if there is not some truth in what I say.

A single 'roomette', as it was called, on both the *Ghan* and the *Indian-Pacific* turned out to be of exceptionally high quality. A wide and comfortable bunk, aligned in the direction of travel at night, turned into an armchair with a foot-rest by day. Upholstery was a peaceful blue — none of your strident British Rail orange here. Space for baggage and toiletries was more than adequate. Every form of ablution, other than a shower, was available on site in stainless steel, mechanically and hygienically sound in every respect. You could take a hot shower at the end of the corridor. I had only one reservation on the *Indian-Pacific*; bunks, still warm from overnight, together with mattresses, bed linen and blankets were turned round into armchairs in the short interval while you were at breakfast, and the bunks, mattresses, bed linen and blankets were still warm with the heat of the previous night when they were opened up again the following evening. I would suppose that such enduring warmth in cramped conditions alongside the absence of any airing at any time during a long journey would have some risk attached to it, hygienically speaking. Further and oddly, 'roomettes' between Melbourne and Adelaide, on the *Overlander*, were less comfortable with a wider gauge, 5'3". This was unexpected; perhaps they crowded more of us into the larger space.

For reasons of economy, no doubt, Australian National Railways have forsaken in Perth, Brisbane and Adelaide the shelter of mainline stations built by the State railways in their early days, their ownership in other hands also being a handicap, I suspect. At Perth the inter-state terminal is now a mile or two from the city centre, a modern tower-block with offices as well as standard gauge and a platform large enough to accommodate the *Indian-Pacific*. In Brisbane for similar reasons the new station where the standard gauge comes to an end is half a mile from the old Central Railway Station. It lives alongside shops and below a large, well-accoutred modern hotel, convenient, if expensive, for those who travel by train. Cheaper by half would be an old Victorian-styled inn across the road. In Melbourne and Sydney inter-state trains still arrive where they always did, at Spencer Street and Central Stations respectively; it is at these places that you can still sense the old thrill of having come a long way and of having arrived at the centre of the purpose of it all, your destination. At Adelaide, whether you arrive from Melbourne in the south-east, or from Port Augusta in the north, your final stopping place is more than a mile from the city centre to the south-west. To be sure standard gauge and 5'3" gauge had to be built as though for 'through' trains, and for trains as lengthy as the *Ghan* and the *Indian-Pacific*, and a clean, low-lined, concrete affair is the result. Arriving there and departing from there is an ascetic, unemotional experience, all in order, taxis and buses duly at hand, commodious and like an airport. And what a pity, you have to remark to yourself beside your patriotic taxi-driver! Passing around the perimeter of the city, along West Terrace and onto North Terrace, you finally catch sight of the old Adelaide Railway Station. None of your run-of-the-mill, modern, prosaic stuff, but an apotheosis of railway stations, pride, confidence, elegance and sensitivity, all concentrated near the banks of the River Torrens, looking across the water to parkland, gardens and the distant terraces and verandas of North Adelaide. If you want to have a clear idea of both the importance of railways to any country in the world in, say, 1880, and also to be aware of the importance of just being alive at that time, if you were white and Australian, go to Adelaide, look at its old central railway station, and swallow it if you can. (Disregard by every effort available the monstrous but oh, so cultural Festival Centre between you and the river. Difficult, but it can be done.) The station façade faces east towards Government House, no slouch either, to be sure, and is seen at its best with morning sunlight upon it. Built of local dun yellow stone, it has the Palladian style and detail of Buckingham Palace, but a quite different effect on its locality, closer to that of the club house of the Royal and Ancient at St Andrew's, patrician and decisive, warm and welcoming, presiding over its own space, and entirely agreeable in its loftiness. In these days the old station still handles local services, but it also houses shops, boutiques and, the ultimate solecism, a casino. One has to admit it; railways in Australia like railways in many other countries paddle about in the backwaters of today's world, counting for little, forever in the suburbs of not only its cities. Adelaide, no different, has followed suit. For me, while shrugging my shoulders with regret, I shall never erase from my imagination a nostalgic wish that I had been among those who, fortunate long ago, had been able to arrive in state in gracious Adelaide beside the River Torrens in the shelter of a charming, palatial building, whose welcome it kept warmly within itself, and whose world looked neither forward nor backwards, content to be what it was.

I admire St Pancras, I continually mourn the absence of Euston, I gape at the gorgeous grandeur of Teutonic Haydarpasa Station across the water from Istanbul at Scutari, I become excited beyond my habit at either the Gare de l'Est or the Gare de Lyon, but give me first, and first of all, the quiet solemnity of the old station at Adelaide, South Australia. There it catches

About to depart from Haydarpasa Station

the throat to wonder at our human past, the way we were then.

The railway station at Bunbury is now also in exile outside the town, as it is too in Alice Springs.

There was one defect on long-distance Australian trains that I feel I should comment on. If your compartment is situated in the last four coaches of a long train — and I found this usually to be the case as far as first-class passengers were concerned — and the train has cause to halt either at a station or for some other reason like a wounded freight train as at Pimba, then the coaches at the rear first jolt powerfully, and then shudder to a stop sharply and decisively, whatever the speed the train has been previously running at. It is as though the application of brakes further forward takes no account of rear coaches having a momentum of their own, which causes them to bang backwards and forwards as brakes are applied elsewhere. The compensations for this particular nuisance are not many, especially if you should be sound asleep before the first bang impinges upon your consciousness. There is one, however. Before any long-distance Australian train sets itself in motion again, a short admonitory blast is blown on its whistle, or whatever electronic device passes for a whistle these days. A second or two later the train creeps forward once more, and once more the rear coaches are smitten by an initial sharp jolt, and then by extended judderings. At least it is good to be forewarned that jolts and judderings are to be served out.

* * *

I have written nothing so far in this chapter about the quality of travel as far as wheels running over tracks are concerned. Buses have a clear disadvantage here in comparison with trains; they are unable to be selective about the kind of track they need to run on. In essence, the relationship between tyre and tarmac is a compulsory compromise. On the other hand, trains have their tracks made for them, and no compromise is in theory necessary. Agreement is assumed. Should this not be so, then the ordinary passenger, first or economy, notices the fact at once; the track becomes a liability, not part of the initial agreement. A bad track is never a good track.

Trains from Vienna onwards, through Hungary, Romania, Turkey, the Soviet Union and China, travelled at no more than a steady speed, and slowly round every curve. No train put any track really to the test, and passengers travelled comfortably throughout, at least as far as the track was concerned. Australian trains, longer and heavier, travelled on the whole at the same steady pace, reaching speeds of more than sixty miles per hour, I would guess, only on the long straights (for instance, we drove 300 miles straight over the Nullabor between Haig and Ooldea). Track engineering also seemed to be of a high standard as trains climbed over and down the Blue Mountains, and on hilly terrain, punctuated by rivers, between Sydney and Brisbane.

Only once did I feel that the tracks we were travelling over were of a seriously inferior quality, and that was in the USA, between Pomona, California, and Yuma, Arizona, either side of the crossing of the Colorado River. It was not because of our thoughts of adventure and romance that no-one slept that night; we were buffeted around, sometimes with excruciating suddenness, and then with persistent regularity; a bumpy ride, to be sure. I had my head banged three times. With the coming of desert once more and straight lines, peace descended again.

However, we arrived in Phoenix, Arizona, breathless and exhausted.

* * *

My first contact with Amtrak in the United States, in San Francisco, whither I had flown from Honolulu, was however of quite a different kind. Just a telephone call, and all was arranged: a seat booked to Los Angeles, for a week later a first-class sleeper from Los Angeles to Tucson, two days later, similarly, from Tucson to New Orleans, and finally, three days later, a seat booked from New Orleans to Atlanta, where I was to arrive the day before my flight home departed from the airport there. All this rigmarole was arranged with care and clarity on the telephone; all I had to do thereafter was to collect the tickets from the Amtrak office, and pay, which I did the next day. Thus, a train journey of some 2,500 miles, with three sets of overnight stops, was arranged without the slightest hitch or hindrance. I was impressed beyond measure, and indeed all turned out to be as it was said it would, on time to the dot throughout. I travelled two nights and four days in all.

The *Sunset Limited* arriving in Tucson for New Orleans, my baggage in the foreground

I took the *Coast Starlight* from San Francisco, or rather Oakland across the Bay, as it turned out, to Los Angeles. The *Coast Starlight* had come overnight from Seattle, near the Canadian border. Trains, other than those for commuters, no longer arrive in San Francisco, and so it was necessary to catch a bus at the Trans-Bay Terminal in Mission Street for Oakland, where a huge train, grey, white, red and blue, arrived at eight forty-five am from the north. I had not expected the train to be organized like a double-decker bus, twice as high as a train normally is and, thank goodness, not as long in proportion. As I was only travelling to Los Angeles by day, I had a window seat on the upper deck; down below were washrooms, further seating accommodation, space for baggage, and one or two specially reserved single compartments. This arrangement, you will realize, needed exploration, and I spent a happy half-hour finding out where I was and what to do. By the time I thought of breakfast, we had passed Jack London Square and were well down San Francisco Bay opposite Palo Alto and Stanford University, and on the way to Silicon Valley and San Jose. Eventually I found myself sitting in the 'diner' as we passed through Gilroy, which my admirable 'blurb' said was the 'garlic capital of the World'. Briefly I pondered upon the origin of that ever-present, often pungent, war-time graffito, 'Kilroy was here', and decided that Kilroy was in fact Gilroy, understandably trying to disguise his odiferous ancestry. Having previously come across no better guess, I ordered bacon and eggs, and felt good.

From Oakland to Los Angeles the tracks followed the same route as the old Spanish mission road, El Camino Real. From 1769 to 1823, Junipero Serra, a Franciscan friar, founded a chain of twenty-one missions and four mission chapels along the road from San Diego to Sonoma. Each was built to be one day's horseback journey from the next, dry hard country still. After passing one of his missions at San Luis Obispo, the old Franciscan journeying south would have caught sight of the Pacific Ocean again, and been flabbergasted these days at his first view of the US Strategic Air Command's Western Missile Test Range, Minutemen galore and Satellite Launch Centers too. The other oddity would have been the presence of gum trees, imported from Australia after his time, to hold the sand dunes and enormous beaches together, I would guess.

As the afternoon declined, the air became white with sand

Mission Church, Carmel, California on the El Camino Real

and spray, while the ocean tumbled ashore with long-range ferocity. I thought of Francis Drake, and how small my journey was compared with his and his crew's. There was no road hereabouts, and only the train for its travellers provides these views, and these thoughts, and the time for them.

Another importation from Australia was an enormous Moreton Bay fig tree, planted in 1877, to be seen on the left while halted at the station at Santa Barbara. It is said that at noon more than 10,000 people can stand in its shade; I wondered how they knew. As the sun set, islands on the horizon became silhouetted in black astride the sea, Santa Rosa and Santa Cruz, and Santa Catalina, too. In the dark we passed through Oxnard, along the San Fernando Valley, passed the Lockheed headquarters at Hollywood-Burbank Airport, Glendale, and wearily at last drew into the Union Passenger Terminal at El Pueblo de Nuestra Senora de la Reina de los Angeles. Sally and Don were waiting.

A week later, thoroughly rested in their company, having caught the famous *Sunset Limited* at ten fifty-five pm from Los Angeles, I woke up in Arizona, in desert country again, reaching Tucson at ten thirty am.

Two days later, I rejoined the *Sunset Limited* and took train through Arizona, New Mexico and Texas. On crossing the Rio Grande we entered Texas in the late afternoon of the first day, and began to sense the approach of a big city. At this point, a leisurely but firm, southern, black voice said over the intercom, 'May I have your attention, please, ladies and gentlemen? This train is about to approach El Paso, Texas. This train is about to approach El Paso, Texas. Before we reach El Paso, Texas, I want to give you all a warning. When we reach El Paso, Texas, the train will stop there for forty minutes. When we reach El Paso, Texas, the train will stop there for forty minutes. You may get down from the train at El Paso, Texas, and walk as far as El Paso station, which you will see on your right. You may walk as far as El Paso station which you will see on your right — but no further. Do not walk outside El Paso station. Do not walk outside El Paso station, I repeat. The train will wait at El Paso station for forty minutes. If you are late getting back to the train, the train will leave without you. I repeat, ladies and gentlemen, if you are late getting back to the train, the train will leave without you. Do not walk outside El Paso station. The train will wait at El Paso station for forty minutes only. If you get off the train and you are late getting back to it, the train will leave without you. You have been warned, ladies and gentlemen.'

Readers, like me at the time, would not wish to be wearied further. I can scarcely believe it at this range, but the announcement was repeated in similar terms and at similar length on three more occasions. Indeed the train had been halted, deliberately I concluded, overlooking a precipitous bank on a long, long curve, so that the full impact of all four announcements might have no likelihood of going amiss. What is more, the voice became increasingly more deliberate, more assertive and more dire on each occasion. When, after an hour we eventually did stop at El Paso, I did not even dream of walking outside El Paso station, nor have ever dreamt of doing so since, as far as I know. I do not believe that anybody else did either. Thus do we become socially conditioned. Incidentally, El Paso proved to be undergoing a cold spell so cold that, having hopped down onto the platform, I hopped back up again, in just the time it takes to make two hops. We didn't lose a soul, thank goodness.

El Paso station is by the way listed in the national Registry of Historic Places, having been designed by the same Chicago firm which had designed Washington's Union Station. Personally I shall not forget it for other reasons.

I had earlier thought of staying a couple of nights in El Paso, but had been advised against it — fortunately so, for it seemed from the train to be widely scattered among the dry Franklin Mountains, and to be of a grim aspect. Its hotels and restaurants had no superficial appeal. Even the neighbouring Mexican city of Cuidad Juarez failed to offer enticement, astride its lengthy hill-top. It was bitterly cold in any case.

Although the station at El Paso would form for me no part of it, a study of Amtrak railway stations, in general and in their modern manifestations, would be a fascinating one. I was able in fact only to lick the surface of one or two of them. Oakland was ordinary beyond no comparison; Los Angeles was delightful, and fittingly a tasteful blend of Spanish and Art Deco styles; Tucson, though larger, enabled me to feel I was playing a part on the side-lines of the station featured in *High Noon*; New Orleans was new too, large and spacious; and Atlanta I saw in the dark, being some way from the city centre, my hotel and its own taxi-rank; my shoulders still recall the fifty-step staircase, up which I had to manhandle myself and my baggage.

'The sun is 'riz, the sun is set; here we are in Texas yet.' The *Sunset Limited* travels 941 miles across Texas, from El Paso to Orange, where it crosses the Sabine River into Louisiana. We left El Paso close to six pm; after dinner in the 'diner', I slept until we had passed San Antonio, the Alamo, and a station said to have had a mission-style exterior, echoing the Alamo's silhouette, while its interior boasted of a 'gilt and polychromed barrel-vault ceiling and broad black marble staircase'. I regretted missing all this as well as our descent from the high plains onto the moist flatlands; the Texas I saw was green, fertile and, in parts, lush, except of course for Houston. I regretted too that Houston did not come as a surprise. The sight of the city's glamour, a sight so common that all the world can recognize it, is now so familiar that it is only momentarily exciting. I was pleased to be able to drive round the centre of the city in a train. (Did you know, by the way, that 'glamour' is really the same word as 'grammar'? It is linked too to the earlier word 'gramarye', used in Shakespeare's day to mean 'occult learning, magic, necromancy'. If you did, might you not think, like me, that glamour, made popular, was more dead than alive?) Even on a dull, cold afternoon, Houston was plainly alive, colourful and graceful. We reached Orange twenty hours after leaving El Paso, 941 miles later.

And so to Acadia, founded by French Canadians, exiled by the British from Nova Scotia after their defeat at Quebec in 1759, their descendants, the Cajuns, giving the whole area a specially Gallic type of culture. And so, fittingly, on to places with names like Lafayette, and Lafitte, Andrew Jackson's piratical supplier at the Battle of New Orleans in 1812, and finally, in the gathering gloom, to the Mississipi River.

It was time about now for a curious spell of schizophrenia. On the one hand, I was thrilled and delighted to see at last the cypress swamps, the graceful plantation homes amid the trees, the wooden houses on stilts, all the traditional sights of the Old South, and, too, the industry, the commerce and the shipping made fast at riverside levées, the quite old and the new combined on the shores of a vast river. All that was exciting and new to me. On the other hand, I found an emotion deep down, of which a fuller account is promised later, but which I had not really felt since I had left Tbilisi four months before. It was an emotion which based itself, I think, upon cultural tone and language. I became convinced of the emotion's strength when I read the simple words of a notice by the river, close to the Cathedral of St Louis in New Orleans. I found the notice stimulated, and then made articulate the depth of my emotional response. It read:

LA SALLE PREND POSSESSION DE LA LOUISIANE

Le 9 avril 1682 René-Robert Cavalier de la Salle prit possession de la vallée du Mississipi du Golfe du Mexique au Canada au nom du roi de France et l'apella 'Louisiane' en honneur du Roi Soleil.

A day later, while in the New Orleans Museum of Art, I found, tacked onto an excellent collection of French Impressionist paintings, a series of prints by Matisse, entitled 'Jazz', published in the 1930s by a Parisian firm called Teriad. I had last seen other prints by Matisse, Chagall, Picasso and others, also published by Teriad, on the Greek island of Lesbos. A Greek called Teriad, born on the island, had become in due course a successful fine art publisher in Paris, and left many of his prized possessions to his native islanders, to be housed eventually in a museum on the island, in a country olive grove, at his expense. The historical thread, which linked together the Cajuns from Nova Scotia, the Sun King in Paris, a museum on Lesbos and the subject of jazz in New Orleans, proved to be more than my kind of rationality could sustain, and I shed a few tears of joy, as I disentangled the thread. Cultural tone and language would do as a base, I decided, but joy was their edifice. More about joy without tears later on, as well as schizophrenia.

My journey from New Orleans to Atlanta by day was uneventful, except for the not unusual pleasure provided by those I met up with, and the scenery. Among the former were a research student of German origin from Brown University, two women teachers returning to work after a break in New Orleans, and a young man who had been at one time an assistant to Billy Graham, and currently could not decide about returning to modern missionary work a third time. The scenery was flat, forested and moist, much as it had been before. I thought I detected signs of abject poverty in some of the wayside shacks, but, if I was correct in this, the poverty was mingled with a lower and middle-class diminished prosperity, betokening a land which is certainly not wealthy but also not heavily populated. The hills began near Birmingham, Alabama, and were closely gathered together with their trees by the time it grew dark and we crossed into Georgia, west of Atlanta.

Accommodation aboard Amtrak had been marginally less comfortable than that in Australia. All toilet and washing facilities for single sleepers were at the end of the corridor, or downstairs. Service, provided as it always had been in the past by courteous and attentive black conductors, who, for good reason, I have no doubt, went about their business as though preoccupied essentially by other things. Their work was plainly arduous, and behind their cheerful exteriors they hid away their individual sets of worries and concerns from us, their passengers. Tipping was *de rigeur*. The underlying rules of their society were vastly different from those encountered in Australia.

The old song's assertion that nothing could be finer than dinner in the 'diner' echoes disarmingly along the corridors which lead into the modest cafeterias of today's Amtrak — with a kind of mournful disbelief, like the RKO gong at the start of a 1930s B-movie. All meals on Amtrak these days are preordained, upon slips of paper on which the customer is required to make his choice with the stub of a pencil, as he takes his seat at table. The slips of paper are of shared design, and remained identical in substance all the way from San Francisco to Atlanta. The choices available were not unlike those provided at any street-corner Macdonald's, and were on the whole just as palatable. In otherwords, there was little to complain about, if you like that sort of thing. The contents of the small bottles of red, rosé and white wine were redeeming features, when not out of stock.

All the way from San Francisco to Atlanta! Al Capone, upon conviction, did the same journey in reverse, under guard, between leaving Atlanta County Jail and reaching Alcatraz. The *Sunset Limited* ran right through to San Francisco in the 1930s. The original train was inaugurated in 1894 for the winter season only, from San Francisco to New Orleans. A second train, the *Overland Limited*, appeared in 1899. In 1913 the *Sunset Limited* began to run on a daily basis all the year round. The expansion of passenger traffic within twenty-four years had been remarkable, and was sustained until 1942, when as a result of war-time pressures it forsook San Francisco for Los Angeles as its western terminal. In 1950, a new train, the *Sunset Limited Streamliner*, replaced the old one, and went into service on a record-breaking forty-two hour schedule, cutting fifteen hours off pre-war times. In 1964, the *Sunset Limited* was made one train with the *Golden State* as far as El Paso, where the *Golden State* turned north for Chicago. The *Golden State* was discontinued in

1968. Since then, the *Sunset Limited* has operated on a reduced schedule, and was taken over from Southern Pacific in 1971 by Amtrak. The rise and fall, not yet complete but imminent, I would guess, of a passenger service from San Francisco to New Orleans is an accurate reflection of what has happened to railways throughout the United States. I was honoured, I must admit, to have travelled the same lines as Al Capone, and take personal comfort from the fact that I had done so in the opposite direction. Mind you, it was expensive, £310 without food and drink, only £100 short of my ever blessed Austrailcard. The journey would have been much cheaper by air, and Al Capone did it for nothing.

The train to Atlanta was not my last train. I leave that piece of information until my last chapter. When I arrived at Atlanta I already knew that I had seen what I had been round the world to see, a sea link on the American side with the English Channel, where I had begun my journey. That sea link I had finally seen on a dull, cold afternoon in New Orleans.

The author's hotel in the French quarter of New Orleans

A straight road, five miles long, runs north from Chartres Street in the centre of town, where my hotel was, to the shores of Lake Pontchartrain. Lake Pontchartrain is no lake in fact, but a gulf, which in turn is part of the Gulf of Mexico. My argument was that the Gulf of Mexico was part of the Atlantic Ocean, and so Lake Pontchartrain would suffice as the symbolic purpose of my journey. I decided, as a fitting end to it all, to walk that five miles, and I did. A long straight walk, it was, through one of the roughest parts of town. It took me an hour and a half to reach its end, and at its end I saw the sea I wanted to see, a piece of the Atlantic Ocean, and a piece of the English Channel. Guess the name of the road. Elysian Fields. Only one more sea to cross.

* * *

So much then for my exploration of the world's matrix within which I grew up, frontiers and their railways. Now for the exploration of the spaces in between. I regret that, as a result, some readers may suffer from a certain jerkiness as the text jumps from place to place. For me personally, the world quickly became a single entity, continuous and uninterrupted.

4

Journeying

The reader would not need to have been unduly perceptive to have noticed that, by the time I had walked the length of Elysian Fields, and was gazing wistfully across the grey lake, I was tired, and wanted to be home again. The weariness of Odysseus, and of others like him, prompted by nagging nostalgia, is well-documented, and calls for no further account of the matter. A desire to return home on my part was by now no oddity, and would be natural for anyone who had a home and had been away from it for more than five months as I had. I had been fortunate in that nagging nostalgia did not affect me before I entered the last lap of my journey. Before I had reached that, such had been the novelty, strangeness, variety, generosity and fun that recurrent thoughts of home had always been a pleasure to encounter, and never caused pain until I knew that home was only one more step across the sea.

Tiredness on its own was another matter. I had been tired on the journey many times. It was rare, for instance, to sleep with old-fashioned soundness on a train, and there were many occasions also when a late arrival at, and an early departure from, a hotel meant that sleep would be only brief. Some quite heavy tasks were unavoidable: humping baggage, embarking and disembarking, trailing in a group behind an eager guide for hours on end, standing when you wanted to sit and sitting when you wanted to stand. Frustration, whatever the circumstances, drains energy. Even though, like me, you enjoy delay, delay itself is a tiring business. No one could be immune to all this, however unconcerned the manner and relaxed the attitude people might pretend.

In addition to tiredness, I knew before I set out that there were two other physical factors which would always concern me and cause me unusual stress, height and depth. Despite this knowledge, I put myself stupidly at risk twice.

Our first afternoon in Vienna was spent on a lightning tour of the city. Following our sunny morning in Salzburg, I was exuberant about all that had happened so far and in the knowledge that so much was to follow, and of course in the sunshine. In fact, careless beyond what is my custom, I became intrepid and rash as well. At the end of our tour, we were taken to the Prater, or fun fair, enticingly at the base of the infamous Wiener Riesenrad or ferris-wheel. Light of heart, we all queued up for a ride. Momentarily I winced, but, carried along by the spirit of the immediate moment, disregarded this early warning. We crowded into a compartment, and some sat down. I stood by a window with my hand lightly on the handrail. Slowly we began to rise in the wide arc followed by the tip of the wheel's diameter, 197' long. It was a slow ride, for periodically we halted so that the compartments below might be filled with other intrepid funseekers. 2'6" a second, they said; that sounds fast, but it did not seem so, with halts every twenty seconds. When our end of the wheel's diameter moved above the horizontal, my mistake became rapidly clearer, and I knew too that not only had we not yet reached the summit but also we had completed no more than a quarter of our circuit. No longer relaxed at the handrail but clinging to it with might and main, and cowering close to the wooden wall in the corner, with eyes tightly shut, within myself I panicked. Sweating, pulse racing and immobile, I was by now competing with a cornered rabbit. I remember nothing of the view that was undoubtedly there, but only the abject nature of my terror. At the summit, only 209' from the ground, we were told, we lurched and halted once more. My companions were enraptured by the city below and out as far as their 360° horizon, while I, I was face to face with my own 360° image in hell. Seconds became hours. Then, slowly, we gathered speed again and began our descent. Slowly panic subsided and terror abated. I stepped down from our compartment at the end with the others, nearly restored to my former self, without the exuberance. I have been a different person since, you may know. I don't go on ferris-wheels any more. And, do you know too, a Wiener Riesenrad was bombed out of existence in 1945, and they rebuilt it in 1946? Oh, what fools we mortals be, all of us!

The lesson I had learnt in Vienna stood me in good stead thereafter. I climbed no minarets in Uzbekhistan or pagodas in China; I took things slowly in Hong Kong, and found that I could manage a walk round the top of Victoria Peak with only the occasional qualm, and I was rigidly resolute in declining the opportunity to climb Ayer's Rock in Australia. I regard my resolution on that occasion as one of my triumphs, vulnerable as I was as the only Pom available in our particular group. Nevertheless I stood my ground. While all the others after an early breakfast left to make their attempt on the summit (867 metres in all), I slept in a bit. I arrived at the base of the rock at the time they were expected to be returning from their climb. Instead of being able to greet a set of conquering heroes, I met up with a disconsolate band of grim-looking folk, more than half our total, who had had to yield in face of a steep, slippery ascent, even in its earliest part, and a strong wind. It was quite warm too. The rock after all, though not regular in its mass, is made up of a rounded lump of granite-like conglomerate, and at some stage, by what means it is not known for certain, it slipped on its side, and so its various layers of strata now lie vertically and no longer horizontally, weathered smooth.

I showed the disappointed ones all the sympathy I could muster amid self-satisfaction, and of course my admiration for those few who were successful in climbing to the top was unbounded. Most of them however, it turned out, had been terrified at various times, particularly on the descent, and admitted to pride but little pleasure in what they had managed to do. The mere sight of the rope, designed to assist climbers on their initial stint and fixed to metal stanchions, receding upwards at 45°, would have deterred me in any case, had I not been adequately deterred already by my experience on the Wiener Riesenrad two and a half months earlier.

The second occasion was in central Turkey, in Cappadocia. An antique land, with its archaeological origins going back to the Assyrians (680-610 BC), the Medes and Persians (610-332 BC) and, with Alexander's conquests, the Capppadocian Kingdom (332 BC-AD 17). The Emperor Tiberius occupied it for Rome in AD 17, and founded the present provincial capital, Kayseri, or in his day, Caesarea. Damaged by the First

The centre of modern Kayseri still boasts the ruins of a Roman aqueduct

Crusade in 1097, it was in essence, mastered by the Seljuk Turks in 1071. As Byzantium began to lose its grip in the area in the second half of the seventh century, the region became a prey to marauding Arab tribesmen from the south.

Volcanic in origin, the land with a base made of tufa became overlaid with other layers of lava, variably thick, of basalt and anderite. Following subsidences, valleys and high uplands became differentiated, and subsequent weathering evolved a unique landscape, particularly in the valleys, where the soft tufa had been shaped into acres of harder, extraordinary sand-like domes and pinnacles, appearing to pass through the earth below, and to reach towards the sky. Occasionally even harder rocks have retained their balance on the top of the tufa, and now appear as the caps of unearthly mushrooms, domes and peaks intermingling. The Turks call these excrescences fairy chimneys. They are unique to the Nesehir valley, dominated on both sides by shaggy, upland cliffs and crags, as indeed all the valleys are. Predominantly dry, other than beside streams, meagre or non-existent in summer and autumn, the area was nevertheless

Rock formations in Cappadocia

habitable and easily adapted to defensive measures when marauders threatened.

In the fourth century Christianity flourished in Cappadocia, and Christian populations spread westwards from there into the dry valleys, where they built homes, churches and monasteries anywhere that took their fancy, inside the soft tufa, amid pinnacles and cliffs. Indeed, even hermits could not be blamed for thinking that a divine hand had constructed a sports ground for the exercise of contemplation and the solitary life.

As schism spread, Byzantium lost its grip and the dangers of murder, rape and pillage increased, the inhabitants of the valleys combined together to build underground cities in the hillsides, more easily defended from attack and not to be despised as places conveniently adapted, socially speaking, to the necessities and comforts of daily life.

We visited one of these cities at Kaymakli, seventy miles west of Kayseri. Inhabited by Christians in the seventh, eighth and ninth centuries, it has the form below ground of a huge apartment building, four storeys deep. Bedrooms, kitchens, store-rooms, chapels and passageways, equipped with beds, air holes, chimneys and altars, provided accommodation for no less than 10,000 people, our guide said. If so, that number of tastes were radically different from mine, even in dire emergency. A large round stone was positioned to roll in front of the city's entrance in that event.

The entrance to the city, despite the presence of its rolling stone, seemed innocent enough, being sufficiently wide, and leading into a large room, forty-watt light bulbs aglow. After an obligatory introductory talk, we were led downwards along a series of corridors and through a sequence of rooms. I was calm enough, even unsuspecting, at this stage. It was when, because of the inevitable complexity of the city's design, or rather lack of it, the group became disorganized, no longer able to keep in touch with its leader, and then became broken up into small detachments, that we realized the possibility of losing our way, and becoming isolated in a maze, which by now had only narrow, cramped passageways, and steps sometimes in series. Wandering vaguely about, without any certainty about our immediate prospects, and missing every point of interest, whether it be an air-duct, a chimney, water cistern or kitchen fire-place (just fancy that), we were forced to crouch down in mid-course along a narrow corridor, which turned out to be a long one, and unlit. Small steps abounded, with raised lips to them, ominously like those across gangways on ships, intended to impeded the passage of flood-water. We became fixed tight, bent double with shoulders and backs jammed against an awkward ceiling; something or someone ahead of us was blocking the way, and, with a queue behind us, we could move neither forwards nor backwards, bent double and unable to straighten up.

Claustrophobic now, as in a Circle Line train crowded to the limit in mid-summer, except in those circumstances you can see and stand, I became fiercely silent, and within myself panicked once more. Seeing no end to our predicament, I tried to relax myself into carelessness. I had moderate success in this attempt, and while contemplating my fate from beyond it, as it were, I heard beyond me too the most extraordinary series of sounds.

'Gee, I can't move an inch. I am banging my head on the top, and my back hurts, bent over like this. Gee, my back hurts. Can you see where my feet are? I can't. Can you just see where my shoulders are, all bunched up? I am crouching down real low. If only I could see my feet. I can't move them. I am just stuck right here. I wish I could see my feet.' This monologue became extended into a continuous flow, and came from an American woman in front of me, nose to tail as we were. As I listened more carefully, I heard a series of American voices proclaiming in detail to the rest of us the physical nature of their predicament. Small conversations ensued as one compared notes with the other. Essentially personalized subjectivity prevailed. Not quite everywhere however. A scattering of nasally twisted Australian voices pierced the damp and fetid air. 'No need to worry. We'll be out of this soon. It will be real beaut when we reach that open air again, won't it? How are you? I'm not crook yet. I'll be all right. No need to worry. We'll be out of this soon. I'm not coming down here again, though, mite.' I smiled for a moment, and then felt that all was hopeless once more. There was only one other sound apart from American commentaries and Australian optimism: a deafening silence from all the British, who in a clear majority thus made all else plain.

As I pondered our various national consciousnesses, the pressures in front eased. My nose ceased to press upon whatever it was pressing upon, and we squeezed forward into a lighted room. I have no need to extend my description much more. The Americans for the most part were relieved but continued to bemoan their fate, the Australians smiled and said, 'Good to be alive, eh? Good on yer, mite,' and the British were just silently glad to be out of it.

I enjoyed the morning sun, when at last we broke free past the rolling stone, as I have never enjoyed morning sun before, warm and splendid. I resolved no more to put my equilibrium at risk, and no more to venture underground. Indeed later I was resolute in declining to visit an underground tomb in Xinjiang (rather like the beehive tombs near Mycenae), and in avoiding the opal caves at Coober Pedy in South Australia. Neither height nor depth, terra firma at ground level was the place for me in future. Mind you, I had learnt something about some Americans and some Australians at Kaymakli, underground.

* * *

The misapprehensions that different languages sneakingly introduce below the surface of consciousness bring prejudices to life, and so may be dangerous. I found it necessary always to be wary of the risk of being misunderstood. An incident took place one or two days after we crossed into China by bus, which I regret still.

We had been travelling slowly and with difficulty all day, and arrived at a small village called Jinte, in Xinjiang, where we were to have lunch. We drew up in the village, as we were by then used to doing, rather past the lunch-hour, at five thirty pm. There, once more, in the open air were rows of metal bowls filled with hot water, soap and towels, for us to refresh ourselves before eating. This open-air show of consideration for cleanliness and comfort, even in the most humble of circumstances, we all understood as entirely genuine, and as a display of hospitality and a prelude to more. Our food was to be served to us inside, in what appeared to be a village hall. The atmosphere was simple and rustic, and what happened came upon me unexpectedly.

A tall, athletic-looking man, handsome and brave-looking, of about my age, walked slowly up and tapped me gently on the chest. Facially his appearance was oriental but not obviously

Han Chinese. I took him to be Uighur. His clothing was simple and on the edge of shabbiness, not a uniform and made of dark blue cotton. The man said, indistinctly, as far as I was concerned, 'Pen Mun Jon.' Initially I did not recognize what he meant. Then he mimed the actions of a soldier, on sentry duty, with a rifle at the ready. He pointed to his left breast where he pretended to boast of a row of medals. The penny dropped, with a resounding crash. He spoke of Pan Mun Jom where the peace talks at the conclusion of the Korean War went on so interminably. My friend had been a soldier in the Chinese army, and had served in Korea at the time of the peace talks, and possibly even at Pan Mun Jom. Guessing that I was about the same age as he, and recognizing the unfamiliar but obvious stance of a fair-haired Anglo-Saxon, he sought me out and explained with dramatic clarity what our link was; he and I had notionally fought on opposite sides, and we had become acquainted, again notionally, at the peace talks. As a matter of fact, he had been there and I hadn't. I understood his intent, and at once, in a similarly wordless manner, I tried to show him that I understood him, and appreciated his gesture. It was a gesture of comradeship, I think, for he answered my smile and my pleasure with those of his own. We shook hands, and were at once on the best of terms. However we could understand nothing more than our comradeship. I would dearly have liked to talk to him about his life and his opinions, and about what he would have liked to discover about me, but that was impossible. I was called in to our meal, and we separated.

He was still on hand when we came out again, and we walked together towards the buses. Before I climbed aboard, we shook hands again. He stood at my window as we prepared to depart. He gazed at me in a wistful fashion. I was mystified by this, and hoping to cheer him up and all too thoughtlessly, as we drew away, I gave him the 'thumbs-up' sign, for me a sign of hope, friendship and confidence. I shall never know what he understood from my thoughtless gesture, for quickly his expression altered to that of a man who was upset, or might even be angry. Now, for sure, I had mystified him, and in consequence we were friends no longer. I regretted then, and shall always regret, the manner of our parting. My thoughtless assumption that everyone, even those who live in Jinte, Xinjiang, know what 'thumbs-up' means had led to a minor tragedy. If only I had just smiled and waved!

Sometimes I think the most important phrase a beginner in any language needs to know first is, 'I am sorry; I do not understand you', and then when he begins to understand, 'More slowly, please'. The essence of learning a foreign language for a traveller, however, is to add enjoyment to travelling. The benefits of being able to speak a language other than your own, even though it be only with a modicum of comfort, are obvious; not only can you make your needs and wants plain to those who can supply them but also you can begin to enjoy the company of those who know the language as a birthright and live in the land where you happen to be. Many of such people naturally wish to practise their English once they know where you come from, and properly so. I found that, if you give them their head and, with all the patience you can muster, allow them to reach the end of their tether in English, and if — and you should be very careful about this 'if' — if you are satisfied that the conversation can be further advanced by your knowledge of how they speak in their own tongue, then, and only then, should you show off what you know, and extend the conversation, change and change about, exploring at will within your limits, and learning all the while. For myself, I have always been ill at ease, at a fundamental level, when I have not taken precautions before entering a country to learn the merest linguistic elements of courtesy and inquiry.

It was with this precaution in mind that I began to learn Italian and modern Greek, the consequence of which, in due course, was that I became tolerably fluent in both languages, as long as travel and reading at home kept me in practice. Modern Greek turned out to have a use, even in Turkey.

The arrangements in Turkey for transporting the baggage of our group from hotel to train, and from train to hotel, were exemplary. A small number of porters, three or four of them, travelled with us and dealt with our baggage on a pre-arranged plan, with separate inter-change buses from those we used ourselves. They were a cheerful and hard-working bunch, and we all liked each other. From time to time, they had meals with us as it suited, and, unfortunately, because of language difficulties, they would group together at a single table. One of the porters spoke Greek, and on finding this out I exchanged a few words with him. On our first evening in Sarikamis, west of Kars, he sat opposite me at dinner, and I found out that he had been born in Athens, and for a time had gone to school there. His parents, because of their Turkish origin, in due course emigrated to Istanbul, where they settled. In any case he had been bilingual from an early age. He naturally wanted to know how it came about that I spoke Greek, and, as all Greeks want to know that, my answer was well used and at hand, accompanied by a small joke or two. Then he told me about the baggage arrangements, and how the group of porters handled it so that it left hotels approximately when we did, and arrived at destinations similarly. It was all most amiable, and he went on to admire my taste for 'raki'. It did not take long, of course, for our English-speaking neighbours to be curious about the mysteries being expounded at the table they shared. Dorothy Walsh, from Melbourne, a most generous traveller and a lovely person, said, 'C'mon, Ian; wot's he sighing?' So, excusing myself for reverting to English, I told her about the porter's Greek, and how he came to speak it. Thereafter, it was automatic, and I have always found it to be so, in similar circumstances, everywhere. I became the table's interpreter. Questions in English had to be translated into Greek, and their Greek answers back again into English, and so on, all the way round the gas-works. This interpreter business fully engages the interest of the participants, and all the energies of the interpreter; conversational exchanges are made which could not be made otherwise, if he were not on hand. It is an entirely good thing for this to happen, and an entirely good thing to be some help in enabling it to happen. I admit to being grateful and gratified myself at the same time. However, for an amateur, and for someone who was on holiday as I was, the benefits of usefulness eventually became overborn by tiredness, and, of course, by the limits of skills and knowledge. Perhaps I should be ashamed to admit it, but I was the one who brought the conversation to an end. I had to apologize all round for not being able to go on further than the limits of my abilities and strength allowed me. In an ideal world, of course, all travellers would be wise enough to take account of the weariness that may overcome amateur linguists when pretending to be interpreters. Possibly one should not attempt to pretend in the first place.

The next morning, for me, things came to a head. We had in our company a diabetic called Bob Williams, who for good reasons preferred to have saccharin in his coffee. He normally kept the saccharin about his person in a small box-like container. He was distressed on the morning in question, at breakfast, because he had mislaid his saccharin container in the restaurant the previous evening, thinking that he had left it behind on the table after dinner. It was no longer there. None of us had any Turkish, and the matter would be difficult for us to explain, even in simple terms, except in English. None of our guides were about. Out of the blue, my Turkish Greek-speaking porter friend appeared. Bob Williams, seeing his chance, asked me if I would ask the porter if he would ask in the kitchen if anyone had found the saccharin container the previous evening. Our amiable conversation that evening, over 'raki', had been, at least to start with, a relaxed affair, and my Greek had unashamedly lacked idiom and precision, as it always did. Now, at breakfast time, I had a different task on hand, and quite an important one from Bob's point of view. By dint of much stumbling, guesswork and sign-language, too, somehow I got the essential information across, and my friend departed for the kitchen. He returned forthwith with the missing saccharin container. There was applause all round, and Bob, greatly relieved, was voluble in his thanks and his smiles, all directed, quite understandably, at my porter friend. I too was relieved both for Bob's sake and for my own, since somehow I had explained my meaning, and the matter, being solved, needed no more effort from me. However, suddenly, no doubt partly as a result of the previous evening's events, I grew cross, and, with detestable self-righteousness, protested at receiving no recognition at all for my part in the recovery of the saccharin. I leave it to the reader to decide whether I was justified in being angry at all, and in my belief that some thanks were due to me, and then in saying so with some asperity. It was after all breakfast-time. Bob speedily restored my equanimity, as I suppose I always knew he would, but momentarily I had not been joking.

Incidentally, at one time, Bob had been an engine-driver, and had done a stint on the *Indian-Pacific* across the Nullabor.

I had done a little in respect of learning Russian, rather too little, to prepare myself for my first visit to the USSR. I had done even less in preparation for visiting China. However, before departure, I had bought a book, entitled *Chinese for beginners, Series 1*, published by China Reconstructs in Beijing

In middle distance, Bob Williams, the former engine-driver on the *Indian-Pacific*, astride Heroes Square, Budapest

in 1972, being encouraged by a paragraph in a note of explanation at the start of the book: 'This book is produced by Guangwha Company; our ability and experience being far from adequate, the present work is bound to contain errors of one kind or another. We sincerely welcome suggestions and criticism from our readers.'

Because of delays en route, our bus journey, after crossing into China from the USSR, from Inning to Shihezi, referred to earlier, in taking some sixteen hours, allowed me to tackle the first chapter or two of the book, by which means I learnt how to say, 'please', 'thank you' and 'good morning', but I was unsure about how to pronounce them, and, in addition, even more unsure about how to pronounce simple sentences in Chinese like 'I want to study Chinese. Can you help me?', the difficulty of tones being a peculiar problem for the English.

An hour or so out of Shihezi the following morning, when our bus halted at the side of the road for what was euphemistically called a 'comfort stop', men on one side and women on the other, I decided to approach our Chinese guide, John, on the matter, and to ask for his help. He happened to be taking a breath of air and to be talking with a colleague, a pretty, little, cheerful person, whose unlikely English name was Blossom. Because of this, I attempted to enlist the help of both of them without interrupting their conversation. First, they were plainly surprised by what I was trying to do; obviously I was unusual. Then, to my surprise in turn, jointly, without conference of any kind, they showed little or no interest in offering help. I was able to check the pronunciation of 'Zhönggüö' and 'zhöngwén', the words for China and Chinese, but little else. Their attitude was in fact resolutely discouraging. And so, easily discouraged, I gave up and returned to my seat in the bus.

For a time I used to ask myself the reason for this attitude, and I have finally concluded that they did not want foreigners to learn even simple Chinese, for risk of intrusion upon their private and national domain. However small the risk, they wanted to remain isolated from my kind of foreign interference in their Chinese lives. To learn even a little Chinese might lead on to learning more, and there would appear to have been some kind of threat in that. I persisted on my own with my solitary efforts, and made little sense of them.

The attitudes adopted in this instance by Blossom and John turned out to be symptomatic of a more general atmosphere which I became sensitive to among all those who attended us en route while we were in China. For instance, waitresses in hotels and restaurants, universally Han Chinese in origin, even in far-off Xinjiang, performed the jobs well enough, but without enthusiasm of any kind. They received little reward for their efforts, I have no doubt, but they never showed the slightest glimmer of interest in any of us as people. We of course were very interested in them. Then, those who tended hotel rooms and made beds, humdrum chores for sure, again did well enough, but totally without enthusiasm. Their main interest seemed to be in gossiping in their little room at the end of the corridor. On one occasion, in Turfan, in a newly-built hotel, I dared to intrude upon this gossip, and made a sign to the assembled crowd that I needed help. Three maids followed me to my room, where I had collected a pile of laundry. By sign language I indicated, pleasantly enough, I thought, that I would like the laundry attended to. A moment's consternation among the girls was followed by an abrupt 'No can do' in Chinese, and they walked out of the room, giggling and chatting, showing no more interest. As a consequence, of course, I did my own laundry. Why else had I brought a spare plug all that way?

It is fair to point out that the position with regard to laundry was quite different in the USSR. On each occasion that I made it, my request was met with a smile and a motherly, gratifying willingness. Sometimes, I gathered, there might be a difficulty in arranging for it to be met. Whatever the difficulty, the laundry was always done on time, either in the hotel or privately in the home of one of the maids. Usually hotel maids were on the elderly side, and treated me as though I were fragile, and in special need of the maternal kind of tenderness. I tried to show my gratitude. Farewells were often touching affairs, showing signs of real friendliness and affection. It was never like that in China, with one exception that I recall with pleasure.

The driver of our bus in Xinjiang made a mark on us that will never fade. He joined us in front of Korgas, on that memorable evening at the border, and made his presence felt at once, even in the dark, as a result of his headgear, a black homburg hat, silhouetted in the bus against the lights outside. Following my personal crisis there and all the commotion of the reception party in the village, he drove us that night some sixty miles to Inning, over some of the worst tracks, designated as roads, that anyone has ever driven over at any time. It had been raining hard thereabouts, and for a stretch of five miles or so, where some kind of reconstruction was in progress, the ruts and the banks were treacherous beyond all previous imagination, muddy, occasionally flooded, and unavoidably narrow and slippery. Below his homburg hat we knew not a hair turned, and his judgement of the road ahead, whose perils could only be glimpsed in feeble headlights, was as sure and as delicate as a cat's at night treading the edge of a wooden fence. His skill in the dark won our admiration from the start.

Two days later, over a mountain pass, after a five inch snow fall, on roads now treacherous again, with rutted ice and at the edge of cliffs and precipices, in heavy traffic, made up of lorries and other buses, amid jams a mile long in both directions, he surpassed even the drive to Inning, continually detached and cool in judgement. As I have already indicated, he had to drive that day, between Inning and Shihezi, sixteen hours. He did it without a flaw.

Driving was no easy matter, even on the best of roads. Traffic, made up of lorries, buses, numerous carts, and periodically cattle and sheep, could be intense, and all of it always travelling at the upper limit of such speed as was possible. His skill in these circumstances too was immense; he could be patient and relaxed one moment, and then intrepid out of all reason the next. We never knew his name, but he was the Emperor of Bus-drivers. Stocky and handsome beneath his hat, with an honest face, aquiline but also broad, with a smile as wide as any in Cheshire, and with glistening, black eyes, facially he was not unlike my soldier friend at Jinte to look at, and I concluded he was Uighur too, perhaps wrongly. Being Moslem, Uighurs wear brimless caps so that they may touch the ground with foreheads in prayer. Not so black homburgs. He drove us for five days in all, from Korgas to Daheyon, the station for Turfan. As far as Shihezi, we had the protection of forerunners, in the form of a People's Liberation Army escort. This protection was both a good and a bad thing as far as the Emperor was concerned.

With army jeeps at the head of our column of six buses, in theory we had right of way whatever the circumstances. Traffic coming from the opposite direction was compelled to give way, while those vehicles going in our direction and whose speed was considered to be too slow had to give way too, however close the ditch. This form of processional grandeur suited the Emperor down to the ground; he was ever ready to follow the army lead wherever it might take us, whatever the risks — provided of course he agreed with it. On one momentous occasion, as we were approaching Urumchi, being still some ten miles out, there was a division in the road. A new, wider approach road was being constructed, which forked off to the right. The Emperor however had plainly used the old road to the left, and preferred it on the reasonable grounds that it was straight and aimed directly at the heart of Urumchi. The new road on the other hand approached the city circuitously, with a long right hook as it were, linking up eventually, we were to discover, with another main road entering from further south, the two in conjunction aspiring to motorway status in due course. New-fangled modernism of this sort was not to the Emperor's taste at all. As a result, as we neared the junction between old and new, he put his foot down and we sped past all and sundry at the blink of an eye, even our army escort. Consternation reigned, we could see, not only among the other buses, for our position was fifth in line, but more importantly among the soldiers, huddled now apprehensively in their jeep, as the Emperor stormed past. Now in the lead, he signified that he was taking the old road to the left, despite signs to the contrary, sure in the knowledge that the others would follow his sensible lead. Which they did not. Scornfully, the army sped past us again, taking the right fork. For a moment we thought the Emperor would persist in pursuing his own choice, and lead us into Urumchi, in solitary triumph, no doubt well ahead of the others. Courage failed him however; imperial tail between imperial legs, he rejoined the column in his former position, fifth in line, line astern. He shrugged his shoulders. What skin off his nose, if the army did not know what was good for it? His judgement had been shrewd in fact; we became ensnarled in a vast traffic jam at the point where the two mains roads met. We lunched late in Urumchi.

 The reader may wonder how it came about that the People's Liberation Army was able so to dominate dense traffic that its every wish became a command for other users of the road. Bedecked in red flags, the leading jeep of our convoy thus advertised its authority, and it was the red flag that turned out to be the crux of the matter. Each bus in the convoy also had a red flag, and when any other vehicle became an obstacle, that vehicle was flagged down, and made to yield. It was a fascinating, if daunting, spectacle; many an overloaded peasant cart was put at risk as a result of a red flag's imperious intervention. We saw one of them at least driven into a ditch, and turn over. Had indeed the red flag supplanted the authority of old, which belonged to the mandarin class, for it thus to have ordinary folk driven from its path as though with whips? Obedience was certainly the order of the day; of that there was no doubt. When our military escort left us for other things, the red flags disappeared too, and our bus became like any other, except for the Emperor's skill. The Emperor, in challenging the flag's authority earlier, had probably taken a calculated risk. He would have been in greater personal danger, had he decided to proceed to Urumchi by the old road on his own. In any event, after that incident, he became even more popular with us.

The Emperor stood out because he always behaved as a separate person in his own right, and not one of a crowd. He even changed his headgear when the sun shone and it became warmer, forsaking his black homburg for a straw-coloured equivalent. Perhaps he was a Uighur, but from Mongolia; I have seen photographs of men wearing homburgs there. One of my regrets is that the photograph I took of him on our last morning in his company was at the end of a roll of film, and failed to materalize. Memory however is vivid enough for no portrait to be needed in his case. He was in addition one of the few who showed pleasure at being thanked for what he had done for us. It was only later I discovered that the Chinese these days consider it bourgeois, rightist and feudal to say 'thank you', 'please' and 'good morning'. I must say I wondered how they could be all three at once. As for learning how to utter such simple courtesies in Chinese, I soon gave up seeking to achieve what recipients would certainly think were but the worst of intentions.

Many Han Chinese however remain eager to learn English. After our late lunch in Urumchi, the Emperor had to go in search of diesel fuel, which he took some time to find. While he was searching, as was my custom when I could, I took a stroll beyond the confines of the hotel where we had eaten. The street outside was a broad two-lane highway, busy by Chinese standards but unencumbered by private cars; even bicycles thereabouts were less frequent than commonly. Pedestrians abounded. As I wandered towards the city centre, two young men politely approached me, and asked an obvious question: was I English, and, if so, could they speak with me? I agreed of course. Only one of them engaged in conversation however. He was a student at the university there and was studying English, hence his interest in me. He spoke most agreeably, with the slightest of American accents, betraying either the origin of his teacher or that of *his* teacher. We spoke about where we came from and what our interests were, and he wanted to know particularly about my journey. For myself, I did not wish to be delayed by conversation too long, for the Emperor might return and wish to be off; in addition, I was lightly-clad, the early morning having been sunny; by now it had become distinctly chilly and was becoming bleak. As a prelude to making my excuses, I remarked on the weather, and asked how it normally was in mid-October. I was at once taken aback by the curiously formal nature of the reply: 'The weather in Urumchi at this time of year is changeable like a woman.' I laughed awkwardly at his text-book simile, albeit enjoying the joke, but he did not think the matter amusing at all, and clearly thought me odd. He stared at me rather as the soldier in Jinte had done. I decided as I took my leave that I would have much to learn about the Chinese, let alone their language. It was more than likely that all would be beyond me.

* * *

Tourist hotels in China, from the point of view of personal comfort, are agreeable places to stay in, though I have been disconcerted on return to find out that the sandals left for guests in each room are not for their comfort, but rather as a means of preventing snail's disease, whatever that is. Bilharzia? If so, I shall wear them more sedulously in future. To have boiling water for tea always at hand is no doubt something which modern hotels worldwide learnt in the first place from the Chinese. Occasionally others had complaints about plumbing, but I never did myself.

The nineteenth century sanitary revolution in Europe and North America, slow at first to reach other parts of the world, has now also spread its benefits worldwide, and these benefits can be relied upon, in my experience, all the way eastwards from London, and so on to London again, at least in those hotels used by travellers who have no special wish to be seen roughing it. Other than in hotels, I would advise particular caution in two respects. First, always be prepared for unpleasant experiences on any train anywhere. There is one exception to this rule, in Australia, where I found facilities unfailingly faultless. Second, avoid at all reasonable cost, if physically possible, all public lavatories east of Budapest as far as Hong Kong. The experiences I had of these establishments, for example, at Bran Castle in Romania, in Istanbul, Ankara, Bukhara, Samarkand, Turfan and Xi'an, were vivid beyond previous imagination, reminding me in each case of the more extreme medieval descriptions of hell. I have been grateful ever since that modern thinking about hell bases itself no longer upon the absence of Harpic but upon the absence of God. I have also wondered from time to time whether spirituality has always depended for its quality upon whatever sanitary conditions were prevalent at the time.

* * *

One of the assumptions we make in Europe and the United States, not unlike those we commonly make about the effects of the sanitary revolution, concerns the post, or the mail, whichever you choose to call it, and in particular post offices. We expect to be able to purchase stamps in prearranged places, probably post offices, and to post whatever we wish to send whithersoever we may wish to send it, also in prearranged places. Finally, we expect what we send in this way to reach the destination sooner or later. We are trained to make these assumptions at an early age, Christmas and birthdays being especially powerful indoctrinators. A small oddity in all this is to be found in the United States. You may do all that you expect to do in the process of posting something just as you may elsewhere, provided that you can find an office which deals in the business of the US Mail. Be warned, though, these offices are not easily found. I never found one when I wanted one by accident, for instance, as you assuredly can in any main street in Britain or Australia. On each occasion I had to use industry and search for what I wanted, as though it were hiding from me. Several enquiries were obligatory before you became in the end successful. Most memorable of all was asking in New Orleans, at the desk in my central hotel, where the nearest office of the US Mail could be found, and being told that it was nine and a half blocks away, that is, two and a quarter miles away. I never found that one.

You have some resource, however. You can obtain stamps from machines nearly everywhere, but you have to pay more for them than their face value. Mail-boxes are also everywhere a commonplace. I still seek an explanation of how it comes about that the US Mail has to be so uncharacteristically self-effacing in the matter of selling stamps to those who want them at their face value.

In the USSR things were nearly normal for someone who is English. The post office in Tbilisi was a grand and obvious building at the corner of Peace Avenue near our Intourist hotel. They sold stamps there as they did at the hotel. The oddity was that postcards could only be obtained at the post office, and nowhere else that I could detect.

Bicycles in Turfan, near the post office

In China, they were not normal at all. While in Turfan, I had occasion to need stamps, having written four postcards and having already in my possession stamps for two of them. Being in town, I looked on the small map, referred to earlier, which hotels provide you with when you hand in your key, and discovered the main post office marked on it. I had to proceed along Qinnian Road, and turn second left onto Jiefang Road. The post office would be along there on the right as you left town. Which it was.

Its aspect was unremarkable as far as I was concerned: a small, two-storeyed building of simple construction, with a single doorway leading into a room the size of an average classroom for thirty pupils. A counter stretched across the full width at about the half-way mark. The floor was made of wood, as was the counter. I recall that the room had no decoration of any kind, and that its general appearance was dreary, and rather dark. The counter had no barrier to it, and behind it there were six women at work, all of them Han Chinese. There was no queue, and I was the only customer at the time that I approached the counter, clutching my four postcards. I saw that one of the women was franking postcards at a table, and throwing them into a bag which was nearby.

I placed my cards on the counter, and looked in her direction. She turned, came to the counter, took my two cards with stamps on them, franked them, and threw them into the bag with the others. I smiled approval, and then, using the simplest of gestures, indicated that the remaining two needed stamps as well, and that I was prepared to buy them from her. Her reaction was not exactly negative, but uncomprehending. I performed my act again. She still did not understand, and turned to her neighbour for advice. They both now advanced on me, and with eloquence explained in a language which I did not understand what their trouble was. It was a simple matter as far as I was concerned, and so I went through my act again, more slowly this time, exhibiting a smiling, pedagogic patience, which was not rude, and gave, I hoped, the whole thing an air of authority. Once more in vain. They then brought other colleagues to their assistance, and before long all six were involved in one way or another, talking to each other and talking to me. There was one thing I am still grateful for: I did not shout at them in English, though much inclined to do so. Obdurate now, I explained once more, desperation added for good measure; all I needed were two stamps for two postcards, so that they could be franked, and properly despatched. Chaos now began to reign amidst obduracy and desperation. I was determined I was not going to fail in getting what I wanted.

Then one of them had an idea. The others nodded in excited agreement, and they offered me a telephone. Now, if it had been possible to think of any instrument that could have added further to the confusion between us, and to my obduracy and desperation, you could not have chosen a more suitable instrument than a telephone. If I was unable to explain my meaning across a counter, how could I possibly manage it over wires, without the valuable recourse to all my acting ability? Words, useless anyway, failed me. I rejected the telephone with a gesture of surprise and scornful amusement. They persisted; the telephone was just the thing, they indicated; it would solve all. They were quite reassuring about it. And so with reluctance, I gave way.

I took up the receiver, resolved to say in the plainest possible language in my own tongue: 'All I want for Christmas is two stamps for two postcards for the UK. Is that clear?' Such idiomatic brevity would show them the absurdity of it all, I was sure. Before I could utter a word, a calm voice at the other end, good breeding exuding from every vowel and consonant, announced in English: 'All you have to do is to go back to your hotel, and buy the stamps you need from the receptionist there.'

I nodded my head, smiled and said of all things, 'Thank you.' How bourgeois, rightist and feudal can you get, I thought subliminally. Then, quickly, astonished, relieved, bewitched and incredulous, I winced a bit, and blinked the mist of unreality from my eyes. Yes, it was all real. I returned the receiver to its bracket, looked towards the six women, who by now were overjoyed at their triumph and grinning broadly, and said, 'Thank you' again. I grinned too, and departed, clumping the while across the floor boards, and of course leaving my face behind. However, I comforted myself with the thought that I would eventually get what I wanted, and so should be grateful. I had enjoyed myself after all.

I have been unable satisfactorily to explain how the mystery voice knew that I was English, and knew too what I was looking for; it may have been a recorded message devised to deal with the same mistaken assumptions which countless other English speakers had made. I can however explain the difficulties of the six postal workers; employed as they were by a state organization, bureaucratically controlled, they knew two things, that as a foreigner I ought only to be in possession of Foreign Exchange Certificates (FECs), and that the national currency (Renminbi) was their only legal tender; if I were to have Renminbi in my possession, and I did, they would have to conclude that I had been operating on the black market, at least officially speaking. In other words, they were not allowed to sell stamps to foreigners, and as good bureaucrats they would allow no trifling with the rules.

By way of explanation, foreigners in China are permitted officially to use FECs only in Friendship Stores, hotels and when paying for journeys by air, or by train, that in 'soft' class only, be it said. These days, however, FECs are commonly accepted nearly everywhere, other than in post offices, as I discovered. Indeed, in Lanzhou I bought excellent leather gloves and a leather travelling bag with FECs in an ordinary shop, receiving my change in Renminbi. Their total cost to me in those circumstances was £3. Those who made similar purchases in Friendship Stores, however, paid roughly the same for them as they might in London. Having to use two currencies like this is a curious business, but no more curious than anything else in China outside the confines of a tourist hotel. In general, creature comforts are well attended to, provided that you stay within the rules. If you like to trespass outside the rules, as I do, beyond what is theoretically allowed and what is accepted as normal for tourists, you will have surprises, and be continually puzzled by what is to Western eyes mysterious and inscrutable. In fact, the real China outside the rules remains just as it has always been, mandarins and all.

My experience in the Turfan post office has also a more widely applicable lesson. The way a country organizes its postal services is unavoidably peculiar to itself, and so idiosyncratic. Travellers need to take account of this fact, and keep a wary eye open when planning to make use of them.

* * *

Like post offices, near the top of the second division of any traveller's concerns is the amount of baggage he requires for comfort on his journey. Judgements about what to take and what not to take are serious enough to be a matter of personal choice, provided that a reasonably accurate picture of the range of weather to be encountered is available. One couple on the trip across Europe and Asia took only summer clothing with them, and by the time they had reached Xinjiang they were continuously and miserably cold. They came to rely on others for extra clothing. As for me and mine — I was not their size — I knew before I started that I would be encountering hot weather in Australia and Fiji, and cold autumnal and wintry weather in China and the eastern United States, and so had to make sure that I was taking a full complement of choices of limited variety with me.

A Californian couple had devised a useful way of lightening their load as their journey advanced. They kept their oldest clothes for travelling in, and upon their reaching the final stages of dirty decrepitude they would throw them away. On one occasion in Romania, however, having discarded a ragged collection of oddments into the 'garbage box' one morning, they found them in their bedroom duly laundered the next. By the end of the argument which ensued, he had 'beaten them down to a dollar'. I discarded some old clothing in Australia without such an expensive result, and in this way made space for presents and other purchases, as I made my way homewards. Incidentally, I took a lounge suit with me in case I should meet up with formal occasions from time to time; I wore it twice.

* * *

Thus far, this chapter has concerned itself with the telling of cautionary tales, to do with heights and depths, language and understanding, China and inscrutability, sanitation, laundry, post offices and baggage. All of these tales have described, in addition, the traveller's environment, and how it may affect him in an involuntary sense, for good or bad. The traveller however need not always be at the mercy of his environment, though I have to admit that much of the pleasure of travelling consists in enjoying and enduring that experience. His own task, it seems to me, is twofold: to suffer any imposed environment as he may, but also to defy domination and to do what he can to be dominant himself. I found there were two ways of doing this.

First, make sure to walk the streets of where you are by yourself or with one other as an ordinary citizen or citizens. It is easy to do this when you are on your own, as I was in Australia and the United States, but not nearly so easy when travelling in a group, particularly in the USSR and China, where tourists have imposed upon them restrictions of various kinds. It seems to me part of the ordinary traveller's duty not to let himself be totally dominated and to challenge restrictions where and when he can. This proved to be easier than I thought it would, but still required an effort of an individual kind.

I have already described walks 'outside limits', as it were, in Baku and Urumchi. Others that I shall refer to later on in the book occurred in Tbilisi and Bukhara. At this point, merely to illustrate the strength of my argument that travellers in groups should break free of limits whenever they can, I describe briefly what I saw, and would not otherwise have seen, on a private walk of my own in Inning in far-off north-west Xinjiang and another with Sally Also more centrally in Shaanxi province.

We had been in China for a night and a morning, staying at the hotel I have referred to before, in Inning, a hotel which had been originally a Russian trading post in wool, surrounded by a high brick wall with only one rather formal entrance, protected by imposing gates. In the morning we had made an official visit, as it were, to a local woollen mill, the north-west corner of Xinjiang being noted for its merino sheep. This fact much delighted our Australian company. The weather had been fearful, reminding anyone from Britain of a cold, rainy, blowy day in January. I decided in the afternoon I would break out of the compound on my own, and walk the streets of Inning to see what was there. I disguised myself in a black, plastic raincoat, made in China, incompletely as it turned out, since my woollen, chequered hat had originated in Scotland. The inhabitants of Inning would give me scarcely a glance until they saw my hat, which caused them to peer curiously.

The rain had stopped and the wind abated, but it was still cold. If you have never advanced beyond the limits of a Russian trading post into a strange Oriental land, where they spoke no English, and wrote incomprehensibly in Arabic script as the Uighurs did, or in complicated characters as the Chinese did, and not sensed that an adventure was at hand, then you may just wish that you had been me. I was nervous, taking strict note of my whereabouts, and the precise location of the hotel. A quiet, tree-lined road bent twice before reaching a T-junction. This was plainly the main street. Should I turn left or right? There being no other evidence but business in both directions, I turned left.

All was grey along that road, it seemed. Only shades made shapes plain. The sky was grey, the buildings, sparse and low, were grey, the people, minute, were grey, and the mud was grey. I had not expected the mud, for the side road had been paved and clean but for a scattering of autumn leaves from plane trees. There was a road, it was clear, for the traffic made that plain enough, not the ruts, the puddles and the glistening mud. The mud dominated the traffic, though. I had worn the wrong shoes, and so I became mud too. There was a pavement as well, broken, temporary and supported by duck-boards. All you can do with mud is look at your feet, and so it was that mud came to dominate the traffic and me.

I came to see other things presently. The buildings, lining both sides of the road, were single-storeyed, with occasional interruptions, coated with plaster and with mud. Some were dwellings entered by an open door at pavement level, and the pavement, with its mud and duck-boards, entered too as though a guest. There were no lights, though the day was close to its end. Interiors were dark and uninviting. But there were shops, though little different from dwellings, with wares on show outside. Tools, spades, shovels, mattocks, hammers, nails, buckets, all the paraphernalia of hardware, manual labour and hard work. Freshly skinned meat, macabre and angular against the flatness and the grey, betokened appetites without queues. Red meat, red flags and red signs now gave life a spring with which to lift the eyes from the grey. Vegetables were green, yellow and brown. Colour, thank goodness, could dawn upon the grey.

Dwellings and shops were side-shows in reality, and received no more than a sideways glance, when the eyes were raised. The traffic and the people, on the rutted, flooded road, after the mud, were the next in compulsory viewing, if only to avoid being splashed; bicycles, pedestrians, in groups or singly, donkey carts in line astern both ways, two carrying coal, old men, young men, driving, pushing, some going nowhere, having nothing, others purposeful and hasty, women with sticks and children as burdens, a floating amalgam of the sluggish slow, earnest whips and whirling wheels. Everybody and everything moved in both directions. There was one car all afternoon. For the rest, they moved and shook like mercury on a flat surface. Slow, slow, quick, quick, slow, I danced in the mud. For some reason at one spot, they were building with bricks. There was even more mud near them.

I walked for an hour, and reached the countryside, a long straight road lined with poplars and cabbages, like the road out of Chatteris in Cambridgeshire, a fruitful land, still worked by animal and by hand. It would be cheerful in the sunshine, I guessed. As I retraced my steps, I did not rejoice. I had never before seen such modesty of existence pervading all. I saw no smile amid the mud. They blinked at me, I nodded, and on they went, doggedly in search of very little, without colour. At a guess, Inning was a town of about 50,000 inhabitants.

The hotel was warm, and I put my feet up and had tea. A grey adventure, it had been.

And so to Xi'an in Shaanxi province. Xi'an was the only city we visited in China which had a metropolitan air to it. Long in years — it had been the capital of China for over a thousand of them, spanning both the Han and Tang dynasties, known then as Changan — its ancient, powerful city walls, still intact and overlooking deep, wide moats all the way round, were lasting monuments both to its former eminence and to its lasting vulnerability to events. Laid out within those walls, in the rectangular manner of the Romans, the old city presented an enticing snare to one of my disposition. We had visited the terracotta warriors in the morning, and were due to visit a cloisonné factory in the afternoon. Tired of buses, their gorging and disgorging, I persuaded Sally Also that we should walk to the factory instead. Our route would lie through the heart of the old city, leaving it by the south gate on the road glorying in the name of Nanguanzhang, where the factory was to be found, if you could find it. We never did. I would always maintain however that we had more mysterious fun on our walk that afternoon than any visitor to a cloisonné factory.

The sun shone out of a cloudless sky, and the air was clean and warm. The sun's benevolence had brought everybody out onto the streets. Narrow pavements, on the whole firmly constructed, were packed with pedestrians in the manner of a narrow Oxford Street, and the road was jammed tight with vehicles of all shapes and sizes, bicycles infiltrating between every manifestation of the internal combustion engine man devised until thirty years ago. Donkey carts were less prevalent than in Inning. Perhaps it was only the traffic which gave Xi'an its metropolitan air. Jostling and bustling flourished, and devil took the hindmost, and even he had to avoid iron pipes and ladders swirling about on shoulders. We learnt about jostling and bustling first of all.

Walking and dodging on the sunny side of the street, we stumbled across the whole world of central China. Roast chestnuts and melon-seed vendors, and purveyors of baked sweet potatoes, umbrellas and sun-shades stalked the pavement between us, or sat on the kerb. Shoe repairers, health shops with men in white coats, hardware merchants, clothing and laundry shops, metal workers, many coloured birds in cages, butchers, steaming dofu workshops, and, most frequently of all, noodle stands, all lapped their way onto the pavement from doorways, past coloured plastic strips. Buying and selling made company for jostling and bustling. We could scarcely think that private enterprise had recently been revitalized. Surely this pandemic, universal marketplace must have been a reality always? This street, the 'cardo' or hinge of the ancient city, could never ever have been a calm symbol of organized, bureaucratic centrality. Its life was plainly immortal, confirming my earlier thought; China could, and would not change, at its roots anyway.

More remarkable than the buying and the selling was the eating. To us perhaps the steaming noodle shops and stalls were sordid and risky, but I longed to taste their wares. Broad noodles, fat noodles, thin noodles, long noodles, truncated noodles, all piping hot, mingled with red sauces, white sauces, yellow sauces, green sauces, brown sauces, all containing bits and pieces of uncertain origin, meat and vegetable mostly, but some fish. I identified pig's ears. Men did the eating on benches at crowded tables, with chopsticks and fingers, women did the cooking and serving, in trousers and ne'er a skirt; both at three o'clock in the afternoon, or any time you liked.

Gradually we approached the south gate, and eventually passed beneath it, a massive, solid, grey stone affair, with towers and a clock, grimmer than any medieval gateway in England.

Beyond was a bridge over the wide, deep, stagnant moat. We were now on the main road south, leading eventually to Szechwan province, but still some way yet from the cloisonné factory. Suddenly Sally disappeared from my right side. She was in the habit of doing this, left or right, and often you turned and expected to see her, and she would not be there, having darted off to investigate something which had taken her fancy. I was not then surprised at her disappearance, until I noticed a heap in the gutter. She had tripped. The pavement, deceptively secure earlier on, had collapsed at this point, she had tripped and fallen, and was now in a heap, in the gutter.

I winced as you will by now have guessed, and thoughts raced urgently like quicksilver through my mind. If she was injured, a broken ankle or even a sprained one, what could we possibly do? An ambulance? How do you ask for an ambulance in Chinese? Two miles at least from our hotel, what chance of a taxi? Hadn't seen a taxi anywhere in China. Was 'taxi' the word for taxi, or a word for something else quite dreadful? There were so many people about, and so much traffic, an injury of any magnitude would be certain to draw a crowd, and crowds were rarely helpful. In a flash I thought of a disastrous incident I had undergone at Madras airport with a crowd. Could Xi'an be even worse than that? What I had read about Chinese hospitals already had me thinking that Sally must avoid a Chinese hospital at any cost. Waiting for medical attention in the first place might last days, they said. All this in a flash.

I had scarcely turned to help, when Sally got up, smiled and said she was all right. Nothing wrong at all. Really? No, nothing. I don't believe you. No, nothing. Let's get on. I blinked, and, showing what solicitation I could in a crowded street, I took her at her word. We got on.

The next moment we saw what happened in gutters. A small child, making use of the slit in his pants at the rear, defecated with childish abandon, rose and got on, like us. Sally's trousers needed dusting.

The world beyond the south gate was a wider world, and indeed the road there aspired to four lanes. Crowds jostled less, wayside eating places could spread themselves, and shops became shops. Traffic flowed freely. Here I first noticed all the fruit and vegetables for sale. It was high autumn, and the produce of the lush countryside which we had seen in the morning spilled prolifically over stalls and pavements, vibrant in a tangled rainbow, aubergine to tomato. The bright, orange red of large ripe persimmon added zest to the jumbled patchwork of well stocked fruit and vegetable stalls.

By now it was hot and dusty. We were both tiring, and our map, small in scale, no longer seemed much help, for it did not mark cloisonné factories. Small hotels and modernized workshops became more numerous, and began to bore us with their concrete and lack of colour. We set ourselves a target; we could afford to walk until four o'clock; at that time we needed to turn back, in order to be ready for a farewell dinner that evening. Which is what happened. We failed to find the factory, and retreated. On our return, they told us that it had not been worth it in any case.

We were never to know. What we did know was that there were two much publicized pagodas in Xi'an, one the Big Wild Goose Pagoda and the other the Small Wild Goose Pagoda. We were undecided at the time about the size of our wild goose chase; we failed to track down the factory, we failed to break an ankle, but we had not failed to catch a glimpse of some of modern China at work. It was very different from Inning. Only a small wild goose chase, then.

For sure, we saw much in the Soviet Union and China that was for ordinary people distressingly limited in terms of opportunity, but we saw no sign of abject poverty in either country, except for one extraordinary instance in China: a group of five or six Tibetans in Lanzhou. With nowhere to go, and nowhere to be, they were slouching despondently across a bridge over the Yellow River; it did not matter to them in which direction; complete with fur hats, long fur coats, and high boots, they had no other possessions than a few rags slung across their shoulders; experienced and hard-bitten travellers, they ranged the land, and, so it was said, lived on nothing. Indeed, we saw no wealth either, other than that which is to be found in the land itself, or beneath it.

Things were of course quite different in Australia and the United States. There I saw a great deal of personal wealth, and, to be sure, most people I met, and even saw from a distance, appeared to live most agreeable lives, threatened only by what they thought of as threatening, death, grief, and the possibility that they would not be able to go to the beach at the weekend.

A street artist in Lanzhou cuts out a paper image of the author

This kind of agreeable living was mine for the asking, too; I asked for it, and received it. I spent my time in those countries travelling in safety and comfort, and receiving frequent respite from that safety and comfort at the welcome, and in the homes, of friends. I cannot pretend that I often thought of the poverty which I had left behind, in such places as Brixton, Brick Lane, Scotland Road, and Handsworth, but I did sometimes, in particular reminding myself that they, and their kind, were places where tourists rarely went. They are not tourist attractions. As a result of these infrequent thoughts, I made a rule for myself: wherever I was in Australia and the United States, I would make certain I saw something, in each place, of a district known locally as blighted by poverty and socially deprived. Not much of a rule, but I tried to keep to it. I failed to find such districts in Perth and Adelaide, which does not mean that they do not exist there, but that I had no-one I could decently ask for their whereabouts.

In fact, there is little to be said about the lessons I learnt from the imposition of this rule, except for what is obvious. Brixton, Brick Lane, Scotland Road and Handsworth are not alone, and are not unique. Most cities in the West, I would guess, have such districts.

The reality enabled me to see a great deal, too. In inner cities railways often traverse the worst bits. In this way I saw in Sydney some of Redfern and Strathfield. There too I walked through Darlinghurst and Woolloomooloo. From the train and tram in Melbourne, I could see bits of Richmond and Burnley, and note the difference between those suburbs and others like Hawthorn and Toorak. In San Francisco, I walked the area west of Union Square, between Mission and Powell. In Los Angeles, Don drove me down Virgil Avenue, and Sally Also along downtown 5th Street. Neither thought it safe to go to Watts. Poor people in Tucson do not live near the city centre, but in semi-rural circumstances, some distance out, on small, sandy lots, where apart from broken down cars assets are few. In New Orleans, I had no need to make any search, because my walk along Elysian Fields took me through one of the worst depressed localities I could ever not wish to see.

What I saw through windows and on my walks was not in any way exceptional. Depressed urban areas were populated mainly by blacks or by immigrants, generally from Greece,

Turkey, Italy and Mexico, depending on the location. Large families, lack of work and hours of idleness were other things they had in common.

No, I learnt nothing new from my observations and brief perambulations. I did become convinced, however, of the differences between us, East and West, principally the different attitudes we adopt towards wealth and poverty. The East attempts to lessen them in favour of mediocrity, and the West allows extremes and a freer but harsher rein. The consequences of both these preferences are easy to see with the naked eye. I never felt in personal danger at any time. One other thing, which may have significance: I remember seeing not one case of obesity between Vienna and Hong Kong.

I failed to understand, or to learn much about one distressing matter which I had prepared myself to face, but could not. I mention it because it puts a blight upon a country which otherwise I hold very dear. The fate of aboriginal Australians remains still an extraordinary excrescence, after 200 years of 'white' development, and no account that I could give of it would do justice to its grotesque nature. In my ignorance, and because I have little right to comment on what is not my immediate personal concern, all I can do is describe in brief what I remember seeing.

In Adelaide, Sydney, Melbourne and Canberra I can remember seeing not one aboriginal Australian, though I was told that there were areas where they lived in those cities. I saw no aboriginal Australians at any time while travelling widely by car in the State of Victoria. I saw many however in Perth and Brisbane, on the fringes, as it were, of 'white' Australia, sometimes in distressing circumstances. For instance, a family group, man, woman, and two children, on the corner of a main street in Brisbane, were drunk and noisy, and desperately poor in appearance. In Alice Springs, the nature of this special problem for Australia became a little clearer. It seemed to me that aboriginal Australians, including all those of mixed blood, made up about fifty percent of the town's population. The white community showed much concern for the welfare of this half of the population, churches, social services, shops and transport services; in addition, they were there, and lived freely there. The juxtaposition of these two societies, however, which at a fundamental level remain radically different, in philosophy and temperament, is not even yet a natural thing, let alone a good one. I could not make sense of it, and felt personally ill at ease for all the time that I was in Alice Springs. It is a harsh conclusion to draw: I felt as comfortable and as safe in Alice Springs as I do in Belfast.

* * *

There can be no doubt at all about the justice of ending this chapter where it began.

For the traveller, tiredness should be his most important concern. What he does to face up to his ever-changing environment, and from time to time to create his own, brings him the satisfaction and enjoyment of his journey. But, if he is tired, and so tired that he thinks only about how tired he is, then his journey becomes little worth, and a hollow shell. There are three factors in keeping a journey full to the brim. First, stay fit. Exercise and an appropriately careful attitude to eating and drinking are vital. A small, personal, well chosen pharmacopoeia is similarly important for emergencies. Second, sleep as much as you can, when there is no point in staying awake, and give up going on an expedition if you are tired, in order to catch up with lost sleep. And, third, keep your fingers crossed. You will need some luck. My own particular good fortune was to have friends at strategically important places like Melbourne, Sydney, San Francisco and Los Angeles, who allowed me to be at ease and to rest in their homes. Such interludes always refreshed me, enabling a new start at each departure. I was always grateful for these interludes as well as for the company of friends.

If it were not for friends, one of the most tiring things about travelling would be other people.

5

Crowds

Meal times are the worst. You never know who you are going to sit next to. Our group travelling from London to Hong Kong was large enough to have considerable variety among its personages but small enough to encourage the development of notoriety among a few of them. These few I would sedulously avoid, if I could. I never sat next to the man from Minnesota, for instance, because he liked to wear a coloured Usbekh cap. Nor the lady who looked like a Roman emperor playing Charles Laughton and announced at breakfast one day that she was beginning to understand the Romans. For preference, I would sit with the two Sallys and Don, but that was not always possible, particularly at breakfast, since the time of our respective risings was so unpredictable.

At dinner one evening a single lady asked if she might sit next to me. Without always succeeding, I try not to be rude in circumstances like this, and so rose, welcomed her and pulled a chair out for her to sit on.

'Gee, a gentleman! My name's Ruby. What's yours?' she said.

Resisting the temptation to ask for a vodka, I told her. A conversation ensued, about the trip, our current hotel and what we did 'back home'.

Ruby was sitting on my right, and so had the advantage of my deaf ear. For obvious reasons, I find a two-headed conversation on my right taxing for my neck, since I have to twist it so that my left ear may give assistance. My neck grows tired after being twisted for a time, and as a consequence I am inclined to adopt a more aggressive manner in such conversations, so as to untwist my neck and give it a rest.

'I wonder if you would tell me something, which I am curious about,' I said. 'Why are Americans always so formal when they talk to strangers?'

This sudden change of tack caused a ruffle on the waters. 'Formal? How do you mean formal? We Americans really like to be friendly. We are not formal at all. You British are the formal ones.'

I recognized all three points, but went on to ask why it was that American friendliness had become such a formal matter.

'What do you mean?' she said.

I was not quite sure actually, but had a go. My neck needed a rest. 'Well,' I said, 'as soon as you sat down, we exchanged names. I gave you both mine, but you gave me only one of yours. Then, I have noticed at breakfast time that the routine for all Americans is exactly the same. You approach, you smile broadly and you say through your smile, "Good moorrneeng. And how are you today?" That, you see, for me is the ultimate of formalized friendliness. I find it as a stranger totally disconcerting. Happy though I usually am to say good morning to all and sundry at breakfast time, that is for me the limit of it. I just cannot smile at such a crisis. I don't feel like smiling, and so I can't. I must ask you; how am I to react to the greeting you all give me, if I am to be true to myself on the one hand, and yet not appear to be abominably rude on the other? For without exception, you all smile, say "good moorneeeng" and ask me how I am today. Because I don't do that, you must think me odd, informal and rude. I am not really rude, you see, but I don't happen to have the key which unlocks the formal approach you always make to me. And another thing; I quite fail to understand the importance you give to your farewell expression, "Have a good day". Utterly confident that at the end of it I shall never know what kind of day I have had, all I can think of saying in response is, "And the same to you".'

Here I paused for a reaction from Ruby. My neck was improving.

'Then, Ruby, remember how we began our conversation just now. Wasn't it the most boring, tedious and formal of obvious discussions? The trip, this hotel and what we do back home? I ask you. Could anything be more predictable and commonplace than that? Am I right? What do you think?'

'I must think about it,' she said, sinking into silence. At least I think she did.

Next morning she appeared at breakfast and sat opposite me, which was good for my left ear. Forbearing to smile, she said, 'Good morning, Mr Sutherland.'

She was a psychologist back home, you see. I had been cruel, and she had taught me a lesson. I smiled and said, 'Good morning.'

It was a valuable lesson. Among other things, I tried thenceforth to have realistic conversations only with those on my left. Nora, our lovable Welsh witch, knowing of my defective right ear, always said that I chose deliberately to sit on her left, and so have the right to ignore her.

The group seen together was plainly a crowd, threatening and incomprehensible to those who looked at it from the outside. When I first met it at Victoria Station, from the outside, as it were, I was at once aghast at the idea of spending six weeks in its company. It took me about three days to see myself as a member of it. Crowds are other people's crowds, I decided at that point.

I came to like my crowd, our group. It contained of course the garrulous and the selfish, the lazy and the inconsiderate, the polite and the rude, the short and the tall, and, to their distress sometimes, the halt and the lame. It also had great compensations. In general, these gave support and courage. In this respect, our couriers — for me, in an immediate sense, Chris Knowles — were vitally important. How they put up with us, our foibles, our complaints and our inconsistencies continuously was close to miraculous. After all, they were running a boarding school, which never stood still for six whole weeks. They were so good at their job that they showed us no glimpse of relief at the end of term, and their relief must have been monumental. Throughout they supported and encouraged us.

In particular, good humour must have been their emollient, and little jokes were ours. I smile still at the thought of Winifred. Winifred was an eighty-year-old from Seattle, who proclaimed that she never needed a towel; she always dried her hands on her hair. She also put it about that she and our eighty-year-old Mr Moore had something going for them, and she would give Mrs Moore on their return home her two cats in exchange. I liked to think that exhibitions of unreasonable arrogance from me added slightly to the joy of nations. Every Australian, for instance, used to be regularly and bluntly informed by me that the Poms would win the Ashes, and 'would wipe the floor with them'. Sally Too would boost my conceit by wishing she could have some of Ian's arrogance when next time she went shopping in Beverly Hills. Others felt encouraged to put it about that I was a former member of Mrs Thatcher's cabinet. Not only are crowds other people's crowds, but also your crowd can only be your crowd. Those who joined us late had quite a difficult time of it, as any new boy knows.

I have felt it sensible to write briefly about 'our crowd' before spending the rest of this chapter writing about other people's, in case I seem hypocritical of their faults and forgetful of ours. From the outside we were a strangely odd bunch. Had I not observed this for myself when I first encountered it on Victoria Station, then we were all to be reminded of it often enough as our journey progressed. We were met at each station as we arrived by a reception committee of some sort. The variety of these committees must have had some meaning, but it was never easy to decide what.

Most dramatic for me was our reception on arrival in Bucharest. We did not draw into the station until after midnight. It had been a long day. Because of delays at the Hungarian frontier and en route, principally at a junction east of the Iron Gates, where the Danube disappeared southwards along the Bulgarian border, we were five hours late in reaching Bucharest. Romanian hospitality on board the train had been lavish too, and we descended onto the platform bedraggled and limp. We lacked distinction of any kind. Yet waiting to welcome us was a vast crowd, hundreds of people. Our passage towards the station exit was lined, three or four deep, by ordinary folk of every shape, age and description. They looked drab, to be honest, unified by drabness under the pale station lights, but how drab were we? They made no sound. There was no applause, no smile, not a word, save those spoken guiltily to a neighbour. Most strange of all was their absorption. They gazed at us, they gazed through us, they had never seen our like before, as though seeing camels for the first time, or like me in my youth gazing at Don Bradman. Something like wonder lit their eyes, and there were we, dragging ourselves along, dull of effort, wearily anxious to be on our way to our next hotel room. I could not be certain about the others, but I became radically self-conscious, no longer able to sustain their gaze without reacting in some way.

I stopped, put my bag down and offered my hand. Someone took it, and smiled. I did too. It was a modestly warming experience. Others joined in. I felt like a politician. The smiles were shy and self-effacing. A few others in the group followed suit. I was embarrassed in a British kind of way, and not many others felt as I did. It was nothing special. I felt sorry for them. How condescending was I being, I wondered. They had such a glum admiration for us. Small efforts gained small responses. They were immovable. This was their pleasure, I sensed, and they were going to enjoy it in their way.

The truth was that they had been waiting for us for five hours, and we in our *déshabille* were their attraction, a crowd of capitalist strangers from the West, travelling in an old-fashioned way in an old-fashioned style, hard currencies oozing from our ears. Not many such passed through Bucharest at that time. Our crowd had attracted another crowd like the honey of unaccustomed notoriety, the notoriety in Romania of the wealthy among the poor.

Our crowd never met their crowd. We passed them by, and were gone. While waiting for our buses, we listened to a three-piece band, two strings and a pipe, playing the sad, plaintive tunes of the Balkan Near East.

We saw little of Bucharest. My memory is of a dusty city with roads and buildings all being replenished at one time, an artificial museum of rustic architecture in a park and a considerable lake, by whose side we had a splendid lunch. The afternoon following our arrival, a steam engine dragged our train up country northwards, past Ploesti, denuded now of its oil wells, to the foothills of the Transylvanian Alps, and to the small alpine resort of Sinaia.

Sinaia provided a reception committee too, but what a contrast! A large crowd again at the station, not quite as large as that in Bucharest. This time all were in festive mood, clapping, laughing, relaxed and clamorously happy; whether at our arrival or because happiness dwelt within them, it was not clear. They had a band too, but this time a dignified affair of the town band sort, playing gypsy dance music. None of us had any difficulty shaking hands with anybody and joining in

![Lunchtime photographers in Bucharest]

Lunchtime photographers in Bucharest

the merriment. They were clearly pleased to see us, and it did not seem that we were anybody special. I admit to having no worries about the inhabitants of Sinaia, but the sadness of the crowd in Bucharest worries me still. I saw no uniformed police about, suggesting compulsion. Just possibly 'stoolies' from the secret police, Securitate, were behind it all. No, no longer just possibly; absolutely certainly.

There was notoriety in coming from the West and in travelling as a large group through communist countries in Europe. Hungarians appeared to sense that notoriety least, and Romanians most, as experiences in Bucharest and Sinaia had emphasized. In Romania families which lived close to the railway tracks would stand outside their dwellings and wave to us as we passed by. It sometimes seemed that the whole nation was somehow aware of our presence, and wished, or was compelled, to show us recognition by some means.

Unusual was the reception we were given in the city of Timisoara, forty miles south of Arad, itself fifteen miles south of Curtici, where we had crossed the border between Hungary and Romania. In order that we might follow the same route

Bran Castle in Transylvania near Sinaia, by repute the home of Dracula

Our welcoming band outside Timisoara, avoiding the hubbub on the station platform

as the original train from Paris to Istanbul in 1883, the Romanian authorities had allowed our chartered train to use the line southwards from Arad to Timisoara. The line however was below a satisfactory standard for regular express services, and was only used on a daily basis by light local traffic. The line onwards from Timisoara, south-eastwards, led to a re-acquaintance with the Danube at the Iron Gates on the border with Yugoslavia, and was of good standard, being used regularly by main line trains from Belgrade, destined as we were for Bucharest. A prestige train like ours rarely if ever passed through Timisoara from the north.

Timisoara was a large place, isolated in a corner of Romania, and situated in the middle of a flat, arid, apparently infertile plain. There was to be no band waiting to greet us at Timisoara station. The inhabitants, many of whom were waiting on the station platform, we saw at once, were desperately poor. They were by no means in the welcoming mood we had become used to. The sun was hot, the station was dusty and unkempt, and women, dressed poorly but in many colours and with beads, crowded round our open windows begging with their children for food and money, as they do in India. People said they were gypsies. With what truth I do not know. A gift of any kind met with demand for more. The occasion offered us a new kind of drama, brilliant, noisy, sad and on the edge of pity and fear. We felt like victims in the drama and became uncomfortable, not without some justice. Suddenly there was bustling, hustling and shouting in the corridor behind us. Young men, threatening passengers in their seats, bounced their way along the train, seeking what they might purloin. There was a brief moment of panic as predators did what they could to bully and steal. Railway guards and attendants came to our aid, and drove the intruders away like crows. Easy pickings had been few if any. The raiding party had been poorly organized, and we had escaped without damage except that to any comfortable sense of security we might have had. Our wealth, such as it was, was more quietly envied in Bucharest, and not envied at all in Sinaia. The colours of Romania were many and varied in texture and tone, not at all unlike the sound of gypsy music. We did not guess that revolution was in the air. It was as though we had said to ourselves, 'Let them eat cake.'

I recollect no crowds in Turkey. Turks go about their business with an apparent lack of social concern, displaying but passing interest in foreigners, and then only when foreigners display an interest in them. I remember a certain formality in their dealings with each other and with us, bordering on secrecy from time to time. This formality allowed for courtesy and friendliness but not self-revelation, a consequence perhaps of male domination of those affairs which take place within the public gaze. Matters of dress typified all; individual non-conformity attracted attention and more than curious gazes. Sally Also wore white trousers once, and we were both made to feel most uncomfortable as a result; a change into something dark solved everything. Formality in dress, implying an underlying precision, also included a male liking for uniforms, whether it be in stark white while on guard at the Ataturk mausoleum in Ankara or in traditional dress for traditional dancing. Other than in Istanbul and Ankara, our arrivals and departures at stations were celebrated by uniformed male dancers, attired in traditional short skirts, with prominent sleeves and collars, long hose and clicking wooden shoes. Fast and rhythmic, to the music of pipes and tambourine, the dances were formal, intricate and masculine. Fierce glares, as bayonets and daggers flashed amid the flopping sleeves, mingled with more gentle countenances as white handkerchiefs fluttered a different pattern about. No crowds other than ourselves attended these celebrations, uniform and a disciplined rhythm prevailed over all, and the formality of performance was the purpose of it. A short bow, and all was concluded with plainly nothing more to do.

Not so Turkish children. They were continuously inexhaustible. Individually and in groups, all showed a consuming interest in foreigners, smiling and chatting with delight at every opportunity, until the age of eleven, that is, when the solemnity of adulthood descended upon them like an oriental dusk. Whether such happiness and gaiety is an absolute among small ones in Turkey, I doubt. Something similar is found in most Mediterranean countries. I have never noticed, for instance, in either Italy or Greece the chaotic, struggling, rabble-rousing attitudes which characterize processions of primary school children in England. Perhaps childhood is a happier thing where the sun shines more often. Turkish children seemed to me to be the happiest of all. The behaviour was like the final beatification of happiness.

Very similar was a group of nine-year-olds I saw at play in their school yard much further east in Bukhara, informal and joyous beyond restraint; and who would want to restrain them? A second group of the same age passed our hotel, in line astern, that afternoon, on their way to some occasion, which it was clear they anticipated with unconfined pleasure, waving and smiling at us with childish abandon as they went. From where could such happiness come, I asked myself. Was it perhaps a consequence of a residual reverence for the hidden traditions of their Moslem past? For such happiness to stretch right across Anatolia and Central Asia as far as Alma Ata made it possible, I thought, even though the practice of Islam at that time could no longer be overtly observed east of the Turkish border. The happiness of all these children affected us too, and surely betokened happy places in which to live as a child.

Travelling through Uzbekhistan and Kazakhstan in the southern USSR was extraordinary, not only for the sights we saw and for the happiness of the children, but also for the character of its people as a whole. For instance, as we would

The vegetable market in Bukhara with Uzbekh salesmen

pass through crowded markets, well stocked with fruit and vegetables, in Bukhara and Samarkand, men and women, young and old, many wearing small, decorated, peakless caps (like that worn by the man from Minnesota), of many races, would smile at us, shake us by the hand and give us gifts of pomegranates and apples. Without quite the frenetic bustle of Xi'an, trade was brisk. Prices were low. I remember no uniforms and no policemen. There was a relaxed friendliness everywhere, and no pretence. People were people.

A number of incidents stand out. Our Intourist guide in Bukhara was a charming and easy person to talk to, and I felt I could ask her any question I liked. She was from Samarkand, not far away, and her family, she said, was Persian. She had married an Uzbekh. I asked her whether there were racial tensions in Bukhara, since there were so many people of different racial origins living there. She said there were not. Both families, for instance, had been quite happy about her marriage to her husband, and she had moved to Bukhara because his work was there. They returned to Samarkand from time to time. Did

I not think it was right for different races to mingle freely? So certain and convincing was she that I had to agree with her. I only wished that such good fortune was more common in other parts of the world. In Bukhara I firmly believed there are now no 'Jews, Turks, Infidels, and Heretics', 'neither Greek nor Jew, circumcision or uncircumcision, Barbarian, Scythian, bond nor free'; people were just people. Events have proved me wrong; my judgement, sincerely held, was at that time superficial and mistaken.

Secondly, in Samarkand, while sight-seeing there, we came to the Bibi-Khanim grand mosque. Its construction, begun in 1399, followed Tamerlane's victorious campaign against India. It was completed five years later, Tamerlane having planned it to exceed in magnificence everything else he had seen in other lands. Architects, artists, and builders had been called in to assist the work from all parts. 200 stone masons had come from Azerbaijan, Persia and India, while 500 labourers cut rock in the mountains for transport to Samarkand. As an indication of the building's size, the rectangular central courtyard measures 130 by 102 metres. Time has been merciless to the building. It began to collapse even during Tamerlane's lifetime. Majestic and impressive ruins survive today. If it were not for the blue, grey, gold and white tiles still clinging to many walls, the buildings would have reminded me, in their decline and scale, of the Baths of Caracalla in Rome. The government has begun extensive restoration work, and intends eventually to have the mosque rebuilt in accord with Tamerlane's original design. We could see from scaffolding that this immense task had already started.

I was surprised that such an effort, demanding vast resources, was thought to be worthwhile in memory of a despicable tyrant long dead. I asked our guide for an explanation. Her reply was simple; 'No, our aim is not to restore the mosque in the name of Tamerlane, or even of Allah, but in the name of all the hundreds of workers who, all those years ago, built it and died for it. It will be their memorial, nobody else's.' Facile, the reader might think, but only facile if you do not have a belief in the communion of the saints who helped to make up your historical past. Soviet citizens in general have such a belief. They would appear to want to be at one with their selection of that past. As for us, we never think of restoring the Baths of Caracalla on the basis of any similar belief. We think only of Caracalla as a symbol of tyranny. Once more, events suggest a different interpretation of this incident. Islam was not asleep but very much awake.

Before belief comes respect. A forceful incident, while we were even further east in Alma Ata, showed how respect for the past might lead on to pride, and then profound belief in the power of heroism. The Soviet Union fought the Great Patriotic War (1941-1945) against the evil of fascism at tremendous cost, especially in lives. Memorials of Glory, as war memorials are called, many vigorous and dramatic in conception, are set up in any town of any size. The memorial in Alma Ata, on the edge of a lovely park, is a particularly fine example of intention made good in practice. Astride a broad plinth, upon which are inscribed the names of battles echoing down the years for those of my age like latter day Passchendaeles, a latter-day Laocoon, with its hero this time triumphant over his enemies, demands the attention of passers-by. Our group stopped, and gazed at the monument in silence. We walked past it, along a formal, rectangular lake with fountains. We were quiet and respectful still, no unseemly group behaviour here, or so we thought. Contributing powerfully to the scene were pairs of young men and women, members of the Young Pioneers and the Young Communist League in their grey uniforms with black and white piping. They were mounting guard over the memorial, and goose-stepping a routine from time to time. We remained respectful and relaxed, many of us in admiration. Hands crept into pockets. At once, a young woman detached herself from the guard, walked slowly up to one of the miscreants, and rebuked him. All hands quickly left pockets, like lizards shaken from the shade. It was not our unaware unseemliness which made the incident memorable; rather, the stern authority of a youthful rebuke and the certainty of its respect for the heroic dead, soon to grow into belief, astonished us at our roots. Many of us remained in admiration. The power of heroism might lead anywhere, we conjectured.

Tashkent, between Samarkand and Alma Ata, is a huge, modern city. Its past as a desert oasis is almost obliterated. An earthquake in 1966 destroyed everything except for a small corner of the city's Moslem past. Planning the city again and rebuilding it in the modern Soviet style has produced a series of very broad streets, wide squares, large department stores, and rows and rows of huge apartment blocks. The use of curves and sudden changes of aspect impresses any casual observer, as does the use of flower beds, still in luxuriant colour when we were there, fountains and long, stately avenues of trees. At the centre of it all, in front of a row of public buildings, in more traditional style, stands a traditional statue of Lenin.

A new underground transport system is currently being developed, two main lines crossing below the city centre. One afternoon we took a ride on a train from Maxim Gorky by way of Lenin, 17 October and Komsomol, and back. At the time I wondered to myself why I had even thought of doing such a thing. Strap-hanging in Tashkent turned out to be in no way different from strap-hanging on London Regional Transport. We were packed in just as tightly, and tactics for entry and exit were just as direct and elementary. I blinked at the absurdity of my seeking to repeat just one more time what I already knew thoroughly from an eternity of times. Not until I had occasion to use a new system on the other side of the world, in Atlanta, Georgia, did I realize that in fact I had done well.

The Atlanta system, more modern in design by some ten years than Tashkent's, was in tone radically different. Although trains ran as smoothly, travelled as quickly and performed as efficiently as each other in both places, in Atlanta design was uncomplicated, plastic, clean-cut and unattributable, on the platform and on the train. In Tashkent the design of trains was similarly functional, but the stations all differed, and had plainly been the subject of careful thought and purposeful architectural differentiation. You stood on a station in Atlanta, named after a geographical locality, and closed your eyes mentally. Standing on a station in Tashkent was instead a mental challenge, and you kept your mental eyes open wide. A little over-decorated and florid, you might say to yourself, but all was most certainly in accord with names and historical references, Gorky, 17 October and Lenin and all the others. London has done something similar with Victoria, Waterloo, Green Park, Charing Cross and elsewhere. Underground railways too, it seems, reflect the kind of society which builds them, and the Soviet Union in Tashkent is notably vigorous in articulating a Soviet view of the past. Incidentally the Russian word for station and terminus is 'vauxhall', because nineteenth century Russian railway planners visited the new station at Vauxhall, and treated it as an example of good practice. Perhaps we should, in answer now, have a few underground stations called after such as Chaucer, Milton, 1707 and the Territorial Army. Could we stand it, I wonder.

To sum up, our time in Uzbekhistan and Kazakhstan had been both happy and interesting. We had learnt that racial harmony seemed to be real. In addition a firm belief in a Soviet and corporate past, that is, in a past made good by a vast amount of heroism among workers and huge sacrifices, strengthened racial harmony, for much of the heroism and many of the sacrifices had been in common cause against tyranny, all the way from Tamerlane to Hitler. Different races made no difference to the righteousness of the fight. Unified beliefs like these, even though they might be only superficially held, were impressive things to encounter. None of us could at that time discount the strength of their public certainty.

In the middle of all this unity there was room for kinds of individualism. The barman who served us coffee in Bukhara spoke excellent English. He had been a school teacher, and had left the profession in order to improve his English. He had taken the job of barman in an Intourist hotel in order to have the chance of speaking English to English people. He was happy that he had done the right thing, and his next ambition was to spend time studying English in England. That might prove to be a long business, he said.

Then, thirteen miles from Alma Ata, in the mountains, an aul, or Kazakh village, had been preserved as a youth camp and a tourist attraction. The village consisted of sixteen yurts, or single room houses, made of wooden frames and covered with grey woollen felt as protection. These mobile homes were also to be seen quite frequently in the wild. In other words there was space in Soviet society for tribal Kazakhs to carry on their traditional way of life without interference. We even tasted some of their traditional food, some of us admitting to no great pleasure while doing so: smoked horse meat, horse's foot, hard sheep's cheese, several unusual varieties of bread and kymiss, that is fermented mare's milk, a delightfully fresh and invigorating drink. Individualism and tribal independence were permitted, among minorities anyway.

Other than on the underground in Tashkent and in various

markets, we saw no crowds in the Soviet Union. On reflection, it would have been interesting to have seen crowd behaviour at a football match or at an athletic meeting. I would assume good behaviour at Soviet football matches is rather like that we used to see on television at May Day parades. Good behaviour and considerable patience, where delay and other frustrations play a part. This is not to say that I believe that the Soviet people are vitally oppressed by some hidden, insidious, internal power, and are likely to behave in a co-operative manner because they are cowed into it. I do not believe that at all. Quite the contrary. Such is the support they give, personally and collectively, to the ideal they believe in, and the unswerving and perhaps unthinking loyalty consequent upon those beliefs, that Soviet crowds could scarcely be anything else but well behaved. Seeing expression of separate loyalties in a crowd, like those which supporters of rival teams from Moscow and Kiev, for instance, might have evinced, would have been immensely interesting, for the strength of local feeling, and even regional feeling in the Soviet Union, is plainly a matter of powerful passion and belief as recent troubles between Armenia and Abzerbaijan, and elsewhere have shown. One of the curiosities of the Soviet Union in its vastness is the manner in which powerful and contrasting local and national feelings have on the surface co-alesced into one. I do not suppose that the expression of local feelings would ever come anywhere near the voluble and sometimes violent explosions which provide the inevitable backcloth to contests between Chelsea and West Ham, and Liverpool and Manchester United, for instance. Crowd behaviour at public contests is surely yet another obvious way of making judgements about national and local tempers and temperaments. There was a time, of course, when English football crowds were well behaved. Perhaps that was when we too had an unswerving, unthinking loyalty consequent upon our national and local beliefs.

* * *

If my impressions of Soviet crowds had to remain a matter of surmise and conjecture for lack of evidence, this was not to be the case as far as Australian crowds were concerned. I saw Australians together in large numbers on many occasions. Direct comparisons are therefore not in order. Nevertheless I can

Sydney, an unusual view of the Opera House, and Bridge from the Botanical Gardens near Mrs Macquarie's Point

hardly imagine Soviet crowds ever behaving as Australian crowds do. If the basic assumption of Soviet society is that the welfare of the people as a whole matters most, then the basic assumption of Australian society is that each Australian matters most.

Manly is a good place to watch Australians, at least those of them whose loyalties reside within the environs of Sydney. It is only a twenty-two-minute ferry ride from Circular Quay, Circular Quay being the hub from which most things, including ferries, depart. Circular Quay is the southern end of Sydney Cove, around which the old city nestles, as well as the Harbour Bridge to the left and the Opera House to the right. A departure from Circular Quay by ferry is anybody's adventure. A ticket, a queue, a ramp, all to be negotiated in a throng of people, upstairs or downstairs, these are the early issues to be faced and settled. You are not good at settling them, but Australians are. Then, all too soon, the fresh excitement of departure, as all and sundry seize and apportion where they want to sit. Nobody predominates, certainly not you, but families, from grandmother to grandchild, are best at making the best of it. You will want to strain to catch the great views of the bridge, the harbour

Manly from Mosman

and the Opera House; others will mainly be concerned with food and drink, snuggled away in plastic bags and hampers. Beer for the men, juice or Coke for the kids, grandma does not want anything, and something else for mum, who is in charge and does everything. There is no disagreement, enjoyment is the thing, everyone knows his or her place, but nobody is less than anybody else. As an unobtrusive Pom, you wonder where you stand. The bridge, the harbour, the Opera House, the water, sparkling and glittering, you do not know which, all are wonderful, just wonderful. And they do not seem to care what you think. But you have to think it.

The ferry turns to starboard, past Mrs Macquarie's Point where she used to like to sit, the Royal Australian Navy in Woolloomooloo Bay, and most other places too, and Taroonga Zoo there to the north below Mosman. Each secluded nook and cranny of the harbour intrigues, but twenty-two minutes are soon over, and you must do it again sometime. They turn to port again past Balmoral Bay, and then sidle in towards Manly Pier.

It is quite a place. When you descend the obligatory ramp, you do not know what to expect. It is like landing in France, in a way. Dieppe, perhaps. The inland esplanade facing a sandy beach, the calm waters of the harbour, the skyline of the big city behind the Mosman headland, and, most important of all, the Sydney Heads and the ocean beyond it, is sunny, broad, white and busy. Yes, quite a place. Restaurants, bars, brasseries, hidden behind Aussie joky names like 'Fishy Plaice', 'Eetalot', and 'C'mon Inn', stretch to left and right. There is a broad avenue straight ahead, aiming directly like an arrow pointed upwards gently in line with a separate kind of brightness. Like the others you are attracted by this separate brightness. People crowd the pavements, but do not jostle. Time is on their side, and they wander contentedly, content to be in Manly and to laugh and shout. They are colourful folk, flopping along in coloured and briefly stated clothing, and thongs, if you know what they are. Knees and legs are brown as toast. Otherwise, pale yellow and pale blue predominate. The avenue has a broad space in the middle, where, unhindered by the traffic, you can eat and drink if it takes your fancy. Try to do nothing on purpose.

Unexpectedly, if like me you are in Manly for the first time, the avenue gives way suddenly to a second esplanade. It is the main esplanade really. It is bigger and brighter, broader and grander, and it has more trees and far more people, and it faces the Pacific Ocean, tumbling in at a distance in low rows of foam. I would guess the sand, low and soft, stretches for a mile in each direction, with a wide, unhindered sweep. Nature's esplanade, this one. The sand is pale yellow, and the sky and the sea are pale blue. So that's the reason. Nature's esplanade makes unanswerable demands. You have to endure the ritual of the ferry boat and the notion of a day out because you come to Manly really to bow your brown knees to the sun, the sea and the sand. Food and drink are only like orchestras in a palm court.

Nature's esplanade in effect houses Nature's court, the spirit of sun, sea and sand, policed by pillars of palm. Each individual Aussie, young and old, knows instinctively about Nature's court. It is a kind of public secret. They would not dream of telling you about it. Singly and together, they worship their birthright in Manly. They were born in Manly, and have every right to it. They are everywhere, scattered on the beach like sand.

That evening, I dined in a Greek restaurant on Oxford Street in Darlinghurst. I enjoyed the food, and speaking Greek to the proprietor and his daughter. I spoke Greek, too, to a bronzed, handsome, dark-haired waitress. In reply, she said abruptly, in your regular Aussie, 'You great galah, I'm not Greek; I come from Manly.' And so she did. And so in a way do they all. The sun, the sea and the sand, you see, are on both sides of the argument, and only half a mile apart. Quite a place.

Another time, when I was in Brisbane, I was to have revealed to me a further eternal truth about Australians. A truth this time I was searching for, and hoping to receive. I was waiting for a bus on Kangaroo Point, so that I might go again to the lovely new Queensland Art Gallery. A man, standing next to me, attracted my attention, and asked me at once, 'Did you gow to the crickut yisterdai?' I said that I had gone, and he asked me what I thought about it. Australia had not done too well, and so I told him. That was not the point, though. That, as I knew full well from experiences of other Australian cricket teams, was not the eternal truth my companion was trying to teach me and I was seeking.

I am certain that nobody would have spoken to me at all if I had been waiting at a bus stop in Wandsworth or Golders Green. Even if a friend of mine had happened to be waiting with me by chance, and I had been parading my MCC tie, his first comment would have been about the tie, not yesterday's cricket. He would only have asked me about that if he had felt like doing so.

That is the point. My friend in England would only have spoken of yesterday's cricket if he had felt like doing so, whereas my Australian companion had been compelled by some unseen pressure to talk to me about cricket. Indeed, he talked about it a second time soon after, with somebody else on the bus. What was important, and what I was seeking for, was not the topic itself but its underlying assumption, the assumption that I would have gone to the cricket yesterday, as anybody in their right senses would, and would have wanted to talk to him about it, as anybody in their right senses would, because he himself had not been there. As an assumption, cricket was important, not only what happened at it. Did I go, in other words?

I do not know what other assumptions white Australians

have about the world they live in, but they have two for certain. One is worship for the sun, the sea and the sand, and the other is an abiding interest in the welfare of their national cricket team. Football, various kinds of it, may well be an interest for the states of the Commonwealth, but cricket and the Melbourne Cup are the nation's affairs, the Melbourne Cup on one day of the year, and cricket the rest of the time. What is more, both men and women share these assumptions.

I was fortunate in being able to watch most of four Test Matches in Australia, on four different grounds, and to watch England play against a State on a fifth. Because of this, I was able to watch not only much cricket but also many Australian crowds. Each time the crowd differed as the cricket did. However, as each match played out its separate drama, the atmosphere provided by each crowd remained constant, in the same way as the ground itself did. Both became for each match unalterable appurtenances. So it always is; the quality of the crowd, the quality of the ground's facilities and the atmosphere of the ground itself make up a constant and consistent backdrop as each cricket drama evolves. In Australia a particular attraction is that each crowd and each ground provide different backdrops. Or better, each drama has a different stage.

The Melbourne Test Match, at the Melbourne Cricket Ground, began on Boxing Day. That in itself made even the journey to the ground a novel experience for me. The festivities of the day before, to be followed by a day watching cricket, what else could somebody like me ask for as a celebration of being alive and well? And then to be watching it at the astonishing MCG, what an icing for the cake!

We took the sixty mile journey from Mount Macedon by car. We had already booked seats on the upper level of the Outer, that is, opposite the Members' Pavilion. We were in no hurry, but began our journey early nevertheless, for both Ken and Pete were concerned about the difficulty of parking the car. I was concerned about the weather. The sun shone with crystal clarity on the Mount, but from close to its top I could see a pall of mist hanging over Melbourne down there sixty miles away. Drizzle had been forecast. A journey to the cricket in England often is accompanied by nagging concern like this, but I had not expected it at the start of summer in Australia. The pall grew thicker as we approached the city, but the tops of skyscrapers, clustered together, are the visitor's first sight of Melbourne from any direction beyond low hills, and they were clear enough. All would be well, perhaps.

Gradually my worries began to dissipate like the cloud, and, as we neared the ground, excitement took over. The MCG is a towering, brick-coloured amphitheatre, four times the size, I would guess, of the Colosseum in Rome in its halcyon days. Without Roman hills, and separated from skyscrapers by a mile or so, it dominates. The railway runs close by, and I had seen it many times. Still it dominated, even more than usual on a Test Match day.

Australians were flooding towards their Colosseum as the Romans did towards theirs, mostly on foot, young and old, men and women, half and half, ambling peacefully in quiet conversation towards the domination. They ambled along paths which lead like spokes towards the hub of it all. We found parking easily enough, and joined those who were using one of the spokes. Pete knew the way, and met up with one of his friends. Cricket was the thing today, and nobody doubted it. And the Aussies would beat the Poms for sure.

We queued in an orderly way, and I thought briefly of queueing for a bus in London. Through the gate and past the outer skin, the MCG, as far as the crowd can go, is concrete: concrete passageways, concrete stairways, concrete lavatories, concrete bars, and concrete food stalls, like a football ground in London. Crowds move slowly here too. There is no space for haste. There is no space either for logic; the crowd jostles for its place in the stream of traffic going whichever way it wants to go. Is this like Rome too, I wondered. Just for a bit, lost in the concrete, Australia becomes anonymous. Separation is impossible. The three of us manage to stay together, and take a staircase to a landing, where there is more concrete and another staircase. We take this other staircase and reach another landing, where there are more stairs and a relaxed, cheerful custodian. He finds us our wooden seats on the front row.

Like many a Roman, we looked down on an arena from a great height. Others of us were even higher up, on a second tier, among the gods. To have booked seats on the front row of the first tier (the first concrete landing had led onto the higher levels of the ground level seats) was a magnificent piece of judgement; all was before us and below us, and, although we were further from the pitch than I had ever been in England, we would still be in touch with the forthcoming drama. We would be able to identify the participants plainly enough, seeing gesticulations if not facial expressions.

The arena was as near as dammit a circle in shape, an even contest between the two contestants, bat and ball, clinical in its exactitude, a place for fair play, and as green and as broad as the month of May. There were only two bare patches, a consequence of the previous Australian Rules football season. There were no visible signs of the Pope's recent visit, however, and his saying Mass on the arena for the crowded Roman Catholic population of Melbourne. A Roman pontiff saying Mass in a Colosseum?

We were early, and there was half an hour yet before play would begin. There was just time for an idle thought or two. Bread and circuses, martyrdom, the Last Supper, a Roman crowd, a thirst for blood, the Rock of the Church, a travelling pontiff, the sand of the arena, an arena of sand, Australia and a Last Supper on sand, and Christmas Day yesterday. What a stained-glass window it would all make! How many levels of meaning could there be? Peace on earth? A Christian world? Unified and at one? Watching cricket? Was it possible, just possible?

At a sudden, my dream was shattered. I was awakened with a start. The crowd, now 58,000 strong, burst into urgent life, and roared an equivocal approval. The England team, distant specks in white, tumbled down the pavilion steps, following the silent umpires, and my dream, into the arena. Thirty seconds later, the Australian opening batsmen followed suit. At that, unequivocal approval, twice the former sound, rent the air. As you know, I could only hear half the noise, and was deafened. Peace on earth? A Christian world? Unified and at one? Not here today, anyway. This was real cricket. We are going to kill the Poms.

Battle royal was presently joined. Gladstone Small ran up to bowl the first ball. All was indeed before us, and I had forgotten my dream until now. It stayed noisy all day, more noisy than any previous experience of mine at a cricket match.

It was a good day's play. A number of things happened to the crowd in the course of it.

Initially, the crowd's massive majority in support of

Australia — I would guess that there were no more than 1,000 England supporters present, vociferous though many of them were — was whole-hearted in its cheering and applause for any Australian achievement, however slight. As Australian wickets began to fall, brief silences would descend, as the unfortunate miscreant departed the scene. The clamour returned as soon as a new hero presented himself, and made his mark by scoring a run or two. Unfortunately for the crowd, miscreants continued to depart, and new heroes to present themselves. Whole-heartedness began to disintegrate.

The seeds of disintegration were sown early on. A thoroughly regrettable incident, brought about by a person in front of us down below, disturbed the crowd. Gladstone Small had just taken the first wicket for England, and the first miscreant had just departed the scene. At the end of his over, Small retired to his position in the field at third man below us near the boundary fence. All English supporters knew him as a thoroughly likeable and cheerful member of the team, but Australians, I suppose, because he is black and has broad, hunched shoulders, found him at first sight an unorthodox member of an English side, wearing his England sweater below an England cap. At the end of the next over, as he returned again to take the ball and bowl once more, the person below us threw a peeled banana onto the field behind him. He turned round at the commotion, saw the banana and, ignoring it, went his way. There was just a hint of uncomfortable laughter at the poor joke nearby, but, within seconds, broad sympathy for the player spread round the ground, and, as he was thrown the ball again, warm applause broke out from every corner. Often crowds, especially large ones, are unruly beasts, but not this one. It detected a mistake in tact, taste and common sense as soon as it had been made, and did all it could to correct the error. Indeed, Gladstone Small remained immune from any further abuse all day, unlike the other Englishmen.

As I have said, this incident disturbed the crowd, and, as wickets continued to fall with the result that in the end Australia were all out for a meagre score, whole-heartedness became totally disintegrated; it fell apart. This had two noticeable consequences. First, Australian players became just as liable to popular abuse as English players, and, second, as failure grew in proportion, so interest in the game as a whole declined, and enthusiasm for minor triumphs, brought about by individual heroes, became more clamorous. This Australian crowd was a fickle one, and remained so throughout the rest of the match. Half of the crowd went home before the close of play on the first day.

England won in three days. I suppose I could have said that the Poms had killed the Aussies, but didn't somehow. We wiped the floor with them, you see. To tell the truth, I was more than a little sad that the match had ended so early. I had enjoyed the MCG. It was very like the Colosseum must have been in days of old.

Those English supporters who insisted on vociferous and ugly behaviour while advocating the English cause were for me a continual embarrassment. If only they would not misuse the Union flag as part of their advocacy, and so wrongfully involve the Scots, and the Welsh, and the Irish in their absurdities! St George alone is answerable. Out of all proportion to their numbers, their congregation in one part of the ground was a persistent and ill-mannered distraction from the main business of the day. I disliked them and was ashamed of them, and could find little fault with their Australian contemporaries who attempted fisticuffs by way of remonstration and rebuke. The local police were rough, and splendid at dealing unceremoniously with a few incidents of violent behaviour. Extraction was an unfailing remedy. I only wish they had been able to extract all of it. A noisome bunch.

Alcohol was not a problem at the MCG. You could not take it into the ground other than surreptitiously, and you could only buy two cans of beer at a time at any of the bars. The barmen always loosened the tops of the cans, so that a full, unopened can might not be used as a missile of war. One result of this method of regulating consumption and the risk of personal injury was that long queues for the purchase of the statutory two cans developed at all bars. You could not get drunk, nor could you watch much of the cricket if you wanted a drink. Before joining a queue, you took careful count of your needs.

I would join such queues from time to time, taking my turn with the others. That was an embarrassment, too.

Since the time that Ken Mappin had made me order a 'take-away' Chinese meal over the phone one evening, on the ground that my 'plummy Pommy voice' would get the best results, I had been well aware that my 'plummy Pommy voice' was a matter for concern in Australia, one way or the other.

Queueing for two cans of beer had me thinking. The barmen dealt with the queues with skill and expediency. Each was able to manage two queues at a time, since each order was the same, and no barmen need lift his head either to provide what was wanted or to receive payment. They kept their heads down, and in that way their queues made good progress. And so, like any honest customer, I had my order and my money ready, and said, 'Two cans of beer, please.'

The barman's head jerked upwards, and all the heads in both queues on both sides of me jerked sideways.

'What's thet?'

'Two cans of beer, please.'

'What beer, mite?'

Already sensitive to the local market in its preference for the local brew, and none of your Fosters or Castlemaine rubbish, I said, 'Victoria Bitter, please.'

'Oh!'

Two second pause.

'There you are, mite,' after spending four times the usual on supplying my needs, you bloody Pom. At least, the ready's right, he thought.

All this was thoroughly disconcerting, especially as the bloody Poms were doing rather well outside on the field, and I did not want to spoil the feast by any ineptitude.

That night at supper I asked my hosts where my fault had lain. After a bout of general and uproarious ribaldry, Margaret, Ken's daughter, advised that I merely say on the morrow, 'Two Vic bitters, thenks.' All would then be well.

And so that is what I said on the morrow. 'Two Vic bitters, thenks,' with a nicely adjusted Aussie twang. Right enough. All was in fact well. I need spoil the feast no more. Nobody looked up, or askance. Don't waste words at the bar is the motto to bear in mind. And don't forget ellipsis; there is no need to say, 'please'.

In Brisbane, where the first Test was played at the 'Gabba', alcohol was no problem either. For nothing was regulated at all there. Cans of beer were freely available. The cricket apart — and I was enthralled by my first Test in Australia — the most astonishing sight on the first day was to see my first beer can battle. I was sitting behind the bowler's arm at the pavilion end, and the vociferous ones were to my right below the scoreboard — looking over long leg, when the bowling was at my end, if you want to be precise about it. In other words, I could see them clearly, though to my good fortune I could not hear them as well as I was to do at the MCG. Of a sudden hundreds of beer cans would be in the air, looping their parabolas over between thirty and sixty yards each, in all directions. From afar it was beautiful, the orange and gold labels of the amber liquid arching in the sun as they tossed here and there. But the weaving and the ducking beneath the beauty plainly showed

Tea-time at the 'Gabba'

that a beer can, when full — and some said they were full of not only beer — was a missile to be avoided on all possible grounds. Your warning might not be more than a second or two, and a pre-emptive strike would find its mark without much trouble. Injury could be substantial, and blood flowed. Anyone apart from me would have been impressed by his first sight, but, as these battles among the vociferous and the stupid came to punctuate the day every hour or so, being impressed gave way to sympathy, and then dislike. Alcohol was in fact a big problem because there were no regulations, I concluded piously.

The 'Gabba' is no Colosseum. Rather, it is the nearest any Australian ground comes, in my view, to St Lawrence, Canterbury. There is more concrete, and much more space for a big crowd, but, without tents, there is a tented flavour to it, and a festival air. There are flags fluttering, and you can have tea with your legs beneath a table and watch the cricket, too, if you have a mind to, and not everybody has. Brisbane is a relaxed, semi-tropical, provincial place, and it has a cricket ground to match. Friendly, smaller than most, and lovely in a rural sense.

The crowds were not large, 12,000 or so on each of the first three days, and they had a smaller effect on me than they were to have in Melbourne. They were as whole-hearted in their support, I suspect, but were not as noisy because of their smaller numbers, and applause for good cricket on either side was more common. Botham's century was spectacular, and they admired it unstintingly. They did not like defeat, though, and I had some sympathy for the lad, who, at the end of the third day's play, saw fit to flip my MCC tie from its resting place on my shirt, as he passed it in the street. Poms, if they are winning, should not show off.

Those I sat next to at the game were quiet to begin with, shy of intruding on my solitude, and then talked most readily. They knew a great deal about cricket, and we had frequent discussions about the finer points. When England got on top on the fourth day, they were sad, and I was glad, and we both laughed. I have a soft spot for Brisbane, for Queensland, and for their cricket supporters.

And a soft spot for Adelaide, too, but the reasons are not quite the same.

The Adelaide Oval is lovely, too, but in no rural sense. Rather, it has a quiet, aloof, classical charm, which, I am bound to say, is not really of this world. The ground itself is an oval, and so, unlike a circle, at once declares a lack of interest in human frailty, or fair play. Then, behind the boundary fence there is a broad, paved track, enabling spectators to walk round the ground, between spectators and players as it were, detaching each from the other. Sheltered accommodation is on one side

The Adelaide Oval and St. Peter's Cathedral

only. If you want to sit in the sun, and it is a hot sun, you can easily do so; half of spectator territory is in the sun, unsheltered from the heaven above. This unsheltered half permits a view of the trees in Pennington Gardens, and St Peter's Cathedral beyond, and, in rather worldly discord, apartment blocks beyond that. The ground, the accommodation and the crowd are in this way detached from ordinary reality. The green of the grass, and the leisured splendour of the space are magnificent, and unreal.

For all these reasons, and for sheer size in addition, the Adelaide crowd is a quiet crowd. That it came close to riot in the 'bodyline series' of 1932/3 means that it must then have believed it had received a monumental and cruel insult, whatever the facts. The Adelaide Oval is not a riotous place, and the untroubled contest I saw there fitted its situation admirably. Two chaps in front of me, who had drunk more than their fair share of rum and Coke by lunch-time, tried hard to make a stir at Graham Dilley's expense, and failed dismally. Nobody else would join in. The vociferous and the stupid were otherwise acres away on the other side, and threw empty beer cans, and also failed dismally. It was not dull, and it was gracious, like the old railway station on the other side of the river.

There was one oddity. Being near the sea, all Test match grounds in Australia have their seagulls. Other than at Adelaide, these seagulls play little or no part in the game. In Adelaide, for some reason, seagulls seem larger and more numerous than anywhere else. They like the Adelaide Oval, too, and they like being 'at the crickut'. Any ball hit further than thirty yards disrupts their peaceful sauntering, and any fielder in pursuit of it disrupts that even more. Thus, the squawking, the twisting, the turning, the swooping and the settling down again are always tremendous. Balls are frequently hit more than thirty yards on the Adelaide Oval wicket. It is as though Furies are allowed into heaven when the seagulls squawk.

It surprised me that no player seemed at all distracted either by the number or by the behaviour of these furious ones. It was all memorable, and became beautiful also, when you grew accustomed to Furies in heaven. Graham Dilley, saving a boundary and returning the ball with grace and accuracy with a swarm of seagulls about his head, gave the lie to any drunken critic, in my book anyway.

I do not wish to enter into local controversy of any kind, and so have difficulty in writing about the Sydney Cricket Ground. For I have somehow to show that the SCG and the MCG are both unique in their own way, have separate characteristics, and are in no way preferable, one to the other. Both suffer wretched disfigurement, in that both have had added to them, in the name of mammon, in recent years, a series of gaunt and thoroughly ugly floodlights. Melbourne has suffered, too, from unification, architecturally speaking, the Colosseum having supplanted several of its former lovely stands, suitably Victorian in origin; Sydney has virtually destroyed its famous Hill, depersonalized each end of the ground and one side with concrete edifices of a sadly nameless sort, but retained its superb pavilion and Ladies' Stand. In spite of these vulgarizations, both the SCG and the MCG remain memorable cricket grounds. If the MCG stands out as a not unworthy substitute for the former Roman Colosseum, then watching cricket at the SCG is like watching a match take place in the Roman forum from half way up the Palatine Hill. It is a wonderful sight, with a separate and unique atmosphere. I believe cricketers themselves like it best of all for that reason. You cannot see the forum, by the way, from the top of the Palatine Hill.

The crowd at the SCG? When I was there, it was whole-hearted and partial, and since Australia won the Fifth Test by a narrow margin, that kind of support did not go unrewarded, on that occasion anyway. It was at the SCG that I finally decided that I definitely would not like it at all if Australia won. That is what the Sydney crowd did for me. There was no dreary animosity, just an immense desire to win. Yet, when I went in search of an aspirin to assuage my companion's headache, it did not prevent the person to whom I addressed my initial enquiry from handing me a couple from his own pocket. People have told me that Sydney is brash, and I expected the crowd at the SCG to be brash. It was not; it was straight-forward and uncomplicated. It wanted to kill the Poms, and did, or so it thought.

I did not have the chance of seeing a good crowd in Perth, because few turned up to watch Western Australia play against England. The WACA is a fine, new ground. It will however take some time before it acquires an atmosphere of its own.

By the way, I watched the floodlights at the MCG perform once, in a World Cup Series match between Australia and the West Indies. I shall not do so again. The imitation of the Roman Colosseum was much too realistic for my liking. I would regret paying money to see such a good imitation more than once. It was not cricket, you see.

* * *

My last crowd was my best crowd and was on the other side of the world. I knew that, if I visited New Orleans, I would have to listen to some jazz. Not that I am in any way knowledgeable, but kinds of jazz had been part of my youth, and so I felt strongly that I should doff my cap, as it were, in the place where part of my youth had begun. Doff my cap? It was not like that at all.

I walked up and down Bourbon Street one evening, and was not amused. The noise terrified, the lights blinded and I could find no corner which reminded me of when I was young. Bourbon Street made me feel rather old, in fact.

So I gave myself dinner at the Old Coffee Pot, where I had done well previously. The Old Coffee Pot chanced to be on the same street as Preservation Hall, an Irish waitress told me. Preservation Hall? I had heard of it, and was intrigued and then delighted to find a queue at its entrance, having finished my dinner. I joined it, inquisitive and doubtful about my prospects. The noise of old-fashioned jazz was creeping through the wall, and the windows, which had only rough blinds over them. The hall looked dark, as dark as the street, decrepit and uninviting. I persisted, though, and in due course was surprised at how cheap the entrance fee was, only $2, collected haphazardly as we moved into a rough and brick-lined foyer.

We were a crowd, the best crowd, packed tight. Being by myself, I could edge this way and that, and, being quite tall, I could see more than most. It was hot, but there was no smoke and no smell of alcohol. Just a crowd of people.

Preservation Hall was in fact a room with about a hundred people in it, crowded on wooden benches, those near the back being raised a fraction. Three walls of the room were lined with other people, who stood as sardines might. I had a choice. I could try and squeeze myself into the back by the back door, or squeeze myself through the side door and along that wall, or stay where I was, peering into the room from outside it.

St. Louis Cathedral, New Orleans, looking toward the old quarter, a musician in the left foreground

St. Louis Cathedral, seen from the old quarter with the modern city beyond

I decided to stay where I was. I could see and hear everything from there.

I did not want to move anyway. I was entranced already by the music. All of them familiar, haunting like a prop for my 'long ago', those bewitching sounds came from musicians who themselves were no longer spritely, having seen it all long ago too: a small, delicate mulatress on the piano, a podgy, half-smiling black the banjo, a little white man the clarinet, paired delightfully with an old black man on the trumpet, a fat younger man the bass horn, a dapper precise drummer, and, the star of them all, an aged, world-weary trombone player, who would burst his cheeks if he could, but was mainly interested in the passage of time as shown on his wrist-watch, and the next interval. The sight of them all, their skill, their wit, their gentle sophistry, their delight in what they did, the dry, humorous singing of the banjo-player, the colour of their instruments, the twinkle of their hands, black and white, and their tunes in formal patterns, all combined were too much for my rational self. My mind left my body, and I became fixed and no longer there, at peace and listening.

The first interval (I stayed past three of them) gave me at last a chance to look at the crowd. It was a good crowd. Everybody was there, all ages, all colours, all sexes, a human unity. I had felt human unity in Uzbekhistan; here I saw it. When the music began again, the trombone-player being the last to return, our conversations with our neighbours slid at once into oblivion, and, not just me now, all of us became entranced again, dedicated, worshipping, like penitents at an altar, joyful, devoted and together. So moved was I that I decided only then that the two hours I spent in Preservation Hall that evening were the best two hours of my journey. I had been moved like that before by music, but never alongside so many others seemingly like me. We were present at a mystery, elevating and unknowable.

I resolved to return to Preservation Hall the following evening, and did. There were different players, and, try as I would, I could not feel again what I had felt before. I went with two Belgians this time, whom I had met at dinner. I was by now a guide, you may know. We heard the group play, *It's a long way to Tipperary*. The Belgians turned to me, and our eyes met in a glitter of understanding. Each knew without bothering, what the others were thinking. Next, they played *The Saints*. And quite right, too.

That First World War song brought it all back again. Where was Europe in all this? In all the crowds I had seen? Would the Belgians and I ever exorcise our schizophrenia? It was all extremely difficult, just as difficult as that picture by Chagall which I had seen in the New Orleans Museum of Art the other day: a cock, an ass, a clown, some musical instruments, a young woman, and a background of sombre blue, purple, black and white. Perhaps Chagall understood. Or Ruby? Could I be European *and* English?

6

Deserts and the Moon

Most people would say that deserts are harsh places. Yet, with time, as we have already seen, they become manageable. Long before the coming of steam and internal combustion engines, the old Silk Road, settling down as a complex of traditional routes between East and West in the Han dynasty (206 BC-AD 220), in due course had its harshness curbed, amenable to horse and camel. You could cross a continent with ordinary safety, long stretches of desert interspersed with rugged mountain ranges. Marco Polo travelled a well-worn route. Time and experience soften, even if they do not make soft.

My own journey took me across several deserts, in very reasonable comfort, it must be said. The Gobi was perhaps the most startling of them, but those in Arizona and central Australia were in no way despicable, even from the window of a train.

Indeed, for the United States, it was the train which eventually provided a life-saving bridge across the deserts of Utah, Colorado, Nevada and Arizona. Before the coming of the train those deserts were places of horror, uncharted and unexplored. The stories of those deserts, for the newly arrived white man anyway, belong to modern times.

Sensible people in the 1830s went west to California, still at that time in Mexican hands, by way of the Spanish trail through old Mexico or by sea. The deserts and the mountains through Utah, Colorado, Nevada and Arizona were vacant spaces of absolute uncertainty. The Spanish had come to California along the coast from the south. The Indians, much earlier than the Spanish, had wandered there, mingling nomadic and pastoral lives as they went. Russians from the north had settled at Fort Ross near the territory known as Oregon.

Dr John Marsh, a widower but a doctor only by fabled repute, came to California by the old Spanish trail, made a living as a doctor in the small dust and mud town of Los Angeles, and then moved north to buy himself a ranch near San Francisco Bay. From his ranch he wrote to friends in the east: 'The difficulty of coming here is imaginary. The route I would recommend is from Independence to the frontier rendezvous on the Green River, then to Soda Spring on Bear River along the Big Salt Lake, thence to Mary's River until you come in sight of the gap in the great mountain, through that gap by a good road and you arrive in the plain of Joaquin, and down that river on a level plain through thousands of elk and horse. Three or four days journey and you come to my house.'

The first party successfully to complete the trip, enticed by Dr Marsh and thoughts of paradise, for the discovery of gold in Eldorado was still seven years away, was led in by John Bidwell, the son of English parents and an explorer at heart. In 1841, at the age of twenty, without the support which had been promised earlier, he set out from Missouri westwards with sixty-eight others, men, women and children. No member of the party had ever been west before. They had no map, nor any detail of the nature of the terrain, or the availability of water, food or forage. They set out without resource except that which was theirs.

The party split at Soda Springs, thirty-two heading for Oregon and thirty-one for California, six already having left it. Bidwell, keeping a diary, wrote as the Californian section came in view of Salt Lake: 'Started early, hoping soon to find fresh water, where we could refresh ourselves and animals, but alas! The sun beamed heavy on our heads as the day advanced and we could see nothing before us but extensive arid plains, glimmering with heat and salt; at length the plains became so impregnated with salt that vegetation entirely ceased; the ground was in many places as white as snow with salt and perfectly smooth — the mid-day sun made us fancy we could see timber upon the plains. We marched forward with unremitted pace till we discovered it was an illusion.' By now it was the middle of August.

They ate their oxen, abandoned their wagons and equipment, and pushed ahead, sometimes until midnight, searching continually for water and food, and the direction in which such rivers as there were flowed. Now leading the party on foot,

Bidwell wrote: 'There were valleys between peaks. Having descended about half a mile, a frightful prospect opened out before us: naked mountains whose summits still retained the snow perhaps of a thousand years. The winds roared — but in the deep, dank gulfs which yawned on every side, profound solitude seemed to reign.' It was now the middle of September.

Killing horses and mules for food, pursued by unfriendly Indians, they became encircled by winter. More mountains, more valleys, more gorges, shoes in tatters, clothes in rags, California became a dream. They had already crossed the Mary's or Humbolt River, down the hollow swamp called the Humbolt Sink, across the Desert Mountains within sight of the Sierra Nevada. Struggling to the top of the eastern slopes of their final challenge, they became lost for a week in a nightmare of mountain crags and gorges.

But, somehow or other, Bidwell brought his party in. On 1 November, seventy days after entering Utah territory and the far west, two scouts returned from their explorations and said that they had come across an Indian who spoke one word of English, 'Marsh'.

Three days later, with his troop of hollow-eyed scarecrows, Bidwell walked onto the ranch of Dr John Marsh. He in his turn wrote back to his friends in the east, and said, '. . . they arrived here directly at my house with no other guide but a letter of mine . . . '

Seven years later, when gold at last, not paradise, was the enticement, the scorching sands of the Humbolt Valley, scattered with a trail of shallow graves, white skeletons of a thousand animals, and countless wagons with their household contents, was described by a forty-niner as 'filled with what the Lord had left over when he made the world, and what the devil wouldn't take to fix up hell'. By a good road, indeed.

The Bidwell party got through with luck on its side, for the extremes of winter had not set in before they began their descent of the western slopes. Others were not so fortunate. The Donner party, for instance, did not reach the Big Salt Lake until 1 September, 1846. They had taken what they had been told was a shorter route. Misled by an unfulfilled promise, they arrived at the eastern base of the Sierra Nevada on 4 November, the towering snow-covered crossing still ahead of them. They were six weeks behind the Bidwell schedule, and they never made it.

An advance party got through by resorting to cannibalism, but failed to return with supplies in time to rescue those marooned behind. The tragedy of the Donner party was not to go unrepeated.

Many died before they even reached the Sierra Nevada as the rush for gold began. The fate of the Donners, and the fearsome nature of the mountains, led one group to take a southern route, avoiding the worst of the mountains but leading through Death Valley and the Mojave desert, joining the safer old Spanish Trail at that point. This party initially called itself the Sand Walking party, but a section of it, as the whole party disintegrated through quarrels and disagreements, became known as the Death Valley party. Death Valley was an unalleviated desolation, eight to fourteen miles wide, one hundred and thirty miles long, and they had to go the length of it. In the centre was a low-lying group of hills, named the Funeral Range. Nothing lived in the valley. There were only wastes of sand and crusted salt flats with mountains on all sides and no trees, no shrubs and not a blade of grass. It was called a 'region of mirage, accursed to all living things, its atmosphere destructive even to the passing bird'.

The Reverend Mr Brier went ahead to look for water, and Mrs Brier was left behind with three little boys to bring up the cattle. She had to carry one of the boys on her back. She blundered on for hours through the dust, the cattle bellowing for water. As night came on, she lost contact with the two men in her group and had to crawl on the ground to keep in touch with the ox tracks. At three in the morning, she came upon her husband's camp, where they had found hot and cold springs. It was Christmas morning. They named the place Furnace Creek.

Next, as death faced them, they abandoned their wagons. 'Twenty miles across naked dunes, the wind driving the sand like shot into the faces and eyes.' Their tongues grew swollen, their lips became cracked, the oxen collapsed on the sand, and never rose again. That night they ate snow, which the men went to fetch from the mountain side. There followed forty-eight hours without water, and they were unable to eat the meat of the oxen they had killed, because they were unable to swallow. Mrs Brier was relentless in pursuit of her goal, California. Their sufferings did not relent. The Mojave Desert was still to come. Men, mere skeletons, lay down and waited for death. Helped by Indians, they found some water amid some shrubs at the base of the mountains, and, looking back over the country they had covered, they gave it the name of Death Valley.

In the end, thirteen men, including the Reverend Mr Brier, lost their lives before reaching their goal at San Francisquito ranch below San Gabriel Mountain. All the women, including Mrs Brier, survived.

With the passage of time the wagons trains became safer, but never completely safe. Good timing, and a degree of luck, were always vital. There was a radical solution, however, to this lack of safety, and a man called Theodore Judah had the vision to see that it was a practical solution as well. He was a railway engineer. Indeed, among other things, he had helped to plan and build the railway across the Niagara Gorge.

In California they wanted a railway to improve communication between Sacramento and the Eldorado goldfields on the western slopes of the Sierra Nevada. Judah and his wife were brought from the east, and Judah was asked to build it. By 1856 he had built what was required, shortening the time taken by wagon and stage coach by twenty-four hours.

Once you have built a railway as far as the Sierra Nevada, is not the next stop to build one across the Sierra Nevada? And with the mountains crossed, is not a railway across the whole continent then inevitable? So Judah thought, and dreamt.

He did all the planning and survey work to accomplish his dream, but others in the end did the building. Like many a dreamer, Judah did not have the financial clout. Charles Crocker was the engineer in practice; three others, Leland Stanford, Collis Huntington and Mark Hopkins, engineered the capital, the acumen and the business organization. Thousands of Chinese coolies, when white Americans failed to work hard enough, were imported, and did the labouring, at the cost of hundreds of lives.

On the day before the tracks laid by the Central Pacific from the west and the Union Pacific from the east made their final link, at Promontory, Utah, Charles Crocker bet that his Chinese workmen could lay ten miles of track in a day, and he won his bet. The tracks made their link on 10 May, 1869. Leland Stanford drove in the last spike. It was Theodore Judah's idea.

So it was that the deserts of the far west, and its mountains, were conquered. The lives of the Donners, the Briers, the Chinese workmen and many others had been spent in the endeavour. Gold had brought California millions of dollars; the railroad could now bring California millions of people, safely and soundly. The first crossings, the finding of gold and the building of a railway were to make the first three chapters in the making of a new civilization.

When the time comes for a railway finally to cross the Gobi Desert and the Tienshan Mountains, linking the USSR with the People's Republic of China, should not we expect to see something similar and just as remarkable? After all, the Chinese can build railways across any kind of country.

* * *

Competition with other railways making the journey to California brought fares down. The fertility of the Joaquin valley and rising property values in southern California, as immigrants crowded in, proved to be just the spur that Los Angeles needed. The city first began to prosper on the back of San Francisco, and then independently. It became its own person well before the end of the century.

It was a result of that prosperity that the railway I travelled on from Los Angeles to New Orleans came to be built. The so-called Gadsden Purchase of 1854 cleared the Arizona and New Mexico frontiers with the new state of Mexico, and space for building a Southern Pacific line across the continent was made plain, across empty desert, except for the occasional Indian settlement and the old Spanish presidio at Tucson. Indeed, Tucson was for a time capital of the Arizona territory (1867-77), and so its inhabitants must have been influential in planning the route of the new railway, which was completed in 1883.

I liked Tucson when I got there, overnight from Los Angeles. Its centre still retains a Spanish feeling. I enjoyed, too, as I have already described, my journey by bus to Nogales across the desert southwards. My only regret was that the bus did not stop at Tamacàcori, an old Spanish settlement, which became a Franciscan mission in 1784. My impression of the former mission buildings there, as our bus passed by, was fleeting but intriguing. They were mostly of red brick, and revealed Romanesque arches still standing against the ruination of time.

Modern Tucson

I willed to go again to Tamacàcori, and examine the ruins more closely.

My only direct and personal experience of the Arizona desert was on a walk I took on my first evening in Tucson.

Tucson is built on the banks of the River Santa Cruz, and where I was staying happened to be close to the river. I set out on my walk along its northern bank westwards. Not for the first time on my journey, a river had no water in it. The banks on both sides were steep and at least ten feet high. At their base was a sandy, stony, flat morass, thirty yards wide. There had been no water on the river bed for months, perhaps years. You could not tell, from the way the sand and stones lay, which way the river flowed. I guessed for myself that it might flow either way, for the water, when eventually it did arrive, might come from mountains in either direction too. Only later did I find

Tucson, as it used to be

out that the Santa Cruz, whichever way it flowed, emptied itself into the desert; it never crossed the Mexican border to the south, and it never reached the River Gila near Phoenix, which flowed westward into the Colorado. The Santa Cruz had a beginning and an end, and both were dry. Its middle was dry too.

This curiosity intrigued me, and so I followed the path along its northern bank westward. The sun was in its afternoon, and was pointing at some low hills on the horizon. You could not call them a range of hills; for they were only bumps on the land, scattered widely, near and far. From their rounded shape it was clear that they had suffered extremes of weathering, wind and sub-zero temperatures. They too intrigued me, as I had not seen their like before. And so I left the river bank along a track which led more directly towards them.

I walked and walked. For one thing, after the train ride, I needed some exercise. The late afternoon light was restful to look at, and the colours which reflected it were mute and gentle, sand yellow, a dun brown, a soft grey and olive green. You could tell too that it had been hot; the air was warm, bouncing from the land.

By the track were tall, pale, faded grasses, the occasional low, desiccated shrub, angular and aloof. I thought some of them were acacias. The low scrub I could not identify, and there were skeletons of trees from time to time, which were strange too. I read later that soapweed, agaves, yuccas, creosote bushes and the mesquite tree were what I was looking at; poetic, romantic names. Nature for me was in the names I read as well as in the scrub I saw. More easily identified were the cactuses, as a type but not in their seventy-five varieties, sometimes regularly spaced over the distance ahead and sometimes in groups. They could be very tall, much taller than I. The ground was hard, white and grey, close by, but like sand in the distant sun. I saw no living thing, man or woman, ant or fly. Apart from the sound of my crunchy steps, there was no sound either. I heard no spirit voices or clash of arms, as Marco Polo did.

I walked for three hours or so, until the sun set. I saw the hills turn from brown to pink, and then to black as the sun peeped briefly from behind them. Bidwell, the Donners and the Briers, for all their sufferings, had been similarly placed. I remembered too the words of Cable and French, describing their experience of the desert: 'The human body, having found its natural swing, becomes strangely unconscious of itself and releases the mind to its normal function of transmuting incident into experience. These are the conditions in which the wayfarer becomes, according to its measure, an observer, a philosopher, a thinker, a poet or a seer.' I began to think that I understood what it all meant, but then had to stop sharply.

It had become suddenly fiercely and brilliantly cold. Transmuting incident into experience? I had been sweating beneath light clothing. Now I was quickly freezing to the core. I turned at once, and made for home with more speed than that with which I had set out. On the walk back two other incidents were transmuted into experience. The tops of the cluster of tall buildings in the centre of Tucson were still visible in the distance, but now inlaid with gold. For them the sun had not yet set, and now a rectangular, regal pattern against the dark evening sky and the mountains became a crown hanging from the heavens. A mile or two later, the moon rose, full and large and orange. I shall have more to write about the moon's relationship with the desert. For now, remember that I walked out of Tucson in the face of the sun, and walked back in the face of the moon, briskly and chilled to the bone. The moon was so bright you could not see the stars later on, after supper.

* * *

I suppose it is no oddity that they discovered gold in California in 1848, and twenty miles north of Bathurst in New South Wales in 1851. Indeed, a man called Hargreaves from California discovered it. Other discoveries in Australia followed quickly in the same year, the most productive being those in Victoria based on Bendigo and Ballarat. The train took me through Bathurst and the Mappins, in the fascinating drives they took with me in rural Victoria behind Mount Macedon, showed me the gold workings near Bendigo and Ballarat. They found them scruffy and debilitating; I found them exciting and evocative. I particularly remember as an elegant symbol of it all the old market at Castlemaine, built in 1862.

Discovering gold first of all stimulated the infrastructure of the parts of Australia that had by 1851 been settled. It then stimulated the growth of population. Immigrants from all over the world flooded into the gold fields, which in their turn stimulated an unofficial white Australia policy. The Chinese, for instance, were sent back home because they worked too hard. (O, my Charles Crocker so soon to come!) As in California, gold in Australia brought wealth and unforeseeable stimulation.

People crossed the sea in their search for Australian gold; deserts did not need to be crossed. Journeys across deserts were made because people wanted to know what lay beyond them. The early convicts thought it was China; later people thought that there was an inland sea to be discovered there; but in the end they just wanted to see how big Australia was. Bidwell and the Donners knew where they were going, but did not know how to get there; before 1860, Oxley, Mitchell, Sturt, Eyre and Leichardt did not know either where they were going, but just wanted to get there.

In 1860, prompted by a £10,000 prize from the South Australia legislature, Stuart set off from Adelaide to find a way across Australia from south to north. He got as far as 18° south, reaching waters that flowed northwards into the Gulf of Carpentaria. In 1862 he went all the way.

However, the great tragedy of Australian desert exploration occurred in 1861, when Robert O'Hara Burke, a policeman, and William John Wills, a scientist from Melbourne observatory, set out with seven others, five horses and sixteen camels for Cooper Creek or Barcoo.

They left behind near the Darling River a substantial party under a man called Wright, to follow on more slowly with supplies. A second group was left behind at Cooper Creek to wait for Wright. Burke, Wills, King and Gray, with one horse and six camels, set out for the Gulf, and reached it. They turned back for their return journey on 23 February, 1861.

Their sufferings, after leaving water behind in the north, can scarcely be imagined. Gray died on 16 April. The others reached Cooper Creek exhausted but hopeful. Earlier that very day, the other party had left, giving up hope of their return and in search of Wright, who had dilly-dallied on the way for no apparent reason. Together, the reunited parties returned to Cooper Creek, but failed to look for Burke, Wills and King, who had wandered off in despair. Only King was found alive in the end. Burke and Wills had died in the desert, which by then must have become their home.

I briefly tell these tragic stories of desert journeys long ago

The Olgas

just to remind myself of my own good fortune; I travelled over and saw deserts in comparative comfort. I was able in this way to enjoy them, and I long to see them again, and to see new ones, too.

It was not always in safety and comfort, however.

Twenty miles west of Ayer's Rock in Australia's Northern Territory you find the Olgas, a cluster of about thirty sandstone monoliths, some over 1,700 feet above the surrounding plain. All have weathered domes like the Rock itself, but are irregular and separated from each other by ravines. We were taken to the western edge of this cluster, and allowed to walk up one of these ravines, the Valley of the Winds. On each side there was a steep, conglomerate wall, studded with coloured pebbles of many sizes. The floor of the ravine was uneven, and, when we were there, pools of water from recent rains were dark with reflections from each side. A yellow moss made the stones, already smooth, more slippery still. Dry stunted shrubs and bushes gathered protectively as the ravine narrowed, and I climbed no further.

It was unbelievably still, hot and sticky. I have not much

taste for lemonade, but drank it avidly when it was offered. Earlier, the day had been clear, and our journey on an unpaved road dusty with red dust. This was a grassy desert growing out of a red sand, and the grass, despite the rain, not green. To the west a black cloud grew strong, and slowly began to dominate even the Olgas. Nervously, our driver summoned us back to the bus. His name was Paul.

He drove back along the winding road at great speed, but not fast enough. First to catch up with us was a wind. No ordinary wind. A hurricane wind. We were now driving on the straight, and the wind blew from directly behind us, and a good thing too. For loose branches and other debris chased us along the road. Had the hurricane blown from our flank, we would have been in serious danger. Instead, it continued to blow from behind, and soon to raise up dust, the bus becoming enveloped in a cloud of brown and grey. Paul could see the road only with difficulty. The ghosts of bushes and trees, blown over and pirouetting now in the wind, appeared and disappeared. We perceived a kind of chaos.

In the nick of time, we reached the tarmac, for at that moment rain began to fall. Like the wind, no ordinary rain. Rain such as we never see in southern England. The Greeks call it 'raining chair legs'. Sheets of it. Our windows were at once awash. Paul's windscreen wiper became a worthless wand. He steered by clinging to the edge of the tarmac. Rain laid the dust to some extent, but combined with the hurricane it began to terrify. We were still miles from our hotel. (No hotel for Sturt and his colleagues.) With a sharp crack, a ventilator in the roof of the bus was blown off its hinges, and we saw it tumble and spin away into the murk. Then, the other ventilator went. Was even the roof safe? It did not matter. The rain poured into the bus in torrents. We all became soaked to the skin in seconds. There was no shelter anywhere, except for a small section behind Paul, where we foregathered. He was a stalwart, of pioneer breed. The storm abated not a scrap, but he stuck to his task, thankful at least that the flooded road ahead was not a muddy quagmire, which could have marooned us in a watery desert.

At last we crept up to our hotel building, halting in dismay for a minute or two, since all was in darkness and hollow-looking. The thirty yards or so we had sauntered after lunch to take our seats in the bus were now a flood, whipped up by the wind and the rain. It might be safer to wait in the bus.

Daring took hold of one or two, and then courage seized the rest of us. We dashed through the relentless rain, and reached the swing doors, which let us in one by one, thoroughly soaked but safe. We had been in danger, I think. None of us spared a thought for Paul, who had still to park his bus and find his own shelter. We had been in danger; we were thinking only of ourselves.

No sunset at Ayer's Rock that night, but a stupendous rainbow instead, as an orange sun just peeped through clouds before setting. The wind abated, and the rain became a drizzle. I had a kangaroo steak for dinner.

The next morning was the morning the others made their attempt on the summit of the Rock. I drove there with Paul later on. He said that he had been really frightened the evening before, but that part of his job was to stay calm whatever the circumstances. He asked me if I would keep my eyes open for the dismembered ventilators, in case they could be fitted back again. It was a hopeless task. Australians are great improvisers however. By the time we took the bus back to Alice Springs its roof was waterproof again. I heard a story of a motorist whose gearbox came adrift halfway across the Nullabor Plain. He secured it with some fencing wire found by the roadside, and made Perth without further mishap. No problem.

The land surrounding Ayer's Rock is completely flat. You can see the Olgas twenty miles away with ease. That morning it was littered with debris, fallen trees and countless broken branches, large and small. It was also marshy in places, and there were pools of red water in traditional watering places. Below the Rock, in narrow gullies, there were even piles of hailstones. Nobody could explain that oddity, as we were all sweating again in the hot and humid air. The sun was shining strongly once more. We were not allowed to trespass; much of the land below the Rock is now reserved for aboriginal use only.

Ayer's Rock lies to the south west of Alice Springs, and is 211 miles away by air. Alice Springs began life in 1872 as an overland telegraph station between Adelaide and the north. Its situation just to the north of a gap in the MacDonnell range of hills, which stretch across nearly all the southern half of the Northern Territory, was of great strategic importance. In forging the gap years ago in the MacDonnell Ranges, the Todd River must have been in its heyday, as part of an inland sea, linking the north with the east. The sea disappeared in prehistory, but the course of the river, into and away from the gap, still survives. These days the railway and the main road also make use of the gap on their way towards a new and bustling town. Formerly a telegraph station and the centre of the Outback cattle industry, Alice Springs is now fast expanding into a manufacturing centre as well as a winter holiday resort. Its progenitor, the Todd River, like the Santa Cruz in Arizona, is for most of the time these days no river at all; it is instead a dry, attractive playground of sand, ending blindly in the desert to north and east.

My first impression of Alice Springs was its new railway station; my second the town itself with its 22,000 population; and my third the Todd River. It 'flowed' past the place where I was staying, and I took a walk along it southwards, towards the gap, the afternoon following my arrival.

Smaller than the Santa Cruz, it is only as wide as a cricket pitch is long. Its banks are low and grassy, pale and spiky, and its sandy walk meanders peacefully amid scattered groves of eucalyptus trees, taking its time and, just for as long as you like, content with itself and you. When the next flood comes, it may have to change its course, but not yet, for floods come hereabouts only from time to time, perhaps years away. The sand is soft and yielding. You can only walk slowly towards the gap. Through the trees, you can see the gap has red, jagged cliffs, but it is a gentle, quiet place, still and warm as air. As I recall that first walk along the river bed and its clean, unpreserved peace, I can scarcely believe that before I left Alice Springs I was to see the Todd River in spate.

Meanwhile I took a day's trip along the western half of the MacDonnell Ranges. It turned out that there were other gaps, all formed in much the same way as the one at Alice Springs, by water erosion in weak places in the rock. There were two differences; these other gaps were full of water, and the red rock of the hills looked higher. Near their base was the normal slope of weathered stones and sand; at the top a crust of pastry, baked hard and burnt long ago, stretching out along the whole ridge, forgotten by the cook.

The water in each of the three gaps was smooth and limpid. Ellery Creek, Glen Helen and Ormiston Gorge offered their own reflections in place of yours. Each place was its own person.

Red River gums at Ellery Creek

Ellery Creek had sharp, sudden cliffs, with red river gums decorating the entrance in timeless patterns of red and white. Glen Helen, broader and less menacing, had time to show off to the sky date palms from Afghan days. Ormiston Gorge, devious like Arcadia in the Peloponnese, was secluded as a monastery might be; two young people dived naked, repeatedly, into the water from the branch of a tree, as the original Australians had done before the whiteys came, seeming to taste eternity. In Ormiston Gorge there was too a solitary ghost gum, nestling against the red cliff, its white bark fitting its trunk like a glove, and its branches like silk, at their tips olive green and silvery, pendulous leaves commenting on the world's elegance. The ghost gum is a most delicate, delicious thing, and so are they all.

It was still humid along the MacDonnell Ranges as it had been at Ayer's Rock, but there were no flies at all. The truth is, quite against what I had been led to believe, I was never bothered by flies in Australia. Nor by kangaroos. I did not see a single kangaroo at any time during a three months' stay, other than in a zoo. I saw no wild camels either, though I did catch a glimpse of some on a camel farm. However, half a dozen attractive wild donkeys did approach us for food as we left Ellery Creek. That did a little to re-establish belief in myth. Much was generally unsettling, though. My time in Alice Springs was unusual in that there had recently been a great deal of rain. Surprisingly for me, and unusually for the town's inhabitants, the desert thereabouts was green and not brown, and the air was humid, even 'sticky', one shopkeeper said. That deserts are always dry is a myth.

Australia is the oldest land of all, and its centre is as old as any of it. The centre, too, leads nowhere in particular, in its present state of development at least. Darwin, after all, and the nature parks of the northern fringe lie on the rim of existence. The centre is a barrier in a psychological sense as well as a physical one. If occasionally you feel cut off from the rest of the world in Brisbane, Sydney, Melbourne, Adelaide and Perth, it is in part due to that vast empty land you always know lies between you and anywhere else. The deserts of the Outback are part of the fabric of the tyranny of distance. Tyranny or not, it is a good life for most people in the cities of Australia, and the centre of the country, to the north, west or east of you,

Wild donkeys near Alice Springs

is a dramatic, romantic place in which to have a holiday, and to begin to understand a little about the dream-time of old. But in the cities, you always have to face one fact; the centre leads nowhere except to the fringe of things, and leading nowhere is an important fact of life for those who are not content with today. The original Australians had never wanted anything to lead them anywhere, and were always content with today, and so had, and still have, a pre-eminent advantage over those who are not. In the United States you need never have been content with today; the deserts always lead you westwards. It was a half moon in Alice Springs, and it shone fitfully through the cloud.

* * *

Turn the mind northwards, across the Equator, to the furthest limits of north-west China. Resplendent in its past, at least the edge of it we saw, the Gobi desert is only now beginning to have a modern history.

The road from Urumchi to Turfan in Xinjiang is an unworldly fantasy. We left Urumchi a little late on a dull afternoon, climbed a road past a huge market selling cattle and everything else, and entered a barren area of black hills. We descended from these and their menace onto a plain which exuded the kind of majesty which invents fairy stories about giants. As we turned gradually to our left, keeping the black hills on that side, we saw to our right a huge lake, lying flat, as flat as its face, for miles and miles. As the clouds began to lift, its colour changed from grey to misty blue. It must have been a shallow lake, and salty, for nothing grew by its side, and the plain was vast and stony anyway, the lake a small depression in the plain's flatness. Beyond the lake was a range of picture-book mountains, peaked and pink, as the afternoon first began to change to dusk. They were high, because their snow seemingly covered half their height, flat against the scenery of the sky. Judging distances was not easy, for the air was not crystal clear. A map showed that the mountains were no more than twenty miles away, perhaps less. No map we had was accurate anyway. The plain was uncultivated, and we passed few people on the road. The black hills, with a rapid change of geological structure, to our left, altered colour to brown, and lighter colours, yellow and grey, would slash their sides from time to time. I took no photographs, for I knew I could not forget our ride that afternoon. We saw no giants, but might have done.

Then, suddenly, we entered unaware a mountain pass, with rushing mountain streams. There must have been a lot of snow somewhere up above. The road narrowed as rocks impinged, the Emperor drove just a little more slowly and we halted for a 'comfort stop', overlooking a grey rocky valley, and some sort of primitive settlement below. Not unlike a small glen in the highlands of Scotland, but more vigorous and nowhere green. The water rushed away with itself, and was noisy where we stopped.

As we descended further, the road grew straighter, and the Emperor drove faster. This and the dusk had us leave the mountains behind us before we were ready for it. I looked back and they were gone. We faced another plain now. We could just see it from our bus windows.

Nobody could explain how it got there. It was not sand, it was not gravel and it was not a mixture of small and large stones, as all other deserts had been, or were to be. It was stones, just stones, and all the same size, about the half of a man's fist, grey, jagged, flint-like, all the same to look at but different individually. It was an eerie sight in the darkening light, for, although the sun had set, we could see that this curiosity stretched for miles and miles; it was all that was visible on each side of the bus. My imagination was, and still is, quite unable to conjure up any explanation. There was no sign of weathering at all, and, because of the steepness of the mountains we had just crossed, one had to assume that the stones were no shallow superficiality, but went deep, very deep indeed. Quite impervious to any water that might come their way, they harboured no vegetation of any kind. I had been able to imagine deserts of sand (and we were to see one near Dunhuang later on) but never deserts of stones, all the same except in detail. Our road was straight but not good. Stones had in the course of time been scattered at random over its surface, and made our journey bumpy. I could not either imagine how you would cross such a desert, if you had to, without a road.

We drove on for an hour at least in these circumstances, and it became very dark, a complete kind of darkness. Only the Emperor's lights at the front, piercing the road ahead, told us anything. A luminosity began to show up on our left side. It was a clear night. The planets and the stars were now shining brightly. The luminosity, white to begin with, changed colour on the horizon to pale orange, and then pink. An astonishing moon, larger than any I had ever seen, because, I suppose, of the huge desert dust, full and complete, crept up from behind its straight line. Orange and pink together, it was the old familiar shape, but benign now and offering benediction in the stillness. The noise of the bus distracted; I would have liked to have stood still and watched. It greeted its flat congregation of stones, and they responded with a sparkle of their own, dry, muted at first, and then scintillating. The desert knows how to shine too. It was one of those times when you know for certain that the world is a beautiful place. Man had not done a thing to help it.

We were lucky. We were to drive another hour yet. As the moon climbed higher and higher and became brighter and brighter, the desert shone more and more. There is always a sense in which nature is a unity and united in effect, but never was it so obviously and so simply so in the moonlight, that evening, in the desert before Turfan. If you can stretch imagination, and think of the moon as part of the earth, that evening we thought of nature as an earthly unity, ours and nobody else's, for the moon's brightness and the brightness of the desert proved to be far too much for the shining of the stars. They ceased their twinkling, and their mockery. The moon and the desert were at one, and we included ourselves in that. This was now no unworldly fantasy. No giants here.

The Emperor rocketed along. There was an odd feeling of going downhill, though the desert still seemed completely flat. Gradually there were signs of life outside the bus, a small light or two from habitations in the distance, a tamarisk, even a row of tamarisks, and some grass by the side of the road. The stones were giving way to sand, and we began to feel that the Emperor saw the end of the journey ahead of him. He was just coasting down the road now.

Fields, and simple forms of cultivation followed. We could not see exactly; it was probably cotton, beans, tomatoes (the Italian sort, growing along the ground), or melons. Or perhaps sorghum, whatever that is; the dictionary tells me it is either a millet or a Chinese sugar cane. Near Turfan, sugar cane, I dare say. Clearly water, regular water, was at hand. It was probably half an hour before we entered town. When we did so, the Emperor began to drive at a stately pace. He was home as it turned out, and our hotel was called the Oasis Hotel. And Turfan was a big place.

When morning came, and the sun shone again with its autumnal warmth, I was surprised once more at the magnitude of the Turfan oasis. No small pond bordered by a few palm trees, this one. A bustling sizeable town, surrounded by fertile land for miles on all sides betokened unusually large supplies of water on a continuing basis.

The town and oasis lie in a depression in the earth's crust nearly 1,000 feet below sea level, while at the same time, at no great distance other than eastwards, lie long ranges of hills and mountains. Bogdo-Ola to the north in the Tienshan range is 22,000 feet high. In this way on three sides Turfan is surrounded by snow. The ordinary wells in Turfan itself yield water of poor quality; no-one drinks it, and no-one, it seems, washes laundry with it. They only use it on the streets, which need it more than laundry, I would say. Supplies of good, fresh, cold water are readily accessible, however, by a method called 'karez', derived ultimately, it is thought, from Persia. The melt from the mountains is led downwards in underground channels. Near the mountains the channels have to be deep, because of the effect of the earth's depression on the flow of water; if the tunnels are not deep enough near the mountains, the water would flood uselessly away at too great a speed on the plain when it reached it. By steady control of the water's slope so that where it is wanted, near and around the town, it is close to the surface, it gushes from its tunnel in a steady and obedient stream. The fertile land beyond the town is punctuated by tomb-like structures; these are in fact accesses to the underground tunnels, which were used in their construction, and now as a means of drawing water. Farmsteads and small villages group themselves round these structures, and 'karez' these days is the Uighur word for 'hamlet'. Drinking water in the town itself, in the old days, used to be sold by Uighur boys from donkey carts. These days, for the most part, it is laid on by public supply, with the result that I still do not really know why they would not do my laundry in the Oasis Hotel. It was lovely to see so much water about in the countryside, bubbling happily along the channels by the road, and then into gardens and fields. They were burly, happy country folk, the Uighurs.

I am not sure about their summers though, when the temperature regularly reaches 130°. According to Cable and French, the bazaar in the Turfan used to have an old-fashioned, oriental look. These days, it has a modern, concrete gallery look on three sides, and a wide, open courtyard with a bridge to help access at the upper level. On the fourth side it leads towards an open space, which has stalls of more ancient, ram-shackled design scattered about. It has acquired a semi-organized appearance. Only when you wander around the stalls and see the variety of goods and the variety of men and women who sell the goods do you really begin to sense the basic, jostling chaos which still belongs to olden days. As well as the galleries, trees and awnings provide shelter from the sun.

I was interested in the carpets and rugs. Before leaving London, I had bought my daughter a large rug from Xinjiang as a present in case I failed to return there. I was eager to see its origins, and there they all were, spread out in the open on the dusty ground. To western tastes their colours are garish,

Above: Selling carpets in Turfan

Below: The monastery and the caves of the thousand Bhuddhas and their valley

The Flaming Mountains and an intrepid photographer

and so Xinjiang carpets sold in London are washed before sale to subdue the bright colours. The salesman in the corner where I was was an old man with a long, white beard, dressed in a long, woollen, dark coat and black, decorated skull-cap. Willingly he showed me his wares, turning them back and forth so that I could see the underside as well. He was not at all offended when I indicated that I could not buy because I was travelling a long distance. I must admit it did not seem a very good excuse in an oasis. Despite that, he readily agreed to have his photograph taken.

The fruit is nearly as colourful as the carpets; varying shades of sultanas, currants and raisins, plums, apricots, peaches, nectarines, mulberries and nuts. Most prolific of all were the melons: bright slices of watermelon, their black seeds set aside for salting and roasting, and slices of cantaloupe of many, many kinds, revealing flesh that is white, green, pink or orange. You can take a slice for just a penny, throwing the rind away as you go. I did not do that; I took the rind back to the hotel wastepaper basket.

Leather goods of many colours, all practical (no trinkets), for young and old, especially boots, saddles and harnesses. Herbs: twenty or thirty different kinds; I recognized fennel, cardamom, saffron, ginger, cinnamon, coriander and sesame.

Silk, cotton and woollen goods, some still in rolls; like the carpets, of vivid colours and put to every conceivable use, patterned and stitched. And a great variety of skull-caps. And second-hand bicycles.

And letter-writers, in a row. There was one, too, I now recall, outside the post office of earlier fame. And outside the hotel, there was some health education, a large notice printed in red, in Uighur, Chinese and English; it said 'To marry late and to have children late is good for health, work and study.' My experience in the post office earlier, combined with the juxtaposition of letter-writers and a complicated, printed health education message, had puzzled me, I must admit. Perhaps it was because Turfan was an oasis town, and had to take anything that came its way.

Like the Cultural Revolution, for instance. Its basically Uighur population has been Moslem for a thousand years, strictly so, and as a result the town used to possess several handsome mosques, handsome at least by repute. In the course of the Cultural Revolution some were destroyed and others put to different use. We were told that two had survived as places of worship. Attendance in any case had dropped dramatically, but was now climbing again. John told us of this unemotionally, in a factual way. Turfan has survived all that has come its way, and so has Islam. What happens to Islamic belief, currently subdued all the way across central Asia, will be of great interest, even to me in my lifetime. They still drink tea and eat pilau.

I speculated too about what might happen if Turfan grapes were to be turned into wine instead of sultanas. By the nature of things Uighurs would not be interested, but, knowing them, the Han Chinese might be. If Australian wine can become a worldwide possession in fifteen years, what might not happen to a subsidized wine industry in Xinjiang, and to its produce? A splendid thought upon which to speculate.

The vineyards lie to the north at the base of some sandstone, conglomerate hills, and it is said that every kind of grape flourishes there. Water from the hills is plentiful, and it rarely rains. The grapes have to be gathered before the scorching summer wind arrives. That wind dries the grapes into sultanas, and that heat would inhibit fermentation, I dare say, but is it not likely that anything the Barossa Valley, for instance, can do, the Flaming Mountains might also attempt with similar success? The sandstone hills have been called the Flaming Mountains because weathering has created numerous narrow, vertical gullies down the side of the hills, and when the sun strikes the side of the hills from the south, the air quivers in the heat, and gives the impression of turning the red sandstone into flickering flames. It is a curious sight from a distance, across the level desert in the afternoon, when the shadows add depth.

Before seeing the Flaming Mountains that afternoon, we had visited the desert site of the ancient city of Kaochang, capital of the province thereabouts in the Han and Tang dynasties, covering the period 100 BC-AD 1500, though it is said that, when the Han dynasty fell, Kaochang was taken over by locals, Buddhist locals it would seem.

The city is now in ruins, its walls and buildings, albeit solid, either stamped mud or baked brick made with straw, collapsing as a result of the weather and the pillaging of local farmers. Its aspect, however, to someone from the West, is entirely Roman, so that you wonder at once whether or not you have by a miracle been returned somehow to Campania. There is a wide central square or forum, with dignified steps and a 'praetorium' at its head. The square has a stately, pillared design, and brick had been used to give architectural effect. The city walls are massive in the Roman manner, and built as a rectangle in defensive terms, with gateways, as you might imagine. Otherwise it was difficult to make much sense of the city in archaeological terms, other than that it had been carefully planned on a large scale, within walls which suggest, I would guess, a population of no less than 25,000. Chinese records say Kaochang was the capital of an area 260 miles by 160, which included twenty other towns. Other evidence shows that, as well as being a fortified centre of trade, it was at one time a place where various religions gathered until Islam eventually succeeded in blotting everything else out, Buddhists, Manichaeans and Nestorians among them. It is even thought that Alexander's soldiers, on leaving their allegiance, travelled as far east as Kaochang, in this way explaining, it is said, how it comes about that so many early pictorial representations of the Buddha look like Apollo. Elementary scepticism took over for me at this point. Turfan people call Kaochang Apsus, and so some like to connect it with the Greek Ephesus. Others call it Dakianus, which makes it, still others say, derive from the name, Decius, a Roman emperor, who persecuted Christians. Scepticism became rather less elementary on receiving this news.

What remains of the city are plainly the remains of the city in its last days. There is no clear record about what happened to it in the end. Perhaps the simplest explanation is that water ran out. The ruins lie in the middle now of a wide, arid area, and are as dry as bones.

Kaochang, to the east of Turfan, had a rival to the west, a place called Jiaohe, or Between the Streams. Jiaohe occupies a defensive position in the hills, on the top of a cliff, with two rivers converging on each side. It only had to have strong fortifications on its northern side, joining the two cliffs together there. The approach to the city is an exciting one, not unlike that on the way up to the sanctuary at Delphi, and similarly awe-inspiring. The bus deposits you at the base of the slope, and you walk along a narrow road upwards, between white, overhanging, hard sandstone rocks. After ten minutes, conscious all the time of steep ravines on both sides, you reach a level

Jiaohe the ancient rival of Kaochang

space, and opposite is the old, ruined gate of Jiaohe. Inside the gate is a smaller city than Kaochang, cramped for space but having nevertheless a spacious central square. We were told that the town had been designed in two halves, one on each side of a central road, to the west manufacture and shops, to the east private dwellings and bigger houses. Evidence for this, on the site at least, did not appear to be strong. On both sides of the central highway there was a jumble of streets, which connected buildings of great variety, many appearing to be like those of other ancient towns, single rooms with large doorways facing a street, in other words, shops. If you liked, you could imagine bakers, tanners, cobblers, tailors, haberdashers, grocers, all plying their trade higgledy-piggledy, in the general throng going to and fro, without order or system of any kind.

Plainly, Jiaohe was strong in the sense that its position was as secure as any position could be. In this sense it must have been a serious rival for Kaochang in times of trouble. In prosperous times, Kaochang on its plain would have far the better chance. In the end, Kaochang conquered Jiaohe, and there was peace until the water gave out on the plain. Jiaohe did not survive either, even though its water did, at the bottom of each ravine.

Before our visit to Kaochang, we had driven up a lovely valley to the north, where a stream flowed southwards and may in the past have been an important source of water for that city. The valley wound upwards in huge bends. At its base the stream meandered vaguely over a flat, alluvial area, of varying width but never more than a quarter of a mile wide. On the inside of each bend, the slope of the scree would be at an angle of 30°; opposite, on the outside of the bend, there were steep, jagged cliffs. These cliffs were of soft sandstone, and the colour of sand predominated in the area, except in the valley where a vibrant green spoke of friendly water. Our road climbed to the top of a cliff on the left hand side of the valley. Far off ahead in the distance we could see the snow-capped mountains of the Tienshan, and, to our left, the first roll of sand-dunes, and a high desert. Down below in the valley by the stream, suddenly there was a crowd of people, many of them on horseback. A film crew was taking a crowd scene, the characters in costume perhaps playing parts in a story of an ancient war between Kaochang and Jiaohe. Ten minutes later, our bus stopped on what was plainly a bus park.

We descended several sequences of steep stairways down the cliff face, and presently came to a terrace, newly made of concrete with a balustrade overlooking the valley, yet still retaining the view of the Heavenly Mountains to the north. It was a lovely, thrilling place. The air in the sun was warm and clear, and in the shade cool and welcome. People lived below in sheltered calm in small houses. Chickens, geese and oranges, I remember. Not a bad place to live.

The steps ended facing south, the valley to our left and the cliff to our right. It was called Bezeklik. There on our right were the entrances to the Caves of the Thousand Buddhas, in the shade now and behind a bend beyond the sight of marauders.

The first thirteen doorways did not lead into caves really; rooms had been built out from the side of the cliff, and three of them had small, shallow domes on their roofs. All the doors were bolted tight. After a space, there were other doorways, seven of them, three larger than the others, all leading into the side of the cliff. Only two of the large doorways were open. Inside, these two caves were about twenty feet square, and had faded frescoes on their ceilings. As far as I can remember in the gloom, the walls were bare. The frescoes gave the caves their name; they consisted of hundreds of tiny paintings of the Buddha, arranged in patterns. You could only just see them, but they were there, and nothing else. There had once been frescoes of grotesques of Indian gods, six-handed demons, human-headed birds and a king on a hunting expedition. In addition, there used to be statues of the legendary Guardians of the World and of the cave's first benefactors. 'By dint of long arduous work, we succeeded in cutting away all these pictures. After twenty months of travelling, they arrived safely in Berlin, where they fill an entire room of the museum . . . . This is one of the few temples whose sum-total of paintings has been brought to Berlin.' So wrote Albert von Le Coq, archaeologist, after his return to Germany following the discovery of the Bezeklik monastery in 1904. He took the statues, too. The monastery had survived more than 1,000 years without the attention of marauders, even Moslem invaders. Closed doors now hide most of the pillaging of Europeans in the twentieth century. The British had their counterpart to von Le Coq in Xinjiang, Sir Aurel Stein, the results of whose depredations are only on public display in the British Museum from time to time, 'recovered', the legend says, from their original resting place, 'having survived intact for a thousand years'.

The steps, the terrace and the balustrade are part of the contribution of the People's Republic towards the preservation of the Bezeklik caves; there was a sandy slope there in von Le Coq's day. Understandably the Chinese authorities are bitter in their complaints about his desecration. Above the monastery the huge sand-dunes watch over everything in simulated detachment, as if they did not care.

These ancient monuments to the former grandeur of the old Silk Road near Turfan are only three among the many which survive along its route. We were to see a fourth near Dunhuang, which mercifully has survived intact, apart from its fabulous library, silk work and frescoes, which are now stored in the British Museum, and the more normal kind of decay which time ensures.

Dunhuang lies about 300 miles south west of Turfan, and was for us an overnight train journey away, the train depositing us some ninety miles or so from the town itself. We missed 300 miles of desert and mountain during the night, but saw on our bus ride to Dunhuang something of what we might have missed, a complete flatness, arid and the colour of red sand, with just the outline of mountains in the distance. As we neared Dunhuang, the flatness was occasionally punctuated by the ruined signs of ancient habitation, a city or a town or two, and, then, tall beacon-like towers, beacons in fact; the name, Dunhuang, means 'blazing beacon'.

Dunhuang itself, when the Silk Road flourished, was a place of decision, for travellers moving westward had to choose there whether to take the southern or northern route round the Taklamakan desert. It must always have had, as it still does in a way, the air of a frontier town, fortified like the Korgas of old.

We had driven south from the railway, and the Mogao grottoes which we had come to see lay fifteen miles further on.

The grottoes, or caves as at Bezeklik, were first hewed out of the side of a sandstone cliff by Buddhist monks in AD 366. The caves were kept in repair and added to over the next 1,000 years in a most remarkable way. As the caves increased in number and the size of the monastery grew, the murals and

The only photograph we were allowed to take at the Magao Caves

painted statues, which resulted over time, can be seen to represent the changing artistic styles and spiritual moods of centuries.

The size of the site was stupefying. I could not guess the length of the cliff. It was large enough to have 484 numbered, separate and different caves, at three levels and in some parts four. The caves were of varying sizes, sometimes more than twelve feet high, and some were linked together by passageways. At a personal level, I could comprehend neither the site's complexity nor the totality of its contents. We were allowed to take no photographs, and so I have no visual means of recollection. We were shown round by a knowledgeable and accomplished guide. I have not been able to remember a single word she said. I was tired, I know, at the time. There survives a brightly coloured kaleidoscope, a jumble without connection, black and white used with great vigour, astonishing carvings of complicated and dramatic figures and buddhas, two reclining hugely, at great length, an impenetrable mythology, a place of ingenuity, craftsmanship and vision, in total incomprehensible to western eyes, except as a monument of an immense, spiritual vigour and serenity. There was just one ceiling, painted with birds in flight, and animals and fish linked by tangles of vegetation and water, which reminded me of the Raphael grotesques in the Vatican, and so Nero's *Domus Aurea*. Such was the painting's stride and confident daring. No monks live there any more.

The present government of China is responsible for protecting the monastery's treasures. Exterior concrete gangways have been constructed at three of the four levels so that entrance to most of the caves is now possible, though I have to say that my fear of heights still had me trembling on a precipitous corner or two. Where the cave entrances had been eroded or looked like collapsing, concrete supports have been constructed, and refurbishing has taken place inside the caves as well. However, means whereby visitors, and particularly foreign visitors, may gain some understanding of the site and its significance have yet to be provided; a simple exhibition hall, offering an introduction to the splendours ahead, seems to me to be of urgent importance, if the memory of a visit to Mogao is not to become an incoherent jumble, as it has in my case.

The main preserver of the caves, however, was a Taoist priest, known widely as Abbot Wang. The Abbot had been a devoted admirer of the Chinese Buddhist pilgrim, Hsuan-tsang, who had journeyed to India and back in the seventh century in pursuit of the original sources of his religion, taking sixteen years to cover his return journey of 1,500 miles. The library at Dunhuang was based on the texts which Hsuan-tsang brought back with him from India. Abbot Wang, at the turn of the last century, saw it as his sacred duty to preserve and, if possible, to enhance the antiquity and sanctity of the monastery. With this in mind, he diverted a stream from the nearby hills so that it could flow along the base of the cliff, and along its banks he planted a grove of poplar trees. The stream and the trees, after a long desert journey, still offer a chance of a pause to the weary traveller, before climbing the stairs to gaze at the wonder housed within the cliff.

It was from Abbot Wang that Sir Aurel Stein bought the ancient library, paintings and artefacts in 1908, persuading him of his shared regard for Hsuan-tsang. Wang used the money to preserve the caves and to beautify their approach. The Chinese believe that Stein's purchases were the equivalent to sacking Dunhuang at the behest of the British Museum and the Government of India. With some justice, one has to say, since the British Museum puts the missing treasure on display only from time to time. In New Delhi, some of Stein's trophies are on permanent display.

Strong winds from the east pile up the sand from the stony plains near Dunhuang, and the result is the mighty sand Desert of Lob to the westward, described by Marco Polo. The edge of this desert is about four miles west of Dunhuang. Before going to the Mogao grottoes, they took us to see the desert. The sand began suddenly.

First, there was a small habitation, a grove of poplar trees and a public lavatory, a sure harbinger of a tourist attraction. Around the corner were strings of camels, and camel-drivers, selling rides at a pound a time. Our group easily succumbed, and so did I.

It was a satisfactorily long ride into the desert, well worth one pound, and easy to forget you were a tourist, and to imagine yourself in days of yore with a thirty-mile stint ahead of you. The inside of your thighs soon told you that it would be an arduous business. You would certainly be bleeding thereabouts before it was over. To stay upright you had to grip the tuft

Camels in the sand, near Dunhang, the author riding last
(by kind permission of Nan Warren)

of hair on top of the camel's first hump. The camel's gait, even at a beginner's pace, was, on the sand, extraordinary, unsteady and unpredictable. The camel itself was encumbered by a cruel 'bit', a piece of wood piercing its nostril on each side. The poor beast would utter a low, plaintive cry, each time the 'bit' was jerked. If it was ever thus, I for one am not at all surprised at the camel's reputation for ill-temper.

Our ride took us through sand-dunes of great size and unimagined height, dwarfing men on camels. So high was the dune I attempted to climb, at the half-way halt we were given, that I gave up, exhausted by its steepness, not from my customary fear of heights.

Except for the camels, we all enjoyed it. The air was good and the sun was warm and soft. We had ridden about a mile, I suppose, before turning back. We turned back at the edge of a small lake, which curved round the foot of the next range of dunes. It was supplied with water from an underground spring. Scrubby trees and grass grew on its banks. Its name was Yueya Lake, the Lake of the Crescent Moon.

On the way back to the train, the moon, three days older now, rose again over the desert in the dark. The desert sparkled.

* * *

Thank goodness, no generalization is possible about deserts. They are not even harsh places, not now. Time has conquered them, encouraged by the bravery of men and women. They are useful now as land routes, safe and reliable, as testing grounds for atomic explosions, as laboratories, as sources of wealth, for agriculture and, even, for holidays and retirement homes. Risks are few, if you take care.

Many things surprised me about the deserts I saw. I can make three remarks in general about what surprised me. First, no desert is like any other; all change their appearance in light and shade; none are boring. Second, there is always so much water about either in the mountains melting downwards or below ground seeping upwards; and it rains, albeit rarely. Third, the moon is a desert creature; nowhere else does the moon come into its own as it does when shining on a desert. So much is this so that, wherever the moon shines, I now think it makes a desert of that place, too.

The last word I leave with a Greek poetess, who grew up about 600 BC by the sea with a desert behind her on land, Sappho, in the north-west corner of the island of Lesbos. I have adapted T.F Higham's translation of a fragment of hers, so as to include the word, moon, in place of its Greek equivalent, Selene. She wrote simply, in her own dialect.

> Bright stars, around the lovely Moon appearing,
> No more their beauty to the night discover
> When she, at full, her silver light ensphering,
> Floods the world over.

7

Water and the Weather

As the reader knows, my journey started in London in the rain. We then received a buffeting while crossing the Channel. In the evening gloom it was still raining when we reached Paris. It had nearly stopped by dinner time. The following morning it was teeming again, and I had to buy an umbrella, having previously thought, quite wrongly, that a hat and a raincoat would suffice for any watery eventuality I might encounter. Quite wrongly, for Paris, like Athens, can produce chair legs, too.

Because of the rain, I enjoyed seeing under cover what Parisians had done to the neighbourhood of Les Halles (nevertheless thinking that what Londoners had done to Covent Garden was somewhat better). I enjoyed, too, my first view of the Pompidou Centre, being fascinated by the extent to which inside space is made available, if you put the lumber of necessities like lifts and passageways on the outside. Whether the Pompidou Centre started the trend for what has now become an architectural commonplace, I do not know. I suspect, however, it is the kind of trend and commonplace which requires caution before too much replication. For instance, the new Bonaventura Hotel in Los Angeles is similarly arranged, and is magnificent in terms of luxury, splendour and the provision of waterfalls, but it proved to be far too much for me. I got lost in no time, thoroughly confused by the vastness of the internal space made available for the hotel's reception area. I looked in vain for where to go next, such was the multiplicity of signs and noticeboards. Then, having lost myself inside the hotel, I also easily lost myself outside it too. At that point, I decided that I had unwittingly experienced in Los Angeles what the French in Paris had called 'technopoly'. Four months earlier, at the Pompidou Centre I had paused to visit an exhibition on the matter, and, without enlightenment of any kind, left nonplussed. No longer, after the Bonaventura.

The rain stopped in time for lunch, which I took in a favourite, secluded spot on the slopes of Montmartre. Afterwards, the view from Sacré Coeur was most unusual. The sun shone brightly now, and it was hot and humid. It was hot enough to make the roofs of the city give off steam after the rain. For half an hour, Paris became ethereal, shrouded in a moving, light mist as far as the vague horizon. How right Parisians have been to prohibit tall buildings from their city centre! Nothing indecent blocked our temporary vision of heaven at that blissful spot.

By the following morning it was teeming again. I had never before purchased a more valuable umbrella. It was cold and blustery. Neither the courteous bank at Montparnasse, where I bought francs for my journey across Europe and Asia, nor the palace at Versailles, where I remembered my first visit in 1938 more easily than any since, can expunge from memory the wretchedness of the day, one sort of Parisian day. The train that evening was like a church offering shelter to weary pilgrims. The champagne on offer came in handy, too.

Every traveller knows that the character of rain matches the character of the place where it rains. Each reflects the other. Water on the road, water on the pavement, water on roofs, water in the puddles give back to the sky its own image, like a married couple well suited to each other but in sombre mood. The familiarity which exists between rain and London, Paris and the English Channel is not one of contempt but one of habit and frequency.

So, I would argue, it is with rain everywhere it rains often, sympathetic but a little sad. As a distant example of this phenomenon, take Anatolia, where it is dry in the summer but frequently wet otherwise. In Erzurum and Sarikamis, the rain was soft and regular. I felt oddly at home. The streets were well prepared for the wet, the gutters functioned efficiently when little else did, and all was by nature the grey colour of the sky. Like the *Madrasah* of the Twin Minarets (Chifte Minare Medresse) in Erzurum, built of dark grey stone in 1253 during the Seljuk period. Arches of its central courtyard were the same shape as

Madrasah of the Twin Minarets, Erzurum. The second minaret rises to the left.

those of any church in England built about the same time, simple and broadly pointed, early English gothic. Like its ancient architecture, the rain in Erzurum had an English quality, gentle, gloomy and slow to anger.

There is a halfway stage between the soft, equable rain of England and northern France, and the angry rain accompanying that violent storm near the Olgas in Central Australia, best represented by the assertive and quietly dominant rain of Los Angeles.

The International Airport in LA is close to the sea, and the main runways are at right-angles to the coast, since the prevailing breezes come in from that direction. Incoming and outgoing aircraft habitually approach from landward and depart over the sea. The airport was laid out in this simple way, with runways lying consistently in the same direction, because the weather in that part of southern California is uncommonly reliable, from day to day, warm and fine all the year round. This reliability contributes massively towards efficiency. Except when the wind alters direction by 180°, and it rains. This happens so infrequently that disruption is the result. Among other things, it brings about a drastic alteration in the whole routine of the airport. Incoming planes have to make their approach over the sea, and outgoing planes have to take off in the direction of the mountains. Enforced change of this kind is monstrously disruptive for everybody, not least for airline passengers, the timing of whose arrival and departure suffers inevitable and chaotic irregularity. Los Angelinos do not dislike rain on its own account; like their weather in general, when it comes it is warm and consistent. They dislike it for what it does to their efficiency, especially at the International Airport. Routine and efficiency are vital components of an otherwise exuberant way of life.

I had a cycle ride with the two Sallys and Don along the cycle-track from Playa del Rey to Redondo Beach and back. The day was bright and warm, as I thought it always would be. The swell of the ocean could not inhibit reflection of blue sky above. Another ride, later on, happened antithetically early in the morning, vastly grey. Proceeding from the Brayton's home in Brentwood in west LA, to the west of Beverly Hills, I wobbled about on my bicycle in the heavy traffic on San Vicente Boulevard, early though we were, until at last we turned right onto quieter residential roads, Sunset Boulevard nearby. Tree-lined, with their sidewalks between abundant grass at the edges and with their dwellings displaying an infinite variety of wealth and charm, these roads wander vaguely about, showing a lack of concern which the rest of LA does not share. They also give an errant cyclist like me some insight into the local opulence and many-sided culture of those who live beside them. Those who sweep streets and water the gardens, by the way, are of Spanish origin. All of us who pass by, in any case, are warned that we risk 'armed response', if we intrude. Guns, not dogs.

Turning corners here and there, a gradual slope westwards on a bend sweeps suddenly downwards. The still air rushes past us, and I remember my youth in the lanes of Leicestershire. No rural ride this, though. The volcanic hills to our right, the Pacific Palisades, where people live and let live on declines of pendulous luxury, break suddenly apart, and there below are the level sea and the level sand. At their edge large houses spread widely here and there, owned by film stars long ago, and sprawling and elegant seaside clubs, which those who still have old money still support. On top of the sandy cliff, we look down on a sandy paradise. Today, though, paradise is persistent grey, sky and sea and sand, all grey. Even the grass is grey. Hispanics water the grass regularly.

We have breakfast in the open air, warmed by gas heaters above our heads, and me on Ocean Avenue, Santa Monica. The sun is not shining, and there may even be a drizzle, but we may still be warm, and eat outside.

An increasingly ominous greyness blanketed the sky. It began to rain oh, so slowly. The sky became brighter for a space, and we thought nothing much would come of it. Unwise among Angelinos, anyway. The ride back was uphill, of course, but without the ominous steepness of our descent. We were in no hurry, and Don knew well how to overcome a hill by stealth. The rain was creeping up on us by stealth, too. By mid-afternoon, a steady, relentless, drenching rain was drowning everything from a leaden sky. There was no avoiding it now. It rained like that until dark. The Hispanic grass waterers went home, knowing they would not be needed again for some time. The wind rose from landward. They had to change things round at the airport. Workers there went home, knowing they would have to change things back again as soon as the wind and rain had had their say.

It was rush hour now. The freeways, always steadfastly constipated on their homeward route at this time, criss-cross each other at convoluted junctions. Rain can only make things worse if you are at the wheel of a car. There is beauty in the rain otherwise. The wet tarmac, spattered and drenching, window-wiping wet, flickers with reflections from orange street lights and whiter headlamps. Red at the rear answers back at the touch of a brake. Near traffic lights you get green and yellow too. If you could only think of it that way, each rainy evening on a freeway in Los Angeles you could have Christmas more often. Don't breathe a word of it to anyone; I enjoyed myself that evening on the back seat of the Brayton's car. Even they did not grumble. Rain does not happen often. It is rather special when it does. Rain is in charge. Efficiency declines.

Very similar is the quality of rain sometimes in Australia. I arrived in Sydney on a wet evening once, and felt then that the rain was more in charge than I was, such was its persevering relentlessness. But three days of it, when I was staying with the Mappins at their home on Mount Macedon in Victoria over New Year, was quite different in effect, despite its similar quality. Incidentally, I have never been in Melbourne in the rain; so unusual therefore were the three days we had of it on the Mount.

Mount Macedon is not a single hill but a collection of them linked together by ridges, weathered smooth in shape. Its steepest, most consistent slope faces north, and southwards, streams of quickly flowing water assemble in the rocky valleys, and cause small lakes to form in pockets, and engineers to collect valuable water in small reservoirs. The stream at the bottom of the Mappin's garden, Stony Creek, leads into one such.

The garden itself, a sheer delight to a guest like me and the object of continual, careful cosseting on the part of its owners, slopes quickly downwards towards the stream, until a thick, tangled barrier of eucalyptus trees halts further intrusion. This barrier, like all of the Mount, is home for wombats, koala bears, kookaburras, parrots, cockatoos, parakeets, magpies and much else belonging to the exotic panoply of Australian birdlife. The morning and evening jokes, which so amused the kookaburras at one extreme, and the tinkling, falling song of the magpies, like a xylophone played in the distance, at the other, entertain the stranger's ear continually, with surprises and variety.

Gum trees in the Mappin's garden

Whatever men and women may do to add further to the beauty of rural Australia, for me, always, the essence of it all is the gum tree, whatever manifestation it chooses for itself. The Mappins have made their garden a lovely place, but the basis of the garden's triumph is not of their doing. The tall, elegant gum trees which surround it and which march like a dense army away across the valley into the distance, are the beginning and end of its loveliness. They are magnificent in their majesty. These particular gum trees, in recession, begin pink, green and white, in sun or shade, and, passing through kinds of olive green, conclude their journey at the valley's edge in blue and pale purple. Tall and straight, each tree is an individual but wears uniform. Peeling bark hangs down from each white trunk like epaulets, and flicks about in the slightest breeze. Branches divide from the trunk, and point increasingly upwards, growing smaller. The trunk divides at last into a smallness of its own, at the top of everything. Leaves crowd round, not in the middle of the tree, but at the end of things in clumps. They hang downwards, olive green on one side and silver on the other, pointed and narrow. And so, in their mop-like shape, they glitter and twinkle in the sunshine and the slightest breeze, just as the strips of bark do. The tall gum tree is a static, living giant. In its structure, it is as solid as a rock — its wood inside is very hard indeed — but all around its topmost branches it has an outer array of lively decoration. The leaves and the bark, stiff and brittle, twist against each other, and make whispering noises. On a dry night, since the leaves of a gum tree fall at no particular season but throughout the year, they can patter about on the roof, and sound like rain. In a crowd, these wonderful trees make a magnificent background for any garden's existence. They like a garden.
    On 2 January, a sunny day, we drove sixty miles north of Mount Macedon to a vineyard. We passed through a patch of dry rocky countryside, as though we were approaching Cappadocia once more, but otherwise it was quiet, graceful, rural stuff, trees, meadows, creeks, dams, a lake, a dead kangaroo on the road, and, finally, in a luscious, green corner of that sunny land, a vineyard, just off the Heathcote-Nagambie road. The Osicka family had founded it when they came from Czechoslovakia in the early 1950s, having already had many years of successful experience as *vignerons* behind them. We

tasted both red and white wine. Ken bought thirty-five litres of the red, which he bottled himself, at a cost of £1.30 a bottle. A full, deep red wine it was. That evening, as we returned home, the rest of the country still had clear blue skies, and we had had a warm day, but there was a long, low cloud over the Mount.

We were taking a pre-prandial drink at the house of a friend by open windows. Suddenly, a wind got up and blew in at us. It was immediately cold, as though from the Antarctic. Bill said at once, 'Cold change; time for some warm clothing, Ian.'

The evening cloud over Mount Macedon in the course of the night must have spread over the whole of the State of Victoria. It then rained, with a cold drift from the south, for three days and nights. By the time it had stopped, Ken measured four inches of it.

No shiny streets and wet cars to dominate on Mount Macedon, as there were in Los Angeles, but the rain had a similar quality. Instead, people and the countryside became shining and wet. It was a time to stay at home, if you could, but the dog still needed to be taken for a walk.

Gum trees can do the description job for me. Because they are designed to shake off the fearsome heat of the Australian sun and store their essential moisture carefully against that heat, they are also designed to shake off, too, every drop of superficial water, so that it may fall straight downwards and be absorbed as soon as possible by the dry earth below. In this way the dry earth soon becomes wet, and so helps to nourish the tree. As a consequence, people walking beneath gum trees in the rain undergo a concentrated kind of rain. The drops are much bigger than average, and appear to fall with their own kind of anger. In addition, the ground beneath is quickly wet and soggy. You have to be carefully and protectively clad, head to toe. It is not a glistening rain. The clouds are low, and even shroud the tops of the tallest trees. It is not a fog, but a thick, saturated, presiding mist. You can see, but no further than the end of the garden or the next bend in the road. The dog, a labrador, loves it. You can see now why the trees are so tall, and why they grow so thickly. The rain, collected at their top, is quickly deposited at their base, and moisture is soon stored away among their roots. The trees above and the roots below combine together to store the water away. When the sun comes out again, and the wind begins to veer away from the cold south, the shade provided by the trees protects the water collected at the roots from any undue heat. The shade does not have the humidity of a tropical rain forest, but the effect of it is similar, I suspect. Trees can flourish and grow old on the resources provided by their own protection. If people with their modern, artificial tastes are quickly dominated by such rain, and hide away, nature does not. It is constructed to make use of rain, and to use it well.

Below the Mount, the land, denuded now of trees, soon dries out again. It has the natural hardness of a desert, and sheds rainwater as plastic sheeting does. Four days after the rain had stopped on that occasion, a warning about the high risk of fire in the countryside north and west of Melbourne was issued. The countryside is a fragile place without trees.

There was scintillating benefit when the sun shone again at last. Australian sunlight is a white sunlight, and after rain its clarity can be as near absolute as the human eye can detect. The unpretending countryside and habitations north of Mount Macedon were especially lovely in these circumstances: the low-roofed, verandaed Victorian farmsteads, Maldon, a gold town, sensitively preserved for little antique shops, Lancefield, with its big corner house at the broad crossing of the ways where flocks of sheep used to be driven to market, and the view of warm and distant Romsey, against blue and distant hills, a view best taken from a pitching, switchback road, shaded by gum trees, Hanging Rock close by. These things are the common things of white Australia, and I believe that I liked them best, in the white sunlight especially.

This kind of contrast, which a rapid change in the weather can provide, is one of the delights of travelling. You fall asleep one evening in the gloom, and, on peering through the blinds next day, you awake to the sun's return, bright and cheerful. It is not an idiosyncratic delight, of course, for such pleasures often occur at home. But at home, the sights are familiar sights, and your delight, at least in part, is due to that familiarity. When travelling, all is always new, and sometimes happens only once. You have to be wide-awake, if you wish to store away the memory of something which happens only once. It is a self-encouraging, circular process. Looking out for what may happen only once is an effective way of keeping wide awake. As I wrote earlier, I shall never forget the impact of our arrival in sunlit Salzburg, after Paris in the rain the day before. Baroque and

Main street, Maldon

blissfully peaceful in hazy, autumn sunshine, Salzburg did not receive its due. A single morning was quite insufficient, and, fully awake, I resolved to return there as soon as I could.

Nor shall I ever forget, a week later, a second sunlit morning, following immediately upon our harrowing experience on entering Bulgaria at the border with Romania, at Ruse. The reader may remember that after that episode we had boarded the good ship *Vlagonev* at Varna late at night, despondent and tired. We had a bad night of it, too; our accommodation had been meagre. The following morning, however, the Bulgarian crew had given us a fair representation of bacon and eggs for breakfast, and in this way had raised our spirits. On deck, we were not to know that a kind of heaven awaited us. It was a splendidly sunny morning, and, there at last, was a sea new to us all, the Black Sea. We were sailing southwards. The rugged Bulgarian coast lay about five miles or so to starboard, and, to port, a broad vastness, a slightly choppy, green-grained sea, like any other sea, but not in reality; it was the Black Sea, in classical times the Pontus Euxinus, the Euxine, the Sea that is Kind to Strangers, the Hospitable Sea.

I went forward. I became exhilarated by the fresh air, by the sight of the sea, and by a host of recollections. All three of these things had the semblance of being instantly new. Most of all, the variety of my recollections surprised me.

All the time mindful that this sea we were seeing for the first time was for us in effect a frontier between Bulgaria and Turkey, I remembered that it was for the ancient people of the Mediterranean the edge of the world. For them the world floated on an enveloping sea which dipped into nothingness beyond the horizon, and on our port side that morning we could see the fabled edge of the world. Some frontier, that one.

Explorers destroyed the fable. Jason and his Argonauts, their adventure told in myth but probably having some basis in fact, penetrated the Bosphorus from the west, and went heroically beyond in search of the so-called Golden Fleece. In fact, the golden Fleece was gold itself, to be found on the distant shore of Colchis. Heracles had been an earlier and divine predecessor ahead of Jason. We now know Colchis as Georgia, and I thought of Jason, his crew and that distant land as the same as that we were to visit within a fortnight. I thought too of that small boat, rowed day and night, clinging to the southern shore and aided by the wind only when it blew from the west.

Jason and the forty-niners, together in heroic endeavour, against unknown odds? For Jason and his crew, gold was the spur, too.

Jason's equivalent of the Sierra Nevada was at the exit from the Bosphorus into the Black Sea. There he faced the *Symplegades*, *Planctae* or *Cyaneae*, whichever you wish to call them (the Clashing, Wandering or Blue Rocks). These are explained as ice floes, adrift in the sea after leaving the frozen rivers of the Russian north. They were said in the myth to crush any ship attempting to pass between them. Jason sent a heron ahead of the *Argo*, and this bird, diverting the Rocks' attention, enabled the boat to sail between them. Perhaps even more fearsome than the Clashing Rocks was the adverse current which flowed out of the sea into the narrow straits. This current, even now, swollen by thaw from rivers to the north, can often run at a speed of five knots. The good ship *Vlagonev* was sailing in a more comfortable direction. When eventually we came to the entrance of the strait, I was surprised at its narrowness. The current at that point must have been truly formidable for a small boat. For the ancients, this narrowness symbolized the end of the known civilized world. They called the sea the Hospitable Sea because that was what they hoped it would be. It rarely was. The same was true of the Straits of Gibraltar at the western end.

The myth of Jason's exploration, once Crete and Mycenae had faded from the scene, led later Greeks into exploring the Black Sea coasts more methodically. They founded a string of colonies there, frequently at the mouth of rivers, and from there they sent home fish, grain and precious metals. From the middle of the seventh century BC these colonies flourished, and for some 300 years triremes plied their peaceful profession back and forth across the temperamental Euxine. As I gazed ahead on the bow of our ferry, I believe that I could hear the rhythmic dash of oars, and even see a string of those wonderful craft, travelling northwards, whose measured beauty research has at last revealed to us. Competition was the essence of it all, and among other things led to the perfection of the trireme. A small town on mainland Greece, Megara, was to have a brilliant idea, and place two colonies at the eastern entrance to the straits, and so to control them in the interests of Megara: Chalcedon first in 676 BC on the southern shore, and, later, to the north, Byzantium in 660 BC. After Turkish conquest, Chalcedon became Scutari or Uskadar, and Byzantium, alias Constantinopolis, likewise Istanbul. So it was that once more an alliance between competition and the accident of choice had an effect on the final history of the world.

By now imagination was free again. Rome, often hesitant, first hoped to use her power over the straits and the sea behind it only for the purposes of trade. Eventually she was forced to control them by use of military might.

The man who caused that decision was one of the world's most daring, dashing and ruthless adventurers, King Mithridates VI of Pontus. Pontus was a fertile tract of land occupying the central section of the southern Black Sea coast. He became king in 120 BC. The recollection of his personality forced itself upon me. He even dared to rival Rome at the height of his power, and to control Asia Minor, the Black Sea and the Aegean. He was half Persian and half Greek by descent, and his first act as king was to accept a call for help from the Greek cities of the Crimea, which could no longer resist on their own pressure from Scythian and Sarmatian tribes to the north. He was so successful in accomplishing his rescue work that he was able to take control of the entire north Black Sea coast. He then set about Cappadocia, Galatia and the Roman province of Asia, enlisting as his allies all the pirates and brigands of the area.

When the Romans attacked, he retreated. When the Romans retreated, in trouble at home, he attacked. Time and time again he made peace (there were, officially speaking, three Mithridatic Wars), and time and time again he invaded once more territory he had just ceded. He was not so much a thorn in the Roman side but a cancer in the stomach, for in his day the nourishment of Rome itself depended upon regular trade with Asia Minor and the shores of the Black Sea. He spread his poison far and wide, winning battles on land and sea, and massacring on all sides those loyal to Rome. In the 'Asiatic Vespers' of 88 BC, 80,000 Italian residents abroad were said to have been slaughtered as the king himself occupied the whole of Asia Minor except for a few places on the south coast, and Rhodes. His tactics were whirlwind tactics.

They were forced to call up Pompey the Great to corner him, defeat him and drive him into exile. He fled to the Crimea. From there he even thought of attacking Rome by way of an incursion along the Danube, collecting support as he went, in the way that Attila was to do later on. In face of his continuing cruelty and ruthlessness, his son and some locals eventually turned on him. He killed himself finally in despair, in 63 BC. Fifty-seven years he had had of it. With his death, Pontus retired for good from bellicosity, and was linked thenceforward with peaceful Bithynia to the west.

As our ferry neared the entrance to the Bosphorus, sure enough, Mithridates' swift ships, crowded with most bloodthirsty-looking ruffians, began to press around us, with screams and jostling. Without our diesel engine I doubt that we would have made it. They would quickly have brought us to a halt, and boarded us. Who could guess what would have happened then? Somehow I had imagined myself into a panic. It was good to see the old peaceful Roman province of Bithynia on our port side. The Younger Pliny, when governor there, had only had trouble with a few harmless but recalcitrant Christians. That was 180 years later, and Rome was really in control by then. I recovered my composure, too, as we left the open sea behind us. A convoy of Roman galleys, laden to the gunwales, were now sailing quietly alongside us in the stream.

The opening of the Bosphorus at its northern end is the shape of a funnel, quickly narrowing into a channel five hundred feet wide. Both sides dip steeply into the water, and at this point the channel must be extremely deep. The atmosphere is stark and barren after the green slopes and habitations of the coastline further back. As the channel becomes narrower still, two fortresses appear at the top of the cliff on each side, Rumeli Kavak to the west and Anadolu Kavak to the east. These were in the first place advance posts for Constantinople, guarding the eastern entrance to the straits. Later, they were handed over to Genoese, who maintained them afterwards. Rumeli Kavak was almost razed to the ground by the Turks as they invested Constantinople in 1452. Anadolu Kavak suffered less damage. The Turks had taken the whole of the Asiatic shore by 1371, and quickly fortified their territory, leaving Anadolu Kavak to fall into ruin on its own account. They also built forts of their own nearer to the city, at the narrowest point of all. A final fort on the European side was completed inside two months in 1452, as a point of pride in the fact that Turks were at last in Europe in full strength. At a single stroke Constantinople was completely cut off from any communication with the Black Sea and beyond, a vital turning point in the history of Europe, its eventual capture in 1453 being only in the end a perfunctory final act.

Soon we were to pass beyond the context of the world at crisis. The stately Roman galleys had already long faded from the scene. I was recalling instead the stability, the bureaucratic arrogance and incompetence of Greco-Roman Byzantium. Then, suddenly, we were riding a sea which divided a splendid land, on both sides the summer palaces of sultans, attracting in their turn the country seaside houses of the wealthy, grand wooden houses with decorated balconies, cool courtyards and fountains, the first built in 1471, and thereafter with increasing frequency until the late eighteenth century. By then, summer houses in their hundreds, large and small, had been built on wooden piles, each with a small landing stage beneath. In the nineteenth century cafés took over at the edge of gracious squares, as public landing stages for transport from the city became popular, at Beshiktash, for instance. So quickly did we enter a different world, a world in which Europe became denied, even though it be built upon a European shore.

Quickly too, a newer city starts. The old Palace of Dolmabahche was razed to the ground after two disastrous fires in 1814 and 1840 and the sultan of the time had the present palace built instead, heavy, monumental and perforce aping European styles now. All sultans except one thereafter made the new Palace of Dolmabahche their official residence. The palace, eventually sanctified by the death of Kemal Ataturk within its precincts on 10 November, 1938, shook me as I looked at it, and I fell at last into an awareness of where I really was. Ahead of us was the Maritime Terminal, and the ferry was going astern in the stream as we floated towards the dock. Ahead, too, at last the skyline of palaces, mosques and minarets, a dream that any traveller wants fulfilled. We were now coming 'to the city', *es tan polin*, Istanbul, in misty noon-day sunshine. A dream come true, and many another dream prompted by sunshine earlier, on a sea which they always used to hope would be Kind to Travellers. I would never want for any greater kindness.

Subconsciously on that glorious morning I had been concerned about one other matter. I knew that the word Bosphorus meant Bull Passage or Cow Passage. I remembered too that the Greek goddess, Io, had, in the myth, attracted amorous attention from Zeus, and he, with Hera's wrath at his elbow, had caused Io to be turned into a cow. It had to be a cow, because Io was closely identified with the moon, and because the new moon, with its horns, was always seen by the ancients as having the semblance of a cow. The tradition was that Io as a cow swam first the Crimean Bosphorus, hence its name, too, and spread her worship into the Black Sea and among the colonies of the distant coasts. All apparently well and good, given some telescoping of time and occasion. Even for a goddess? Would it not have been more sensible for a cow to swim with the spiritual current rather than against it? This was the starting point of my concern. Then, is it not the case that the moon in the heavens travels westwards, in pursuit of the sun? In addition, moon worship was not only Io's affair but the affair of Isis in Egypt, Astarte in Syria, and, further off, Kali in India. Surely, I asked myself, it was much more likely that moon worship spread westward. The ancient Greeks, always great assimilators of other people's wares, welcomed in due course a new goddess, Io, to Olympus from the east, from across the Bosphorus between Asia and Europe, quickly having Zeus fall in love with her, at Hera's wrath, turning her into a cow and having her travel back again whence she came.

I have to admit that the full significance of the Io myth did not occur to me until I saw the desert sparkle in response to the rising moon in front of Turfan. The divine cow, I now believe, first passed over the Bosphorus from Asia, swimming with the stream as it were, and then travelled westwards, taking Olympus by storm. Figuratively speaking, that is. As she did the rest of us in our time, and Sappho in hers.

* * *

As the reader already knows, we left Istanbul for the east by train from Haydarpasa Station in Uskadar on the Asiatic side. The station is ideally placed on the seafront, gazing across the water towards the European city, Topkapi, the mosques and the minarets. Built by Germans, the station has a contrary European grandeur, like the Palace of Dolmabahce, grand but out of place, except as a station. As the train leaves, it skirts the northern shore of the Sea of Marmara, or Propontis, as the Greeks called it, Ahead of the Sea which is Kind to Travellers.

For us that evening, as the sun set, the sea was the colour of bronze, flat and shining. On the sea there floated black islands, the Princes Islands, ideal for monks and churches in Byzantine days, and for those who fell from grace and were sent into exile. For us they were the last romantic places hiding in a brazen sea. We were saying goodbye to Europe, and they were a last, brief glimpse of a Mediterranean world.

Sea however is a universal thing, a universal water. We saw it in that state next in Baku, where the Caspian is enclosed, and then in Hong Kong, where it is hot and humid. I personally went on to Fremantle and Bunbury in Western Australia, where they call it the Indian Ocean. All these seas partook of sea's universality. They were unexceptionable.

A particular sea however is enclosed by the Bass Strait between the State of Victoria and Tasmania. The reason for this is plain on a map. At some stage in its geological history, Tasmania moved away from the mainland of Australia, leaving behind Port Phillip Bay, where the city of Melbourne was sited, and a string of islands between Tasmania itself and the mainland, the Furneaux group to the east, facing the Tasman Sea, and the larger King Island, some thirty-five miles long, to the west, facing the Great Australian Bight. In addition to the islands, the movement left behind a shelf hidden below the sea, with the result that the depth of the Tasman Sea on the one side and the Bight on the other is in sharp contrast to the shallowness of the waters between Tasmania and the mainland. The northern coast of Tasmania is in general about 160 miles from the coast of Victoria. This gap and the shallows are called after a naval explorer of the coast, the Bass Strait.

One of the coincidental pleasures of being able to stay with the Mappins was that they lived in two different locations, one on Mount Macedon and the other in Hawthorn near Melbourne. In addition, because of the generosity of a friend, they had available a third. This was a holiday house by the sea on the Bass Strait, which their friend permitted them to use almost at will. The house was in an isolated spot called Skene's Creek, on a side road some three hundred yards from the sea. Skene's Creek was in turn three miles or so from a small fishing port going by the delightful name of Apollo Bay. This port is sheltered to the west by a headland called Cape Otway. Cape Otway is the second most southerly point in Australia, Wilson's

Apollo Bay Harbour

Promontory on the other side of Port Phillip Bay being the first. In other words, because I was allowed to join the Mappins for a week while they stayed at their friend's holiday home at Skene's Creek, I was able to take quite a close look at conditions in the Bass Strait, and the nature of the coastline nearby.

There was something obviously English about it, about the sea certainly. Not the North Sea or the English Channel, but the Atlantic off the north Devon coast on a sunny day, close to the Bristol Channel. It was continually a restless sea. I do not think, in seven days, I saw it calm once. The tide too was a strongly flooding and ebbing tide, leaving long stretches of watery sand quite bare twice a day. The relationship between the sea and the sky had an English quality, too. On a sunny day — and the sun shone for some part at least of each day — there would be a bluster in the air, and unthreatening clouds over King Island on the horizon. King Island was never visible, though I kept thinking it would be. Even Tasmania did not seem too far away. You would say there was an enclosed feeling about the sea, though there would never be any visible enclosure. The sea had a trapped kind of turbulence. Out of the sun, it was grey and pale green.

What was especially un-English was its blueness when the sun shone. Because of this, I knew for certain I was not in England, especially from the top of the bending road at Skene's Creek. From there you might think that you were in some secluded spot by an Ionian shore in southern Italy. The tide, however, ruined that impression, when you were near to it. It was a tidal shore, rocky at its roots near the land. Flat, smooth rocks, though, and slippery with a thin, black slime, if you did not take care, worn regularly in different ways and smoothed twice a day by a rough tide, attacking and retreating continually. The rock appeared to be a variable limestone, which meant that there were many rock pools full of water, left behind by the ebbing tide. Varied pools, the shape of pieces in a jigsaw puzzle, sometimes deep, were full of colourful weeds, urchins and molluscs, and the black slime. Walking along the shore at any time was a delight, especially for the dog, and especially if you like the wind to blow the cobwebs away. As so often in Australia, I concluded the sea and the shore were English, but not English.

The coastline itself is another matter. No English, or even Irish, coastline this one, despite place-names like Torquay and

Lorne. The Otway Range, limestone hills covered with impenetrable eucalyptus forests, provide a barrier between the farming land of the interior and the sea. They are high hills, with steep, eroded valleys, only denuded of trees on windy headlands, and drop in precipices towards the shore. As a result the coastline is heavily indented, sandy beaches alternating with sharply projecting cliff heads. For these geographical reasons, it was a coastline which from the earliest times was only sparsely populated. With the coming of the white man, coves and calm spots below the cliffs became known to sea captains tackling the Bass Strait and small settlements, like that at Apollo Bay, began where ships put in to shelter from the weather. Coal ships would call in at Apollo Bay as they passed along the tortuous sea passage from the east, towards Geelong and Melbourne. Small farms began in clearings, and the ships on their return voyages would bring back supplies to the farmers and their families. Life on the coast was hard, rugged and dangerous, starvation on the one hand and fire, flood and landslip on the other. There was no possible philosophy other than the philosophy of survival and the elements.

Unexpectedly, the depression of the 1930s brought relief. Capital expenditure on a new exploratory road was to provide, first of all, employment. That it did, and also, slowly and painfully, a fine, corniche road, the Great Ocean Road, was built between Geelong and Apollo Bay along the winding coast. The road, a triumph of engineering for the time, not only helped to solve a few economic problems but also provided at last a secure lifeline for the seaside settlements. Beyond Apollo Bay there is still a short three mile section of the road to be completed in the dense forest of trees behind Cape Otway. Understandably and for good reason, Victorians are proud of their Great Ocean Road. As it happened, it helped a lot of them too. For they now have speedy access from Melbourne to a completely unspoilt seaside playground, to be compared with the Cilento peninsula in southern Italy or Highway One along Big Sur in California. The source of it all, the Road, is fortunately to be found in a distant corner of the world, which so far remains delightfully unspoilt. Meanwhile the underlying philosophy of the area has drifted in the direction of elemental hedonism. Unspoilt hedonism in the long term? What a hope!

To the west of Cape Otway, the cliffs with their sandy

indentations continue in an informal, rugged way, like life itself thereabouts. Facing the weather more than their companions further east, and open, too, to whatever may come their way from off the Great Australian Bight, they are wild places and not inhabited, except for the occasional occupant of holiday shed-like homes. As part of his Christmas present to me, Peter Mappin gave me a 360° panoramic photograph which he took himself, of one of these indentations, Crayfish Bay by name. I am thus continually fortunate in having a precise record for my memory of something particular and good. White sand shelving down to calm water, calm only because the ocean waves dash themselves to death on the flat rocks further out; the sea a Mediterranean blue within the small lagoon, but nearly wild purple beyond it; clouds stretched like a distant scum across the sea's wine-dark edge, thicker over the spot where King Island probably is; yellow succulents near the edge of the sea-worn sand, pale grasses and white flowers further back; gorse-like bushes with spiky yellow flowers scatter themselves around; the air blowing billows all about; twenty-five feet behind, where the sand stops in banks, the cliff, like a crescent moon, holding the beach in its grip, all shrouded with shades of green, such greens as cause you to wish you had your paint-box with you; and, isolated, the steep, white, sand path down which we came from the car above parked on bare grass amid pink and blue flowers. All particular and good. Round the corner of the cliff, they discovered the skeleton of a dinosaur in a cave. No change in Crayfish Bay. There are other dinosaurs there, you know. It was only the car which did not fit.

Beyond Crayfish Bay the road clings to the cliff top, and wonderful views over the sea occur every mile or so. The hills flatten out, and a high plateau, undulating only slightly, drops suddenly in terrifying precipices towards beaches which are continually stormy. The strata of the limestone are horizontal now, and the cliffs show their age with parallel striations, young at the top, old at the bottom, and sand, sandy red and grey. Often at the base there is a long stretch of reddish sand. Just as often, the sea pounds the root of the land with swaying, frothy, surging abandon, never ceasing its timeless rhythms. In the beginning, of course, the sea eroded and built the cliffs. Now the cliffs have a harder limestone at their base, and so can resist the sea's advances. The ensuing struggle is mesmerizing.

Five of the Twelve Apostles

Mesmerizing too are the shapes the struggle has settled for. At a spot called the Twelve Apostles, rocks the same height as the cliff, twelve in number, stand and guard the shore, struggling and resisting on their own. From a headland you can count all twelve. Their horizontal lines match each other, and the cliff's too; a limestone family, the children sent to sea to earn a living for their parents.

Twenty miles of coastline beyond Cape Otway form the Port Campbell National Park. Port Campbell is another inlet like Apollo Bay, where beleaguered ships could shelter. Before reaching Port Campbell, other scenic wonders occur. At Loch Ard Gorge, the cliff lower down had suffered internal contortions, and the result is a puzzled cliff, not knowing which way to look, the sea running fiercely all about, into inlets, into caves, through gaps in the cliff, like a bridge, arching the land back and forth. You lose a sense of direction. The wind buffets

London Bridge, near Loch Ard Gorge, destroyed by bad weather in the winter of 1990

about, and you wonder if chaos was as beautiful. The cliff top is a wild place, and, should you trip, your chances of surviving are just about even. On a headland there is a cemetery commemorating the loss, in a storm, of a ship, the *Loch Ard*, together with all hands and all passengers, except for two small children who were found still alive in a cave when the storm abated. Their family was returning to Melbourne after a trip home to England. I cannot recall the exact date of the wreck. It was about 1870. It was an emotional place. Such losses on this stretch of coast, and in the Bass Strait itself, were frequent, even regular at one time. Fifty vessels have at one time or another foundered on the coast of the National Park alone. Where two oceans meet, there will always be such a danger. Seafarers still fear the Bass Strait.

Beyond Port Campbell the cliff is lower still, and, I suspect, softer. At a certain point the sea has eaten into it, and, from a narrow entrance, has carved out a huge bay for itself. Once inside, the sea is calmer, and so allows small islands to stand at attention on their own, scattered all about. They call it the Bay of Islands.

As the miles pass, the cliff turns to sand, and you reach a tidal estuary with long marshes behind. The road has a bridge. It might be Norfolk, somewhere near Brancaster. It is just as flat and beautiful, as wide now as the sky itself.

I was to find a contrast between the wild scenery and superb beaches on either side of Cape Otway and the sophisticated beach-side playground north of Sydney, where the inhabitants of that city have built no temples but worship the sun, the sea and the sand with abstracted, prostrate devotion. In mathematical terms, these beaches are to me all sub-sets of the ocean beach at Manly. They are not Manly; they are smaller, but the same. Perhaps it was the grey day which was at fault when I visited Whale Bay, Avalon Bay and Palm Beach. For sure, they were fine beaches but I found that I could not admire them as Australians do. They had become too close and basically trivial for me, like a dining car on a train which serves only hot-dogs. I have worshipped the sun in my time, but rarely, I think, in a trivializing crowd. The reader may, for instance, remember my feelings of separateness in Manly. The Australian and his beach, the worship the one gives to the other, remain for me a mystery. There is an arrogance about the worship, which any believer is entitled to feel but not, I think, to impose on others. I remember in this connection the remarks of a helicopter pilot from Sydney on television. He was flying over Lake Menindee in Central New South Wales, close to the Darling River. The lake had a long, sandy beach; strewn upon it were lake-side debris and a few desolate human beings. It looked a boring beach to me, perhaps my definition of boredom. He said to his television audience, 'Look, they have a beach, too. What a lovely beach! Anyway, better than any I have ever seen in Italy.' Australian beaches are, for sure, fine beaches. Perhaps it was only the arrogance associated with them which put me off. It was also a grey day.

We had had a lovely time that other day, though, along the Great Ocean Road east of Cape Otway. Our return to Skene's Creek was further enhanced by a new, large, painted notice, recently installed outside the pavilion on the Reserve at Apollo Bay. Australians often call areas designated for sporting activity 'The Reserve'. I was interested to note that the Brisbane

Melbourne across the River Yarra, showing Flinders Street station at ground level

Cricket Ground, the 'Gabba', is sited on an area once described on a map of the city dated 1850 as 'reserved for leisure activity'. The notice on the pavilion at the Apollo Bay Reserve was quite simple: 'Apollo Bay is Cricket.' I was not one to disagree with that at all. They were going to play a team of Poms the next day.

* * *

I left Australia on 26 January, Australia Day. I had been in the country for some three months, and believed that I had come to know something about it and its people. One thing for sure, I wanted to return. I had enjoyed myself, particularly in the company of the Mappins and their friends. Yet I left Australia with ambivalence about the depth of my affection for it. I enjoyed the countryside and the coast, wherever and whenever I came across it, immensely. I enjoyed the warm weather, though it turned out to be much wetter than I expected, or, I believe, than any Australian would have predicted. City life was vibrant and hugely confident and cheerful, and, inevitably and

Melbourne, Iron-work and a train looking toward Flinders Street station

agreeably provincial on the fringes. I enjoyed all the botanical gardens in every city I went to, and the art galleries, particularly in Melbourne, Canberra and Brisbane. Where then was the source of my ambivalence? I think there were two sources. First, I felt deeply uncomfortable everywhere about the position of aboriginal Australians in white Australia. And since their position there will not radically alter in my lifetime, I feel I am bound to retain that deep discomfort as long as I live. Second, I believe Australia as a whole is in too much of a hurry. A new country in an old land as the world grows smaller has immense problems, some inherited, some created and others being created. As a portent, they have built a new temple on the top of a hill in Canberra to house Parliament afresh, forsaking the old building for a new one. In that temple they house a hasty, commonwealth god, in a hurry. If I were an Australian, whatever my colour or origin, I do not believe I would trust what is happening there. More of that later.

Jack's Place, Malolo Lailai, Fiji

Fiji was quite another matter. I had never been there before. A travel agent in Melbourne had booked me into a holiday complex called Plantation Island on Malolo Lailai for three nights, having told me that I would be happier there than I would be at Jack's Place nearby, which I had myself preferred. In any event, I wanted to be on a small island, as far away as possible from any kind of urban existence. I needed a radical change, I thought.

The holiday complex was most comfortable, and a rather sophisticated place, with two restaurants, a dance floor, a long American bar and a swimming pool. What was more, my accommodation was of the splendid sort, detached and looking towards the lagoon at the front and a tropical garden at the back. I had no better accommodation in any other place. Unfortunately, none of that was really what I wanted. I had to be content however, since all had already been paid for in Melbourne. On the evening of my arrival, I strolled along to Jack's Place, three'quarters of the way round the lagoon, to see what it was like. It was much more to my taste, casual and higgledy-piggledy, and no swimming pool. The sea was only fifty feet away at high tide, after all. The water in the swimming pool at the holiday complex, by the way, was unbearably hot, and nobody swam in it for that reason. They did not dance much on the dance floor either; the dance floor was too hot. Thinking it was a good idea, somebody had transported a form of urban existence in Sydney to Malolo Lailai, and called it Plantation Island. A bad idea, in my view.

I would take lunch at Jack's Place. You could sit in the shade there, and sit in the shade for a long time, untroubled by anyone except for a bare-foot waiter dressed only in a cloth called a *nulu*. He was continuously solicitous for your welfare as soon as your can of lager looked ready for replacement. Usually the tide was out, and an unpretentious yacht, two hundred feet away, balanced at the slope, was the only sign of humanity. Plantation Island, praise be, was hidden away among the palm trees to the left. Malolo Lailai, with its low, bare hills, gripped the lagoon in a pincer-like grasp, but gently and without cliffs. The lagoon's entrance was wide enough for you to see the reef clearly a mile or so away, pounded by the swell of the Pacific Ocean outside, a dark blue line on the horizon, fringed at the reef in white. The lagoon itself was a wide blue, reflecting perfectly the colour of the sky. I usually thought little as I drank my lager. There was no need to think at all, in fact; I just liked looking, looking at that distant dark blue line. It was always there, secure and straight. This was what I had wanted. The troubles of the ocean, or anything else for that matter, were at least a mile away. Lunch was, for three days, a simple curry.

It was all very hot everywhere. When the tide was in, you could swim, pleasantly but without invigoration, in water the same temperature as your blood. You felt only briefly cooler when your swim was over, and you dried out in the sun. There was always a slight breeze off the sea when the tide was in. Then I liked to lie on the sand, and gaze upwards through the dark fronds of coconut palms at the eternal blueness beyond. The compound leaves swayed back and forth in the slight breeze, saying that they needed to hide eternity from you in case you found it too strong a matter. They tinkled together like eucalyptus trees on Mount Macedon, but they did not sparkle. Theirs was a more intense business; their sun was hotter still. Their tall trunks, bending slightly, never absolutely straight, marked their age upwards in rings, only at the top permitting fronds and coconuts to grow. They had to store moisture from a great depth, and pump it upwards; there was rarely any rain from above on Malolo Lailai, only on the main islands. I supposed they drew their water from the sand, which drew water in turn from the sea nearby. I learnt somewhat slowly that coconut palms grow mainly close to the lagoon or the ocean in lines, like soldiers, if you see them from a distance.

I would take my walks on Malolo Lailai slowly for obvious reasons, dressed in shorts, a singlet and sandals, protected by a floppy hat and layers of sun lotion. The sun in January was as hot as I have known it anywhere. Once I walked to the top of the hill behind Plantation Island in order to see the mainland across the sea from there. It was an excellent and exciting view, well worth the perspiration. The hill itself was a harsh place, stony, with long, dry grass and prickly scrub. Gently, downwards it became marshy and dark green at the level of the sea, and coconut palms lined the tidal beach. Across the sea, about eight miles away, lay the long, grey blue line of the mainland. At that distance it seemed a gracious, elegant land, with high mountains strung across its centre. Heavy clouds hung about their tops, and it was clearly raining hard on their other side. A dreamland, if you live your life away on arid Malolo Lailai.

Another hot walk which I enjoyed was first along the lagoon, and then through a sandy gap in the surrounding hills. In this gap you stumble across the debris of centuries, not a plastic container in sight. (Too hot for plastic containers and their purveyors.) Dead things only. The trunks of trees, long fallen, spiky cactus plants, grey green, long dead or seemingly so, other remnants of other living things, birds mostly, dry bones, the pale white compound leaves of palm trees, and straggling grasses, tough and prone to trip you up if you take no care, and the vague, multifarious detritus of the sea, trapped inland by the force of hurricane winds. And fine-grained, shell-white sand. Rain perhaps once in a hundred years? More often than that, but you would scarcely notice it if you lived in this dry land with water all around you.

Wise folk fly to Malolo Lailai from Nandi, the airport on the mainland where you land from Sydney. The landing strip on Malolo Lailai is made of stones and is short by any standards. The plane you fly in is a light one, with room for only six passengers. You discover how wise you are on the outward leg, for, from a mere 1,000 feet, you seem to skip across land, coast and sea, but learn their shape. Beneath it all, the blue-green of coral water beguiles the eyes, allowing puzzled land only fractured space. Malolo Lailai is like a horseshoe. You know you are wise because by now you realize that there will be return leg, too.

The aircraft flies in to Malolo Lailai every two hours or so, and you join a group of five others, and wait too, early so as not to be late. Native Fijians, who alone support the tourist industry on Malolo Lailai, have already told you by their behaviour how it might happen that you may be late. They learnt bureaucracy from the British, and retain its procedures but dislike its use. The result is that they can be found to talk a lot of vague nonsense about what is or is not planned. For good reason, they move slowly, too. They charm you with smiles and abandonedly relaxed behaviour. I mislaid my pocket book when in some haste on arrival, and upon discovery they returned it to me intact with a broad comprehending grin, which was the most winning of all. Thank goodness, bureaucracy is not in their lifeblood. You are wise though to take care that you are not late. Incidentally, I remember no trace on Malolo Lailai of the political antipathies between Indian and native Fijians, which caused such disturbance only a few weeks after my departure. Our plane in fact arrived promptly. We had had no need to be early.

In Nandi, though I did not remark it at the time, mainly Indians were working the airport.

I had four hours to wait there for my flight to Honolulu. The only incident which enabled me to alleviate boredom concerned a fellow passenger, waiting too. He carried with him a parcel shaped like a cricket bat. I eyed him once or twice as we passed each other, this way and that. Eventually I abandoned restraint and asked him about his parcel. Yes, it was a cricket bat. He had bought it in Sydney. He had spent some four weeks in Australia, and perforce had watched a lot of cricket on television. In this way, unbelievably, he had grown to like the game, and had become quite knowledgeable about it. I asked him if I could feel the weight and balance of his bat. He was delighted to let me do so. I showed him how to play defensively forward, and defensively back. Where did he come from? Chicago. A cricket bat in Chicago? Why, yes, why not? He was going to teach his buddies about this new game he had discovered, and play cricket with them in their local park. Would I, please, come and coach them when I had time? I played defensively forward once more, and we both laughed. It had also rained very hard while we waited in Nandi. Not cricket weather.

* * *

In conclusion, I return abruptly to Alice Springs. I experienced there the highlight of my journey, as far as water and the weather were concerned.

We had just returned from Ayer's Rock, and I had dinner in pleasant company on a warm, close evening. I went to bed, tired, relaxed and with nothing but idle thoughts in my head.

Sometime after midnight, I was awoken by the noise of a tearing wind. Presently it began to rain, a crackling and boisterous accompaniment for the wind. Then, there was what seemed like a distant roll of thunder, but only for a second or two. Suddenly, the noise of immediate thunder began to burst over the nearby hills, huge and seeming to shake the foundations of the tiny building in which I was abed. I was on the point of climbing out to inspect what was going on, when the noise of thunder ceased, and flashes of lighting took their place. I did not know the danger, and so I stayed in bed. It all then became enormously strange. So many were the flashes of lightning that it seemed that they were continuous. My room became bright as though it were day-time, lit by a white sun, as if in the desert after a dust storm. The whiteness was strong enough to be a glare. I could tell the time and read a book, but did not feel like doing so. The wind died away suddenly, but the rain was as fierce as ever. There was now no sound of thunder at all. Inexplicable, I thought, continuous lightning but no sound of thunder. The storm now settled down to this routine. I became used to it, but did not sleep, dozing a little from time to time. After about two hours the rain slackened, and the lightning became gradually more intermittent. At that, the sound of thunder returned, harsh and full of threat, but more within the realm of my experience. And so it ended. The storm receded, and I slept soundly once more.

The following morning was a special treat. All was clear and bright, the storm a bad dream. No, not so. There, outside, in the courtyard there were puddles, and the sand beyond the entrance, near the road, was wet. Below the gum trees, across the road, it was best of all. The Todd River, last seen dry as a bone, silent and soft in the desert heat, was now in flood, moving joyfully towards the gap in the hills. At last, a river in the desert full of water. Sparkling and blue, it was a magical river. I could not have been luckier. I had found a final text for my chapter on the water and the weather. They make magic when they combine, do water and the weather.

8

The Awesome Demon

In his *Symposium*, Plato has Socrates recalling a conversation he once had with a kindly witch from Mantinea, called Diotima. She had told him about Love, or Eros, how he was born of a god for a father, Poros or the god of Plenty, and of the lowliest of women for a mother, Penia with the name of Poverty. Love was therefore half god and half human, or to use Diotima's word a daimon or demon. It is in this sense that I would like the reader to understand the meaning of the title of this chapter; I do not mean 'demon' as a devil or as a malignant spirit, but as a quality which has both divine and human characteristics. As a god, the character is concerned for beauty, goodness and truth, and, as a human, he is inconsistent, unreliable and mischievous, rather as Eros is.

I use the word 'awesome' in the title to describe the demon, because the possibility of his suddenly appearing at any time during the course of a journey should summon in the traveller apprehension, reverence and the need for humility. If possible, as you go your way you should prepare yourself for his coming, and try to proceed in expectant mood.

I had previously met with a number of awesome demons on my travels, for instance, at Mycenae, at Tiryns, in the *agora* in Athens and on the Capitol in Rome, in Assisi and at Torcello near Venice. They live near rivers, rivers like the Thames and the Loire, and in marshes by the sea. Sometimes you have a premonition; sometimes they take you unawares. Sometimes you recognize them at once; sometimes you can only be certain of a presence when you have departed the scene and upon reflection. I hope the reader will discover as I have done;

recognition of an awesome demon at work depends entirely upon you, your mood at the time and how open you can keep your mind, your eyes and your ears, attendant upon receiving all that you sense. Travel is in the business of mystery, thinking, seeing and hearing all at once. Demons like it best that way.

I expected to encounter many awesome demons on my journey. I prepared myself beforehand as far as possible, but I was also ready to be taken unawares from time to time. Expectations, I knew, were all-important.

Take Samarkand, for instance. James Elroy Flecker's brother, H.L.O. Flecker, had been my first headmaster, professionally speaking, at Christ's Hospital, and, on that emotional ground at least, I considered myself well prepared for a visit to Samarkand. I was even prepared to take into account Flecker's warning: 'For lust of knowing what should not be known, we take the Golden Road to Samarkand.' The idea that one was entering mysterious territory fitted exactly my expectation that I might meet an awesome demon there.

Prehistoric in its origins, the site of the future city, first, provided food for hunters like Cromagnon folk in central France. Then, a far-ranging pastoral community took over, on the edge of mountains, at the crossing of the River Zarafshan but where the land above was dry, and, at last, a city by the middle of the fifth century BC, on trade routes travelling north, south, east and west. This city, called first Afrasiab after a mythical king, was the city which Alexander the Great fought over from 329-327 BC. On his death, it became part of the Seleucid kingdom, yielding eventually to a succession of central Asian imperial dynasties. In the spring of AD 1220, the hordes of Genghis Khan overran the valley of the Zarafshan. A contemporary historian wrote, 'They pitied no one, slaughtering men, women and children. They slit open the wombs of pregnant women and killed the foetuses. The flames of the massacre spread far and wide, and evil covered everything like a cloud driven by the wind.' Afrasiab was razed to the ground, and new Samarkand took its place, the capital of Tamerlane's Mongol empire. From its base, Tamerlane waged war for thirty-five years, and won an empire which stretched from the Volga to the Ganges, and from the Tienshan mountains to the Bosphorus. This was the combination, historical depth linked with imperial height, which had built up my expectations.

I have already given some description of the grand mosque, *Bibi-Khanim*, which the state is currently restoring, not in the name of Tamerlane, not in the name of Allah, but in the name of all its original craftsmen and labourers. Before visiting the mosque, we had earlier gone to the Registan Square. Registan, meaning 'place of sand', is the heart of ancient Samarkand, a commercial and artisan centre, its forum. It is fringed on three sides by three superb buildings, patterned all over with white, gold and blue tiles, each with twin minarets and blue-tiled domes at the front corners, and a huge blue-tiled dome behind. A wide, pointed lancet archway, diminished only by the huge blue domes, announces the entrance of each building. All three are *madrasahs* or schools, and have names and dates as follows: *Ulughbek madrasah* (AD 1417-1420), *Sherdor madrasah* (AD 1619-1636) and *Tillya-Kari madrasah* (AD 1647-1660). Each was damaged by earthquake, war and time, and have been recently restored at state expense. The *Ulughbek madrasah* is by far the most delicate in decoration. It was a school of advanced religious studies, and so an example of an early Islamic university. It used to have fifty dormitory cells, and so provided accommodation for one hundred students. *Sherdor* means 'bearing lions', which decoration shows as correct, and *Tillya-Kari* means 'gilded', just as correct. The total effect of the three buildings is splendid, stately and colourful, brilliantly colourful. A bright sun glinted off the tiles. In a corner of the square is the *Chorsu*, built 200 years ago and a place for the selling of skull-caps.

After the Registan Square, we went on to the *Guri-Emir*, or 'grave of the Emir', Tamerlane's mausoleum. In 1404, Tamerlane had it built for a favourite grandson, killed in battle. However he himself died the following year and was buried there too, as were two of his sons later on, and Ulughbek, a grandson, of whom more later. The mausoleum is not as large as you might imagine. It is dominated by a fluted, onion-shaped dome, made of decorated blue tiles, on top of a tall drum with elegant, script-like patterns on its sides. The drum and dome are large, and I think out of proportion with the size of the building as a whole. Inside it is dark, and Tamerlane's tomb is a low, dark grey slab raised above a paved floor in a brick-lined cell, rather like an undercroft in an English cathedral. In its smallness, even humility, it is all in strong contrast with the magnificent Bibi-Khanim not far away. Even in his greatness and his death,

Tamerlane seems to have had an underlying faith in Allah, lord of all.

Before lunch, we went on to Ulughbek's astronomical observatory, built in 1428-9 above Samarkand on its hilly outskirts. It was destroyed after his death, and has been reconstructed in modern times. The most astonishing feature was an open-air, giant marble sextant. With a radius of forty-six feet and an arc of seventy feet in length, it was installed in a curved trench along the meridian. With this and other devices, Ulughbek and his colleagues were able to compile with astonishing accuracy 'a table of stars', containing the co-ordinates of 1,018 of them, all without other optical instrumentation of any kind. Ulughbek's estimate for the length of our year was only a minute out.

In the afternoon, on to *Shakhi-Zinda*, 'the living king', a necropolis on the south-eastern slope of old Afrasiab. The group of tombs, twenty in all, stretch along an enclosed street-like gallery, and grew gradually to its existing state over 900 years, from the eleventh to the nineteenth century, so representing a condensed history of architectural styles. From its elegant, tiled portal, lancet arch within lancet arch, steps mount upwards. First, a twin-domed mausoleum in memory of a mathematician from Ulughbek's school and his wife, a young person from the east. A long flight of steps leads on to a more open form of gallery. Here Tamerlane's wife and sister are buried. Nearby is an earlier tomb belonging to Kusam ibn-Abbas, a holy man of the early days after the Arab conquest. One day, after a sermon, he is said to have taken his own head from his shoulders, placed it under his arm and retired into a cave where he is said still to live. He was 'the living king' after whom the necropolis is named. On its rocky, irregular hill, the whole complex intrigues and puzzles, especially in its variety of style and decoration, carved terracotta, carved wood, mosaic, and ornamental glazed brick. So varied was it all, in fact, that I became dazed in the sunlight, and could no longer concentrate. Of all things, we had to go on to the *Bibi-Khanim*. It had been a long and exhausting day. At its conclusion, we visited a large and lively market near the mosque. There I had reason to enter and make use of what was, as far as I was concerned, the last word in dirty public lavatories.

As a matter of fact, during our visit to Samarkand we had

seen only some of the monuments which belonged to only one part of that city's long history. A single day had been quite insufficient even for that restricted programme. There was so much else to see which went undiscovered. And the result? I met up with no awesome demons in Samarkand. I am sure nevertheless that they exist there, and have only to be discovered. I would not be surprised, for instance, if some of them do not lurk radiant in the old city of Afrasiab, whose art and whose ruins still to some extent survive. Then again, much happened in Samarkand after Tamerlane's time. I felt we totally neglected too the possibilities of the 500 years which followed that. In addition, I would like to have known details of how the city's inhabitants came to change their method of government, from an Islamic despotism to republicanism within the Soviet Union. In detail and in sequence, I left Samarkand thirsting to know more. Nothing less than a whole week's stay would suffice for any future visit that I may make. I wonder what the reader's interpretation of an ancient Usbekh legend may be. At a time of invasion and massacre, a golden book hidden in a golden casket was buried by the people in ground outside the city. The people believe that in the course of time a true warrior will arrive, discover the treasure and return it to the people. Maybe, if you could look inside the golden casket and the golden book, you would find a demon who could tell you what should not be known in Samarkand. On the other hand, some believe that the true warrior has already arrived in the person of Lenin, and it is he who has already returned the casket and the book to the people. For me, Samarkand was a disappointment; my expectations before arrival were in the end unfulfilled. In truth, I had arrived ill-prepared, and departed having learned too little.

* * *

Mount Li is some twenty-five miles east of Xi'an. Mount Li is the site of the mausoleum of the First Emperor of China, Qin Shi Huangdi. He died in 210 BC, at the age of fifty, during one of his journeys through the provinces. At his death, they took the body home. Because of the terror he inspired, there were no onlookers on the journey. A contemporary historian wrote, 'It was summer, and to disguise the stench of the corpse the escort was told to load the cart with salted fish.' So it was that the First Emperor of China was laid to rest. Or not, as he himself rather hoped. He had spent his life in search of immortality, and because he failed in his search and was continually anxious about dying, he had built himself a tomb where he believed he might live for ever, a tomb together with its environs, servants and a defensive army as magnificent in death as his palace and his court had been in life.

In 1974, some farmers on Mount Li, as they were digging, broke accidentally into an underground pit. To their astonishment the pit was crowded, line upon line, with an army of terracotta warriors. In a vanguard were 200 bowmen and crossbowmen, disrupters of the enemy before the infantry behind made their charge. These corridors below ground had been skilfully built, and had withstood earthquake and pillage since their closure sometime around 210 BC. The walls were made of rammed earth, each chamber was paved with brick, and a wooden roof was supported by pillars and beams. The roof in turn was covered by a woven mat and clay, to impede water from seeping down. This discovery, now known as Pit No 1, has over the years been meticulously restored and preserved by Chinese archaeologists beneath a large hanger-like building.

Qin Shi Huangdi's buried army was, of course, in reality a sham, but no hollow sham. Soon after the discovery of Pit No 1, two other pits were discovered nearby, Pit No 2 in 1976 encompassing chariots and cavalry, 1,400 warriors and ninety chariots, and Pit No 3 in 1977, where bronze weapons were found and perhaps the headquarters of the commander-in-chief, many officers among its sixty-eight figures. Since then, and since the discovery of a bronze chariot pit, iron tools and leg-irons, and graves belonging to the convicts set to work on the museum in 221 BC, controversy has reigned, particularly about the possibility of locating the ultimate sham, the burial palace of the First Emperor. The Chinese are taking worldwide excitement with great calm, and plainly do not intend to rush the job. Their culture, like every member of the terracotta army, tells them that there is no need at all to hurry. All will come to pass if you stand firm and wait.

If there was to be any sense of climax at any stage of our long train journey from London to Xi'an, that was almost certain to be on our visit to Mount Li. We had just stepped off the train for the last time at Xi'an. In any case, the terracotta army had

Our welcome to Xi'an.

been much publicized worldwide, and the Queen had only a day or two ago completed her visit to the site.

They took us there by bus through a modest countryside of farms, maize, chickens and pigs. The road was still a country road, and the traffic appeared slight, thought bicycles and small carts were common enough. The day was fine and misty.

At once, the crowd at Mount Li took us by surprise. We were not by any means the only foreign tourists there. Our bus was one among many, but we were outnumbered many times over by the Chinese themselves. Mount Li with its army, already a tourist attraction, had surprisingly allowed an informal market to base itself and increase within the museum precincts. Once we had disembarked from our bus, independent fruit stalls crowded the sides of the avenue upwards, the bright orange local persimmon piled high in rows on all sides in the open. Near the hangar, soon to appear at the top, other goods were on

A tourist market near the Terracotta Warrior Exhibition.

boisterous sale, brightly-coloured clothing, mostly red, Chairman Mao caps, red star badges, badges of many kinds proclaiming socialist wisdom, the sparkling clutter of cheap souvenirs, more delicate jewellery, and needlework, fine and coarse, old and young, large and small, nowhere expensive. The market was open and competitive. To the side, food stalls and official shops, both more refined than in Xi'an itself, displayed a willingness behind the counter which was just as aggressively reluctant. (Was this reluctance the result of employment by the state on the one hand, and the boisterous, lively selling outside in the open stalls the result of a free market on the other, you asked yourself without really ever finding out the answer.)

We handed our tickets in, keeping the other half as a bona fide souvenir, passed through the entrance gateway, and there, suddenly, was a huge and molten crowd, flowing at random. We queued where we could, as though for a bus in Piccadilly in the rush hour. Gradually those ahead were allowed in, and soon enough we were too, but not before bemoaning the absence at Mount Li of any kind of queueing discipline. We were, so to speak, forcibly allowed in. The objects of our journey were inside the hanger outside which we had been queueing.

There was no denying it. The first sight of those rows and rows of soldiers, standing still, silent and aloof, in their hundreds, six feet below ground level in their excavated trenches, took the breath away. First, it was their stillness, and then it was the brownness of it all. I suppose I had expected a terracotta red. Everything was mud brown, though the warriors themselves had a blue-grey tinge to their brownness. Close to, this was revealed as a kind of patina. Each soldier, grim of aspect, had never moved, never stood to attention, never been at ease, but always straight. The uniformity of their stillness was the first thing about them. Then, you could see, as you looked more closely, even from the parapet where you stood, that they had individuality too, as all soldiers do, a steadfast individuality. But stillness overrode both individuality and uniformity. They were as still as death, and dead in truth. Dead in the midst of their valour. It was the crowd which was alive, and moved, and jostled, and craned, and took photographs against precise instructions not to. The soldiers had no life, no spirit in them. We had, though. Soon, I began to feel superior. I could disobey, but I did not of course. I was not dead, yet. The roof of the hanger could never stand for heaven. I felt superior in the presence of death.

Wisely, the authorities have erected two large exhibition rooms outside the hanger, where they have put on show exact scale models of each type of solider, privates, archers, crossbowmen, officers and generals. In these exhibition rooms I was able to look carefully and long. Crowds are not so keen on replicas. Each exhibit, too, had attached a note in English, valuable mementos of the Queen's recent visit. The craftsmanship applied to each individual and each character in the lifeless drama is certainly impressive, first for its scale and, second, for its conscientiousness in terms of detail. Each soldier, high or low in rank, is separate in some sense or other. Head-dress, shape of head, lines on face or lips, armour, uniform, all have an identifiable separateness. Even their footwear is specially made, and can have nails in the soles, if kneeling like a crossbowman. Many have their clothing modelled to fall in folds. But not always; exact craftsmanship is not universal. Some clothing is not modelled and hangs stiffly, deprived of natural shape. Hands are often out of scale and too large. Feet and legs, even though covered against the cold, are gross and clumsy. Most significantly of all, postures have little in the way of variation. An infantryman stands regularly and firmly on two feet, in solid equilibrium. Similarly, crossbowmen stand or kneel without variety, archers stand with right hands raised to hold an arrow, and charioteers stand solidly on their heels in stolid balance, hands on rein without semblance of any tension. Details though they may be, all these defects detract from the quality of the total effect. Most revealing of all is the posture of cavalry horses. They stand as though cast for ever to witness a Trooping of the Colour, four-square, immobile, without life or any potential for movement. As I gazed at the replicas, I could not help recalling, among other things, the careful balance of the Bronze Charioteer at Delphi, the lively vigour of the Panathenaeic Procession on the friezes of the Parthenon, and the galloping chariots on the small coins of fifth-century Syracuse, all portraying in classical simplicity of implied motion the drama of horsemanship in action, and all designed and crafted 300 years before the terracotta army and its horses. There is indeed a classical poise about all of the terracotta army, but it is the poise of death. It has never been alive, and has a craftsmanship to match.

I felt awe in face of the terracotta army. Its scale and its silent unity were formidable, and concentrated attention. There was a weirdness about it, and there was no laughter among the crowd. I made no sacrifice, however; there was no demon to accompany our awe.

You can not say that the soldiers and their accoutrements are beautiful; they are half-beautiful, superficially so, like their patina. Nor are they true to life; they are only true to a vertical kind of non-life. Above all, there is no goodness; no imperial goodness dwelt among them. Qin Shi Huangdi, I am convinced, was a thoroughly evil man, self-centred, tyrannical and cruel. For instance, the discovery of a meteorite in 211 BC worried his superstitious nature greatly. When it was reported that someone had inscribed on the stone, 'After Qin Shi Huangdi's death, the land will be divided', he had all the people living in the neighbourhood killed, and the stone pulverized. Instead, he had poems about the Immortals sung in his court each day. Other people's lives were nothing to him. There were only men in his terracotta army. What place did womenfolk have among those over whom he ruled? We know little, but we do know that, when he died, all his concubines were buried with him, alive.

A tea room in a Buddhist Temple in Lanzhou.

Philosophy, scholarship and religion of a popular kind were abandoned in the time of the First Emperor of China. All was dedicated to the absolute will of an absolute ruler, who was lord of all under heaven. There are many more astonishing things still to be discovered in the mausoleum on Mount Li, for sure. However, I for one am willing to wager that they will have some beauty among them, little truth and no goodness. The people suffered greatly. You can see it on the faces of the terracotta soldiers.

Incidentally, in case the reader thinks that I became quite insensitive to the quality of things Chinese, we had seen the day before our visit to Mount Li some quite delightful bronze horses, galloping in full vigour, at the Gansu Provincial Museum in Lanzhou, albeit of later date than those in the mausoleum.

* * *

The walk that Sally and I took through the streets of Xi'an on the afternoon following our visit to Mount Li was for me far more entertaining than our visit there. Another walk we took together four weeks earlier in Istanbul far exceeded both for entertainment, and, more important than that, offered an appearance of an awesome demon.

We had decided to forsake our group that day, and 'do' Istanbul on foot, as far as we could. Our first target, naturally enough, was Santa Sophia, the Emperor Justinian's church, 'such as had not been seen since Adam'. On a sunny morning we walked across the Galata Bridge from our hotel, up the narrow winding incline of the Ankara Cadese, to the square and gardens around that vast monument to Imperial grandeur, erected in the name of God's holy wisdom. These days, the ground level of its foundations are a good nine feet below the level of the street. Inside, we experienced the hugeness of its internal space, its marble-lined walls, bronze doors, arches, columns and domes, and in particular mosaics restored in gold after iconoclasticism. Emblems from Islamic days distracted us. It was a muddle. You could not focus on anything. A congregation, procession and music, no longer possible in fact, would have given the building some chance of being itself. Without them, it is a hollow monument. It was tawdry, too, and for me spelt no magic. I was glad to have seen it, but I doubt that I shall go again so directly, first of all.

Outside, we walked round the base of the church, through the Imperial Gateway, into the seraglio belonging to the Palace of Topkapi, hoping to see another church of later date, but smaller and less daunting, Saint Irene. It was bluntly shut, so shut that you would think that it would never open again. It was nevertheless a place of dignity, and of lovely, narrow, pink Roman brick. You would not think that the Turks had later used it as an arsenal.

We then made enquiries from the tourist information desk about the whereabouts of the Mosaic Museum, much praised in the tourist literature. It too was closed, we were told, and so we never found out where it was.

Then, to a Turkish coffee in the sun, to plan what to do next. Sally was most understanding about my enthusiasm for Byzantium, and so let me have my head. I knew I needed to see the great Walls of Theodosius, breached in 1453, and the question was how to combine that, more than six miles away to the west, with some other visit, for we had the notion that, after lunch, we would walk down the hill on the other side of the city to the Golden Horn, and so back to our hotel by boat. We selected the Kaniye Camii, 200 yards inside the Walls I wanted to see and towards their northern end, and so within walking distance of the Golden Horn. If we could manage it that way, we would then be in a position to discount our earlier disappointments.

An incident, threatening at the time but delightful in retrospect, interrupted progress for a time. We began looking for transport in the wide square outside Santa Sophia, and eventually came across a sleepy old cab with a driver to match, pondering the pavement abstractedly. Having no Turkish, I approached him and showed him our map, pointing to the square inside the Walls close to where we wanted to go. He peered at the map with what I now recall as a complete lack of comprehension. Even if I had known how to say, 'Kaniye Camii gitmek istiyorum', which I most certainly did not, I doubt that he would have made much attempt to understand what I was saying. He gestured vaguely, and we climbed into his cab and drove off. I tried to follow on our map where we were going, but soon lost my way as crowded street followed crowded street. Progress was however slow, and tension increased. Presently we arrived somewhere, and he indicated that we should descend. I paid him, very little it seemed to me, and he drove off. It was plain at once that he had deposited us nowhere near where we wanted to be, and certainly nowhere near the Walls at all. All that was in fact plain was the proximity of a huge mosque across the street, to which our driver had briefly drawn our attention before driving off.

Nonplussed and frustrated, we stood in the shade, out of the hot sun, and suggested lunch to each other. There was an attractive-looking restaurant nearby. At that moment, two young Turkish men made their exit from its door, and, seeing our puzzlement, asked to look at our map. They at once pointed to the Mosque of Suleìman the Great. Did we want to be there, they queried with just a look. No, most certainly not, was our easy answer. Clearly, our cab driver had been unable to read, and everyone wants to go to the Mosque of Suleìman the Great, anyway, he must have thought. Where, then, was their next question. I pointed to the square near the Walls. They smiled, nodded and asked us to get into their car, parked by the pavement outside the restaurant. I suppose we showed some hesitation. They reassured us, and pointed again to the map and the square near the Walls. We all got in, and were driven off at great speed. Straight as a die we went along a broad boulevard, Fevsipasa Cadese by name. Direct conversation being impossible, I whispered to Sally that I thought we would be all right. She was non-committal. They took us at least four miles and then put us down on the corner of a large, bustling, chaotic square, unreliably portrayed on our famous map. Was chaos preferable to lunch, I asked myself. I dared not look at Sally. We thanked them. I tried to offer money. They rejected that at once, with courtesy and broad smiles. They were a lovely pair, I decided at last. They must have wished us luck as they drove off. There was no need. The Walls were straight ahead, and a sign on a corner just to our right read, 'To the Kaniye Museum'.

We walked as the sign directed, along a narrow suburban street, and then turned right, following another sign down a hill. There, ahead was a peach of a building. The advertised museum was in fact in origin a Byzantine church. An open narthex or porch supported by pillars and round arches, faced us. Above, the outside corners of a cruciform nave, topped by

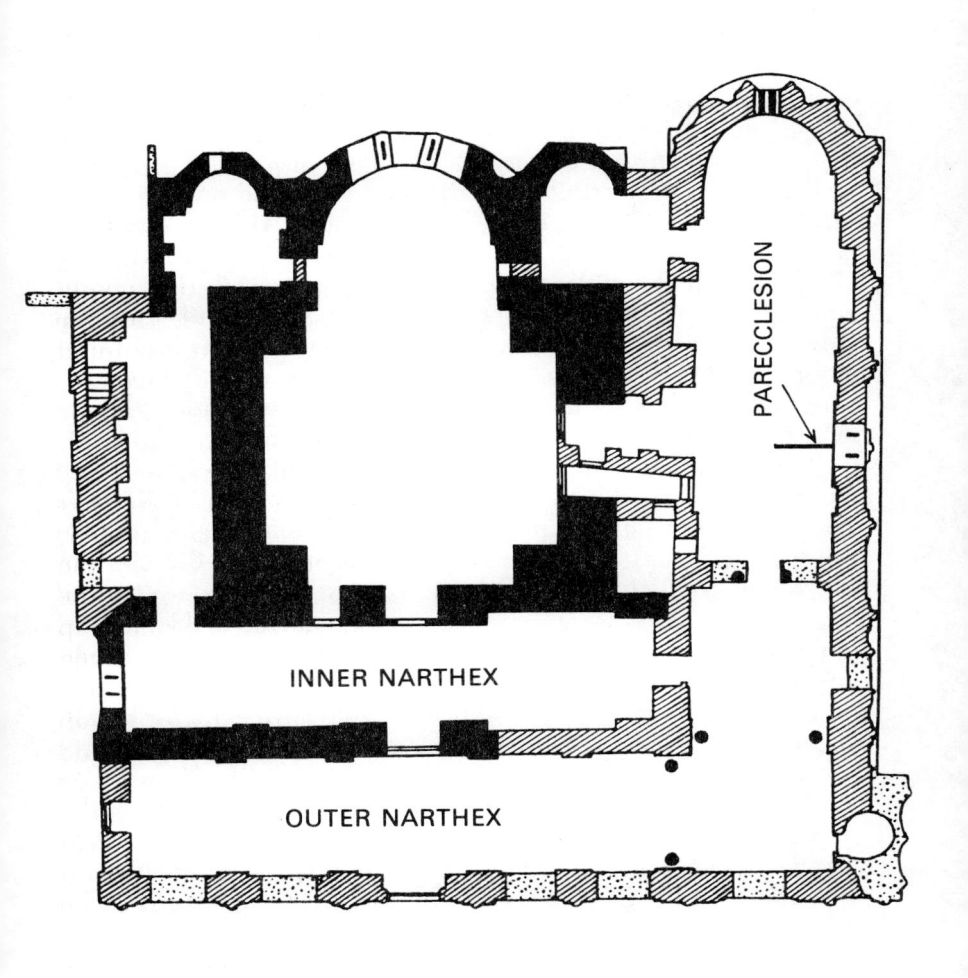

Ground-plan of St. Saviour in Chora
Black: twelfth century reconstruction
Shaded areas: fourteenth century additions.

a shallow, tiled cupola, supported in its turn by a shallow drum, with twelve narrow-arched windows, even-spaced. Since it was still before noon, the west face was in shade, whereas the dome was in bright sunlight. You stretched your eyes to see better. Cool, pink brickwork, in light and shade, made me think of ripening peaches on a tree.

Strides lengthened downwards, and we found ourselves in a sunlit square. We could now see a minaret. It had once been a mosque, and the Turks have now made it into a museum. The square had cobbles in long steps down towards the church, and a small Turkish fountain in front. They had scattered flowering shrubs round about, red and gold, and an old gas-lamp painted white leaned inwards at the edge, with cool, Turkish wooden verandas surveying the scene behind. There was no other soul in sight, except for a quiet cat.

The church, its name Saint Saviour in Chora, did not dominate. It was like a very old grandfather, so old that you could tell that everything else thereabouts was young in comparison, and, on the whole, in the mind of the church, worthy of kindly but scant regard. The charm of the square did not hold us back for more than a moment. Quickly inside, unawares, I met the demon. At once all became revealed, and my spirits rose beyond the roof.

We passed through a double narthex into a small main church, older and confirmed of cruciform shape, with an apse probably added slightly later, and smaller apses, cut off like chapels, on each side. The demon by now had done his work thoroughly. It was like returning home by accident. I became blissfully happy. What Sally made of my burblings, I cannot think.

Imagination flooded past eyes and mind. The old church, with its thick walls, comfortable with its dome above, and its four equidistant corners, with light entering dimly only from the drum, the door and the apse, was certainly of early date, built by Justinian (AD 527-565), I thought. It had also plainly suffered damage in its early centuries from earthquake and neglect. Large areas of wall and dome had had to be restored in recent years (by the Byzantine Institute of America, I later learned), and were now bare of decoration. There were however three mosaics still surviving, but of a much later date than the main substance of the church, classical in style, elegant but more human than Justinian's austerity. On one side Mary, and on the other, Jesus, both standing, and over the doorway a picture of the death of Mary, hallowed in a surround of gold. How could I explain newer mosaics in an older building? To the inner narthex, then. Perhaps I could find a clue there.

The inner narthex, enclosed but for doors in and out and small windows at each end, is to all intents and purposes intact, remaining as it was intended but for slight damage from damp and the depredations of time. Its ceilings and walls are lined with mosaics that were placed there at the time of its construction. It was thus in the first place an addition to the earlier church, and then contemporary with its renovation and redecoration. Mosaics of Peter and Paul, standing, flank the entrance to the church, and above the door, in the tympanum, there is a mosaic of a man in gaudy official dress and head-dress, kneeling and offering back to a seated Christ a model of a church. The church being handed back is the reconstructed Saint Saviour in Chora. Here, then, was the clue I was searching for. The gaudy individual portrays Theodore Metochites, the first minister of Andronicus II Palaeologus (AD 1282-1328). I remembered having seen previously representations of the picture in books. The mosaics in the renewed church and those in the inner narthex have a similar date, something like AD 1320, when the reforming cultural zeal of Andronicus II was at its height. Saint Saviour in Chora is therefore in main substance a monument to the Byzantine Renaissance of that period. Other mosaics show Mary interceding with Christ on behalf of the sick, and representations of a selection of Christ's miracles on their behalf. As a symbol of it all, the small cupola at the southern end contains at its centre a medallion of Christ Pantocrater (Greek for Emperor), surrounded on the curved sides by representations of the twelve tribes of Israel and the patriarchs, who form part of the genealogy of Christ. At the northern end, in the cupola, Mary with her child are at the centre, with Moses, the prophets and the Kings of Israel surrounding them. There can be fewer more concise history lessons about the relationship between the Old and New Testaments than the mosaics in the inner narthex of Saint Saviour in Chora, nor indeed more interesting architectural detail drawn as a background, or more delicate and decorative borders, separating one from the other. I tried to drink it all in, as well as I could. It was a special place.

The outer narthex, though obviously later for simple practical reasons, is in the same style in a rather more spacious setting. The mosaics tell stories from the gospels of Matthew and Luke. Over the entrance is a figure of Christ, symbolizing the realm of the living in the square outside, and over the exit into the inner narthex, a figure of Mary, signifying the realm of the infinite within. Everywhere a masterly and moving experience. Particularly moving for me was a portrait of Andronicus II on the curve of one of the arches. He had been responsible, too, for another meeting I had with the demon in Monemvasia in the southern Peloponese; it had been he who had built there Santa Sophia, that wonderful monument to the final flowering of Byzantium astride the top of a huge cliff overlooking the sea.

The one oddity at Saint Saviour in Chora is the parecclesion, a surprising sepulchral corridor ending in an apse, built also by Metochites, at a slight angle to the south side of the church. The style of its brickwork externally, and its intricate arching internally, covered with frescoes concerned with the Resurrection, to my mind do not harmonize with the rest of Metochites's reconstruction. Was it a modernizing attempt? Or perhaps its subject matter made a good argument for building something different. The oddity remains a problem for me. After all, Saint Saviour in Chora is only a small building; sketch plans in guidebooks suggest thirty-six feet square.

My imagination on the other hand had earlier led me personally into error, as I was to find out later. Though the original church had indeed been built in Justinian's day or before, there had also been a major reconstruction after damage between 1081 and 1118, which the mother-in-law of Alexis I Comnenus initiated, most probably causing the complete rebuilding of the central dome. I have to admit however that I enjoy my fallible imagination, and blame the demon for fostering its enthusiasm.

Exhausted but jubilant, we looked at last for lunch, and found it after a frustrating interval; melon, butter beans, fish and some superb bread.

There followed a leisurely walk northward along the Walls, inside and outside, and the sight of some lovely children with their smiling mothers on the steps of small houses. And so, as planned, down to the shore of the Golden Horn, limpid and blue beneath a cloudless sky, but smelling dreadfully. We took a small boat-taxi as soon as possible. The water bubbled steadily as we crossed to the other side. The air smelt of sulphur. Our helmsman by his looks could well have been Charon himself, taking us over the evil-smelling Styx. His fee was just as small. His pride and joy however was a little model aeroplane, which he had made of wood, with a propeller which worked. We were allowed to handle it. It had really been a thoroughly enjoyable day.

* * *

The demon who lives in the ancient city of Ani in Turkish Armenia was of quite a different character. I had hoped that I might meet him there. Friends had spoken of him before I set out.

Ani is in eastern Anatolia, and lies just thirty-one miles east of Kars, which in its turn was forty miles from Sarikamis, where we were staying. We made the journey by bus through high upland scenery. Military encampments were all about, and so was military business. As the road approached the frontier with the USSR, security became strict. We had already been instructed to take no cameras with us outside the bus. If we did, they would certainly be confiscated. The country we passed through had been fought over since time immemorial, most recently by the Turks and the Russians prior to the signing of the Treaty of Brest-Litovsk in 1918. It was a corner of the world where pressure had continually collided in conflict, perhaps for longer periods than any other such. Similar conflict over Poland, Israel and Ireland has, for instance, been more recent.

Armenia and Armenians occupied the land over which the struggles wandered, and for a long time survived them, somehow or other. A second factor which singled the Armenians out for special treatment was their Christianity. Converted early in the fourth century, they decided to go their own way in AD 511, being among those who held a strong heretical belief in the single nature of Christ (not man, if he was of one substance with the Father, as far as they were concerned), and so separated for good from the Orthodox church of the West. Hard-working and conscientious, Christian Armenia prospered despite the disappearance of the Byzantines, and conquest by Arabs in 772, recapture by Byzantium in 1045, soon followed by the conquest of Seljuk Turks in 1064, and those more orthodox Christians, the Georgians, in the early part of the thirteenth century. Armenia was in fact astride the shortest trade route between East and West, and, whatever happened, that was good for business. Convinced Christians and good businessmen, they did well for a time.

After various dynastic troubles, Ani became the capital of Armenia in 961. The town could be easily defended, and it grew in size. Numerous large churches were built, often original in concept and design. Our long bus-ride from Sarikamis caused our expectations to grow as well, and we built upon our imaginations, even though the road was a rough one.

You pass through a small village, dry dung piled high in the yard for winter fuel, and there in front is a huge wall; you can see that it is in ruins at the top, but it is still high enough to dominate the place where the bus is parked. You can sense too that it is a thick wall. Not just thick, it is a double wall, for good measure. As you walk through the main gate, you see first the double thickness, and that twin towers on each side have crumbled, and, then, on high, emblazoned large, a lion passant in base relief on a huge stone. You recall the two lions of Mycenae, and expectations increase further.

I met the demon when I first discovered the nature of the site. It was a thrilling shock. The big walls are more than a mile in length, still standing, if incomplete. A second gate, 200 yards to the right, has two sturdy round towers, still seemingly intact. There are also other towers fortifying the inner wall, which has regular large, curved niches on its inside. I could find no convincing explanation for these. Perhaps they were wall-strengtheners; perhaps they offered shelter for defending troops when missiles threatened from outside. Impressive though the wall was, the site's most impressive feature appeared at each end of the wall. Here, at both ends, two chasms yawned, down which rough rivers tumbled. The chasms were both narrow, no more than 200 yards wide at their broadest, wandering about and following rock-strewn river beds. The sides of the chasms were steep, like cliffs. I for one did not think of scrambling down them, or even peering over. They were at least as high as the Riesenrad in Vienna (197'), and just as terrifying. The chasms met at the rivers' confluence, and, at that point, on the city's side was one of its highest places, its citadel. The site then is the shape of a rough triangle, like that at Jiaohe in Xinjiang, rivers on two sides and pointing south in both instances, with a wall protecting the third side to the north. Ani however is much larger than Jaiohe, being, at an estimate from a sketch map, 100,000 square yards in approximate area. A possible population of something like 70,000, do you think, with numerous others outside the walls? No guidebook tells you.

The River Arpa is the larger of the two rivers, and flows southwards on the eastern side. Across the River Arpa lies the Soviet Union. A Soviet military camp, no doubt with sensors and towers continually alert, looks across the chasm. It was another shock and a thrill. At once, the demon was all around, across on the other side, down deep below where the rivers rushed and astride the lofty walls away behind us, in the spirit of a lion waiting for missiles.

There was a third factor in addition to the site's size and situation, a potent factor, possessed by any place where people once lived, worked and died, and where all is now deserted and for the most part in ruins. The ruins are the people's only monument, and spell out their aspirations. Ani is for me as numinous as Mycenae. Remnants of at least ten of the churches of Ani survive. Their signal, scattered presence is awesome. The suffering of their people had something to do with it.

We had time to look at only four of the churches.

One of the difficulties for those attempting to describe any of the architectural features of Ani is that there would appear to be no general consensus about the plan of the city nor of the location of several of its ruins. Another is that there appear to be no reliable guidebooks, and, for good measure, few good photographs. The eager tourist has to rely largely on his own resources.

For instance, I can not reliably identify from any document the name or location of the church about which I wish to write first. All I have available is my own sketch plan and the few notes which I put together after our visit. Tall and foreshortened, as far as traditional Romanesque design is concerned, it was nevertheless a three-aisled basilican church, with a main apse towards what was probably its eastern end, but whose narthex was in ruins. I made no note of any tall, externally decorated drum and conical dome, but, since these are a common, if not traditional, feature of Armenian churches, I suspect that such a drum and conical dome should have been included in my plan, spanning the main aisle and supported by pillars and arches close to the apse. Overall, however, what was particularly notable was the clarity of the church's internal frescoes, still to a large extent surprisingly intact, detailing the life of a Cappadocian, Saint Gregory, who first introduced Christianity to the Armenians. Having already visited Cappadocia, I thought I could identify a later, more primitive Cappadocian style in the frescoes. The date of the church was said to be about AD 1000, and so such a link was then a possibility. Internally, the church had a Roman feeling, not unlike that of Santa Maria in Cosmedin in Rome, but it was not Roman. It was paler and cooler. It had great height, it looked upwards as well as towards the apse; it aspired to be more than just a processional church. I was most unclear about whether the architecture had been copied from western traditions. The building said more than just that.

My second church has a name, the Church of Saint Gregory of Abugamrents. It was a round church in the memorial manner, not unlike the Seljuk tombs we had seen in Erzurum. Dated in the tenth century, again it appeared taller than you would expect, its drum and cone being nevertheless of traditional design. I especially enjoyed its circular interior. More delicate than anything Norman, and smaller than round churches in Rome, like Santa Costanza, without their light and the colour of their mosaics. The pillared arcade round the central space was gloomy in its elegance. Windows were few and narrow. Later, the church was used as a funeral chapel by an important Ani family, we were told. The building is now in poor repair.

Third is the city's Cathedral, most exciting of all, since it began to isolate for me an identifiable Armenian spirit. Like the other two churches, the Cathedral was built of a dark, reddish stone, which glowed warmly where it faced the light. Built originally between AD 989 and 1001, it was sacked by the Turks in 1064 and converted into a mosque (a collapsed minaret can be seen nearby). It was restored by Georgians at the start of the thirteenth century. Externally, at first, it appears to be a simple, rectangular building with high walls. Closer to, it is decorated with slit windows, some with small bulbous tops, and overall with slender, blank arcading, the arches reaching to the top of each wall. This latter device adds distinction and grace to an otherwise dull geometrical shape. Spaces are kept blank except for Armenian lettering carved in elegant paragraphs. As you enter through the main door, you at once see sky in the circular space where a drum and a dome once rested on wide arches and four sturdy pillars. As a result, the building is now lighter than originally intended. Nevertheless, a large central apse, flanked by two small chapels, contributes to a secure notion of what a remarkable building it must have been in its heyday. Internally speaking, it is still simple, spacious, lofty, dignified and coherent. I have seen no building like it in the West. Inside the Cathedral, the demon is at rest.

I found my fourth church just as remarkable, though for quite different reasons, since it now lies in ruins. It lay in ruins, in fact, only a few years after it was built. The finished building collapsed. Its name is the Church of Saint Gregory of Gagik, and it was built around AD 1000. My thesis is that the building collapsed because it was overambitious in design. It was said to have been modelled on a similar large church at Zwarthnotz in Soviet Armenia. As far as I could make out from the ruins, its plan was circular, and much larger than the Church of Saint Gregory of Abugamrents, though built about the same time. Along the inner wall were elegant blank arcades, with pillars of classical design. A true arcade then ran all the way round a central space, some of whose pillars survive amid the ruins, topped by strange Ionic capitals. Holding up the dome were plainly four huge pillars, not, as often, monolithic, but made of blocks of stone hewn smooth, so huge you would have thought they could have held anything up. In extension, though, my thesis is that these pillars were meant to support a drum and conical dome of such vastness that, in the end, as pieces of engineering they were fundamentally insecure, and so allowed everything to fall into ruin soon after completion. Even today, as a pile of incoherent stone, carved and careful in small pieces, the ruins spell out an aspiring energy, imaginative and adventurous. The fault of aspiring too high however is inescapable and well documented. Hereabouts, the demon is in a restless state, and encourages dismay and disappointment. You have to ask yourself once more about the final fate of Turkish Armenia. It was certainly a devastating, cruel fate, but by how much was it prompted, and then urged on by an unwillingness to conform, and by excessive zeal for an idealism on high on the part of those who suffered it? You begin to wonder, too, about the fate of Armenians who now live in Soviet Armenia. The church at Zwarthnotz also survives at ground level only.

Mind you, Ani itself was deserted by its citizens, as Tamerlane's hordes began their marauding in the area in the early fourteenth century. You could not blame them for doing that. No doubt, these days, if you are an Armenian, some of those who descend from those hordes still live in Azerbaijan. Meanwhile, Soviet Armenia is on the other side of the chasm and the River Arpa. On this side, there is no authoritative guide to a city wonderfully surviving amid its ruins.

* * *

Church of Metexi, Tbilisi.

At about the same time as Georgians were restoring the Cathedral at Ani, they were building a new church of their own near Tiflis, now Tbilisi, their capital. The Church of Metexi

Church of Metexi, Tbilisi.

(1278-89), when we saw it on a bright, sunny morning, standing tall and grey on its own small hill overlooking the River Kura across to the hills opposite and back northwards towards the city, gave me a sudden shock, for I had not expected it. It sprang upon us. Then it excited me, for I realized that there would soon be more like it as we journeyed round Tbilisi.

At first sight, externally speaking, the Church of Metexi reminds one of Ani and Armenia. It has a tall, slit-windowed drum and a conical dome, it is a taller and more compact building than you would expect to see in the West, and it has an uncomplicated directness. Then, looking closer, you notice that it has a character of its own. The cone is less steep, the ground plan is more complicated, and the walls, built of dressed stone, eschew decoration as far as possible; there is modest, slender arcading on the drum and a dog's tooth design beneath the eaves. The slit windows on the main walls are simply constructed, and the porch is stark in its simplicity. It is a tall, balanced building, designed with great care.

You had to imagine its internal structure, for its doors were bolted, the church being no longer used to worship in. Inside, it would have three aisles, ending in three apses, the centre apse being larger than the other two. Four pillars with arches would support the dome, and allow for a cruciform ground-plan. It would be dark, and seem foreshortened and very tall. Armenia, yet not Armenia.

Most assuredly so, for Georgia had been converted to Christianity 200 years later than Armenia, and then not without a struggle in its hinterland. Christianity was used as part of the unifying process among Georgians as a whole, and, when converted, they adhered strictly to orthodoxy, never joining Armenia in its heresy. You could see that the builders of the Church of Metexi had dared nothing rash.

While driving around Tbilisi that morning, as we sped down a broad, river-side boulevard, our guide pointed fleetingly to a small, basilica-like building, obviously of some antiquity, to our left. On we went elsewhere, but later I had the chance to ask her about it. She said it was formerly a church, of sixth century date, but now an artist used it as a studio. Could I go on my own to see it? Yes, of course. If the artist is there, he will let you see the inside. She gave me directions about how to get there from our hotel.

The Sixth Century Church of Ančisxati in Tbilisi.

That afternoon, I set off on my own, to see what I could find. It was Saturday. Tbilisi folk were on the streets in large numbers, many arm in arm as though partaking of an early *passeggiata*. I lost my sense of direction once, but in the end found what I was looking for. It was delightful. A simple, rectangular, three-aisled building of brick and stone, with a taller nave, three small windows on each side of it, three others at the east end, and no apse. The main door at the west end had an arch with a large slab across its pillars supporting the arch, as you often see in rural Greece. The whole thing had the honest savour of the Mediterranean, utterly derived from there. Its name was Ančisxati. There was a small yard at the back, with a 'No Parking' sign and a tree, flanked by wooden Turkish houses of a later date. Unfortunately, the artist was not about, indulging in the *passeggiata*, no doubt. The demon poked his head round a corner and smiled.

I turned happily back to the hotel, and took a photograph of Lenin's statue in the square from behind a bus. Then, I had the idea of purchasing a bottle of vodka, to celebrate with

Porch of the Church of Ančisxati, facing Turkish-style domestic wooden balconies

friends my earlier good fortune. I prepared a gracious request in my best Russian, 'Could I have a bottle of vodka, please?', turned a corner, and there, down a step or two, was a Georgian version of an 'off-licence'. Down the steps I went, courage brimming over. Georgians were buying wine and, apparently, spirits, bottle by bottle, at a low counter, from a red-haired lady of small stature, in a white overall. I looked for vodka on the shelves, wired off as a protection against pilferers, and saw none. Nothing daunted, I joined the queue, eyed askance, or so I thought, by the locals. When in due course I reached the counter, I produced my elegant request with purposeful poise, again so I thought. My answer however was blunt, not to say, abrupt.

'NIET.'

How you leave an 'off-licence' with any dignity in the face of such brevity, defeated me entirely. Having no further response available, not even a 'Why not?', I returned to the street feeling abused and hurt. Of course, my enthusiasm had erased from memory the Gorbachev anti-vodka campaign. The lady with the red hair had probably felt just as abused and hurt as I had. Plainly an honest soul, she knew that tourists bought their vodka from Berioska shops, no longer from 'off-licences', where it was not available to anybody anyway. Who did I think I was?

King Mirian, who unified Georgia in the fourteenth century and was responsible for initiating its conversion to Christianity, wrote to the Emperor Constantine, asking him to send to Georgia not only priests but also architects skilled in the construction of churches. The Church of Ančisxati, as a basilican church, was in direct line of succession from those first architects. The Georgian instinct, however, was for centralized planning, focussing attention on the centre of a church's cruciform shape. Such a church was the Church of Dzvari, built between 586 and 605, near Mirian's ancient Georgian capital of Mcxeta, north of Tbilisi in the foothills of the Caucasus mountains.

Built at the top of a hill near the confluence of the rivers Kura and Aragvi, at a point where a huge wooden cross had once stood in the open air, it stands now, a cross itself, for a unified ground plan, external completeness, and a carefully constructed internal space, with four small chapels filling each junction of the cruciform shape. A wide drum and dome offer an unusually large area for the church's congregation. Though smaller, the church is as complete in concept as San Vitale in Ravenna, yet quite different in totality. It does not have the mesmerizing effect of an internal arcade. It stand stable on its own and as a symbol of the Cross. Inside, the church is now bare of decoration; outside there are small carved features on each facade, and a remarkable sculpture over the west door, two angels in flight holding a cross, not occurring anywhere else in the Byzantine world.

Church of Dzvari, near Mcxeta.

For me, as soon as we were climbing the rocky path towards the church from our bus, I knew the demon might be present inside. The statement which the hill itself made, at the junction of two rivers again, amid the low mountains of the southern Caucasus, was plain enough. The unity of the building and its shape as a memorial of great antiquity caused the spine to shiver. I began to mutter to myself. The shadows of the space inside were likewise harmonious and strong. There was a crowd of us inside, and there we all became compulsively silent as we perceived where we were. I still have no words for the experience. The architect of the Church of Dzvari had built with rare originality. He must have been Georgian, through and through.

Slowly, a choir began to assemble in one of the square spaces in rows, those at the back standing on benches. Men and women, all were dressed in black. As we were already silent, the choir's conductor had no need to call us to order. Light from the windows behind shone brightly, and suddenly the choir ceased to exist in the shadow of the light. Even the building ceased to exist. Sound only. The sound of unaccompanied human voices in harmony burst upon all ears and minds, and captured the universe without a struggle. Sound enveloped everything as a tide in flood. I was unable to think. I can remember only standing and hearing.

They sang for half an hour. They sang church music, music from the tradition of the Georgian Orthodox Church. Sometimes it overflowed with sadness, sometimes with triumph and jubilation. Underlying all was pattern, the pattern of sounds in harmony, the pattern of varied rhythms in measured treads, and the pattern of sense and intelligibility, often complex. Our guides apart, none of us understood a word, but we all understood the music. First, it was tuneful. Then, it told us of tradition, of history and of emotion. And, finally, with soloists adding personality at points of intensity, it told us of our common existence in a church on a hill. Without understanding a word, we recognized it all by intuition, and because the music made demands upon us. All became overcome by individual kinds of reverence. Somehow we shared both joy and sadness. As for the building, it had heard it all before. It had some of us feel at one with the communion of saints.

When the singing was over we moved outside, and looked across the valleys all around. Only while doing this, did I realize that I had just had an encounter with the most powerful awesome demon of all, the demon who, though being immortal, never introduces himself. Unconsciously at first, we had just witnessed the beautiful, good and true all at once, overwhelmed until released.

The reader may remember that I had been similarly abstracted while listening to jazz at Preservation Hall in New Orleans, where the demon had also been present, but before I had introduced him as an important character in the course of my story. I would however draw a distinction between these two meetings. In New Orleans the demon invited us all to share with him and the musicians their own pleasure in what they were doing; at Dzvari, the demon was a more austere character, and we had to make our own approach into his presence, as separate individuals. At the church on the hill, we appeared as supplicants, not being warmly invited to a party as we were in Preservation Hall.

There was one other occasion when a demon interested in music presented himself. This was much further east, in Turfan, in far-off Xinjiang. It was a warm, moonlit evening, and we had congregated in the open air after dinner round a rustic platform, wooden pillars at each corner supporting a simple roof. There were a few electric lights. A simple open air stage. A performance was plainly imminent.

And what a performance it was! A group of Uighurs, men and women, some twenty strong, sprang from the darkness into view and collected themselves in a semi-circle, musicians on each wing. They bowed, and began. Their instruments were a strange collection; I counted two lutes with long necks, one bowed with twelve strings and the other plucked, a long four-stringed fiddle, a hand drum, a tambourine, an elementary dulcimer, two or three recorder-like pipes, and castanets. Sometimes, the musicians would dance too, but for the most part they accompanied a colourful group of dancers and singers, dressed in silks and braids, small caps and boots for the men, long hair and long dresses for the women, red, green, gold and black predominating.

The Uighurs are a proud race, and they dance with their heads held high, with great vivacity, good humour, flirtatiousness and vigour in the use of high heels and clapping hands. At once for us, their spectators, their performance was exotic, and yet homely. Their basic rhythms were those of their Moslem origins, half concealing in the background a tinkling chant from the lutes and tambourines which spoke of China. In the old days, they used to sing and dance in this way at the small courts of their rural kings. Tradition has it that they learnt their craft from those who came to visit from Persia, Kashmir, Afghanistan and Central Asia. The craft has now become a tradition in its own right, and it continues as a delight to those who came to watch and listen on the edge of the Gobi and Taklamakan deserts. The songs tell tales of love and rivalry, and speak, too, of springtime and summer, and of movement and jollity. Their

Cathedral Church at Mcxeta, the former Georgian Capital, the Church of Dzvari on the hill beyond.

performance treated us to a novel feeling, that of being present at an ancient royal occasion, an occasion celebrating fraternity and equality, in the open air, beneath the moon. Exotic and homely.

So homely was it that one of our number, one of the younger ones, was invited to join the dancing. And a very good job she made of it, too. She was on her honeymoon. Soon we were all clapping and tapping our feet in time with the lively rhythms. By now, the demon was among us. He was joining in, too. A friendly, convivial chap, this one. The whole performance lasted no more than forty minutes. The Uighurs, with their flashing smiles and their darting eyes, had captured our hearts with their friendliness and, indeed, their brevity.

It was the spine-tingling music at Dzvari, from the Georgian Orthodox tradition, which led me into this digression about similar occasions when my spine had been tingled, quite different in style and content. Quite different also was the cathedral church of Sveti-Cxoveli at Mcxeta, the ancient capital of Georgia, down below, along the valley at the confluence of the two rivers. From its site on its small plain, you can see the church at Dzvari on the top of its hill. It is a fascinating juxtaposition.

Sveti-Cxoveli is the cathedral church of the patriarch, and still in use as a place of worship, though I have to say that there were few people to be seen worshipping there when we made our visit. The oldest functioning church in Georgia, it was built on the site of a tomb belonging to a Cappadocian Jewess called Sidonia, earlier converted to Christianity. Over the tomb, so it was said, a life-giving tree had sown itself spontaneously, sprouted and flourished, many people being miraculously cured by its effect. The church of the life-giving tree in the valley was thus twinned with the church of the Holy Cross on the hill. The church of the life-giving tree was finished in 1029, 450 years later than its twinned companion.

The cathedral is a well balanced construction on a rectangular ground plan, with an elongated east-west axis. Because of its length, the effect of its conical dome, placed towards the eastern end, is less dominant than usual. Made of a warm, pale stone, all the church's many external faces are decorated with long, elegant, incised arches, in balance and carefully calculated. Windows are narrow, single slits within each arch. Compared with any church of similar eminence in the West, Sveti-Cxoveli would be in proportion shorter and taller, but without any appearance of being stunted.

Inside, I lost hold of reality once more. Suddenly, I was in Normandy; three aisles, a large central apse, two others balancing on each side, and soaring pillars completed by proud arches bulging slightly outwards. The effect was so obviously Romanesque. Indeed, I must have been somehow, I thought, miraculously returned to the Abbey church in Bernay. Closer inspection revealed details of decoration and construction which would have been out of place there, but, nevertheless, in general, the over-riding impression was one of a late Romanesque building in northern France. And, what is more, exactly contemporary as well. Georgia had been cut off from mainstream developments in the West for centuries, and so the similarity was a problem. I concluded that my impression could only be due to coincidence, and to nothing else. Certainly, outside, Sveti-Cxoveli was the epitome of Georgian stylishness. Nearby, on the River Kura, Lenin had had caused to be built in 1921 the

Two fortified sixteenth Century churches in the lower Caucasus.

first Transcaucasian hydro-electric dam. Irrationally, I thought about the life-giving tree once more.

I loved the churches of Tbilisi and its environs. There are, praise be, many more yet to be seen. In sympathy with Armenia, yet quite distinct. In sympathy with the Romanesque, too. I hope to be back.

* * *

Lenin once said that socialism was a combination of electricity and democracy. Sounding old-fashioned now, such political sentiment must have had a dramatic effect on the lives of ordinary people all along the southern border of the Soviet Union between Afghanistan, Tibet and China. A striking account of their earlier poverty and oppression under Islamic emirs before the October Revolution is to be found in the Museum of Regional Studies in Bukhara, where a direct lie is given to those who suggest that progress in Soviet society has everywhere been sluggish and patchy. Indeed, throughout our journey through the southern republics we were continually impressed with the confidence and cheerfulness of the people who lived there. Given that the description of life in and around Bukhara before 1917 in the museum is broadly accurate, confidence and cheerfulness are no mean achievements, where once misery, cruelty and starvation were once a commonplace. People may not have become rich, but they have become happier.

The Museum of Regional Studies is housed in the Ark Fortress, a fearsome citadel and palace in the centre of old Bukhara, a fortress where fierce fighting took place between the contending parties at the time of the revolution of 1917. Old Bukhara lies eight miles away from its railway station. I have often wondered why the great Trans-Caspian railway was built so far away from such a long-established centre of trade. Perhaps its emirs were as apprehensive of industrial progress within their domain as the University of Cambridge had once been, demanding that progress be kept away, more than an arm's length. Like the University, the emirs ran a good business. Bukhara as an oasis had been a centre for trade for more than 2,000 years. A full array of conquerors, such as Alexander the Great and Tamerlane, had passed their way through Bukhara, yet the city had always survived, continuing to purvey its silks, astrakhan skins and metal-work. Bukhara carpets came from the south, and were marketed in the place from which they got their name. The lower reaches of the Zarafshan river provided the oasis with an agricultural base. As a result, the emirs flourished on the backs of their labourers, and old Bukhara now survives as a city of outstanding beauty, mosques, minarets, *madrasahs* and mausoleums round every corner. We were shown the sights on our first afternoon there.

The Ark Fortress provided a starkly strange introduction. The *Ismail Samani* mausoleum and the *Char-Minar madrasah*, built of mud-coloured bricks, survive to this day intact though built 1,000 years ago, both strangely and soundly elegant in shape, not aspiring to the heavens as buildings do in Samarkand. You find them in a park, near the ancient walls and a modern market. More elegant still was the gracious facade of an unknown *madrasah* built in the seventeenth century. Tall, wooden pillars astride a balustrade, support a curved, patterned roof, an open narthex for the premises behind. Adding to the charm were the long reflections of the building in an ornamental lake, still and

Seventeenth century *madrasah* in Bukhara.

perfect in combined calm and colour.

   Our hotel, the Bukhoro, Uzbekh for Bukhara, lay outside the old town, near the modern city's administrative centre, with its wide avenues. New Bukhara, its factories and residential zones, lie towards the railway. Modern administrators have kept the old and new quite separate; neither detracts from the other. Administrators in other countries might well wish they had such space in which to be wise. I enjoyed our introduction to the sights of old Bukhara, and resolved to visit them again, if I could, on my own.

   Next day the weather was brilliant once more. At the sights which we had visited the day before, I would find myself nearer to their spirit if I were not in a crowd. The view from the top of the hotel showed me the direction in which the minarets and blue domes were to be found, and I set out, curious and excited. I had with me the customary sketch map provided by the hotel, but nothing else. The names of streets were shown on the map, and I expected that I would recognize them wherever they were displayed.

   As I left the open spaces of the administrative area, I took note of the position of the sun, so that I could use it as a guide if need be. It was climbing towards the south, on my left hand, and in line with the tallest of the office buildings. I had taken a rough 'fix' on the position of the Bukhoro.

   First, a lane presented itself open over dry ground on the left side, with a distant view of the southern walls. Then, a junction at which I had either to maintain my outward movement towards the wall or to dive towards the centre, into what was plainly a maze of narrow streets. I chose the latter. Soon the streets, no longer paved, became rutted with cart tracks and craters where puddles would form whenever it rained. There were no pavements at the side. The houses in jagged rows were all single-storeyed, and for the most part made of wattle and daub, often painted white but sometimes a light brown colour. All had flat roofs, sometimes with shallow domes. There were few windows facing the street, only doors leading into small courtyards, where there would be fig trees and vines. These streets, curving naturally this way and that, had formed themselves long ago. The houses had certainly been homes in the time of the emirs, for they spoke of wariness and suspicion. But they were wary and suspicious no longer; doors would be wide open, and women worked inside at their chores. There were few people in the streets, occasionally someone with two plastic bags, in balance, each laden to the brim, plain without advertisement, white or brown. These plastic bags were the only signs of modernity but for electricity cables held aloft on wooden poles, no longer needed for arcading *madrasahs*. There was a dusty peace overall, no motor vehicles and no bicycles, the bright sun angling deep shadows on the ground. I was beginning to enjoy myself, already unmindful of the sights I was seeking. I just followed my nose. The air was clean, and there were no smells.

I merely strolled in the peace, and grew slowly warm. I put on my sun-hat to collect the sweat and to keep my spectacles clean, contented poverty all around. At least, it seemed contented. Nobody gave me a disturbing glance of any kind. They went about their business purposefully and without haste. They had things to do. There were no children. Strange, no children.

I turned right, with the sun behind me. The aspect changed. I was in a trading area, small shops, mechanics, electricians, metal workers, hardware merchants, a bakery, a granary, some fruit but nothing else to eat, all in agreeable chaos. More formal was a covered market. No modern market this one but going back to Turkish times, a bazaar. At the intersection of streets, there were conglomerations of these covered areas, sheltered also by shallow domes. Stalls of a permanent kind were set up inside, for jewellery here, for skull-caps there, and silk and cotton everywhere. No moneychangers nor ere a bank. It was more crowded in the market, but no bustle. People strolled like me, and did not purchase either. Still they did not look at me.

I sauntered past the markets, becoming dazed by this new kind of magic. A stranger, dressed in strange clothes, wearing spectacles and no skull-cap, tall and fair, not dark as they were, I was accepted as entirely normal. I was no exception, just a thin part of a thin crowd. I began to feel embarrassed by this acceptance, enjoying it nevertheless. I suppose I felt that I was the only one having no real purpose there. That was the shame of it, not the enjoyment.

The streets and passageways became inextricable. Surprise became routine. A small square and a fountain dry of water in its centre focussed on a small ancient building with twin towers and a blue-tiled dome. Then, tall wooden arcades at street corners, roofs supported by tall wooden poles. Next, a second square, larger and not dominated by anything, in a state of quiet disorderliness. A dark passageway with strong light at its end. And there, suddenly, best of all; an ornamental pond, cricket pitch square in shape and size, a low parapet round its edge, sheltered by trees, deep and dark green, reflecting the trees and only the blue sky in pieces. Round the pond, there was a broad space for strolling side by side, like a college quadrangle. Not much strolling though, far more sitting. Sitting on the parapet, sitting on sundry benches and, especially, sitting on the edge of platforms, supping tea from small glass beakers. You rest your elbows and your tea on a second platform, smaller than the first and placed on top of it. Low tables placed on low tables for sitting on in rows. Tea houses at the back of the square behind, two of them, with their static, fixed accommodation for customers. Space inside was not capacious and gloomy. Customers chose the open air, and sat, and smoked, and talked, and supped tea. No sign at all of emotion. Men only; not a woman or a child in sight. There were beards galore, and a uniformity of skull-caps. Old, thin, wrinkled faces peered from eyes which had seen too much and would not open wide. The younger faces were broader and fatter, whose eyes had seen rather little and darted to and fro. Conversation certainly, but no smiles or gesticulations. It was all serious stuff. I wanted to join them. I would have liked to sit down in the shade after my walk, and drink tea too, and say nothing. However, faced with this secretive crowd of menfolk, I could no longer be embarrassed by acceptance and was made shy of intruding. It was the caution which stops you joining a group because, though friendly, it is preoccupied. Anyway, it would never be possible to know what they knew. So I stayed away, trying in vain to absorb the atmosphere from the outside. They did not give me a glance even then.

It was a good time, full of interest, even though full too of introspection. Reluctantly, I left the pond and its tea-drinkers, and the trees and the talk. The sun was right behind me now, and I was aware of taking a wide, circular route, in a clockwise direction. I was also aware that I was somehow going to miss seeing the sights I had come on my own to see. I was going to fail in attaining my objective, but even without that I had already drunk deep from a cup brimful of satisfaction. I had

A corner of old Bukhara, which I failed to find on my solitary walk.

been in old Bukhara and seen it as it really is, and had been calm, relaxed and old-fashioned, very old-fashioned. Its inhabitants seemed entirely content with their lot and their old-fashionedness, albeit without the emirs. I would dearly have liked to have known more than I had seen. They were rooted in their old-fashionedness, and any change would be very slow in coming, if it ever did.

I turned toward the east, thinking now of the train we had to catch that afternoon. I knew I was leaving the sights I had come to see behind me. It would add another hour to my walk, if I turned about. I had still to find my way back to the hotel. The area I had now reached was part of the old town but neglected, on the edge of redevelopment perhaps. Where domestic walls had broken down, at least I could see how they had been constructed. Wattle and daub it was, but of quite an advanced kind, using a solid, intricate wooden framework as a basis for thick layers of mud and plaster. The dry climate had enabled the builders of old to build soundly, from shrewd experience of what made things permanent, old-fashioned though their skill was. Attitudes and architecture, both of one mind, I decided.

Suddenly I found myself walking along a broad avenue once more. I was back in the neighbourhood of the administrators' complex. Pleasant, cheerful cries abruptly rent the air. Children in white collars and black smocks burst from their bounds, a well-built, modern primary school, into their playground. They combined exuberance and playfulness. They ran and shouted everywhere. There was even a corner for very small children to do the same. So, that was where the children were, nearly all of them from the neighbourhood. So, that was why the streets of old Bukhara were so quiet and thoughtful. Efficient primary schools and nurseries.

As I strolled, I wondered again. Where were all their mothers and fathers? Not, that morning, in old Bukhara. Almost certainly at their workplace in new Bukhara, having left the children at school on their way. Could then old Bukhara, as I first thought it could, really survive the blast of the modern world, separated and detached from it as it was? Not for long, I thought, certainly not for another 1,000 years. The old-fashioned ways would decay surely, unless some sudden disaster happened to the modern world, and that was scarcely thinkable.

So once more I drank from the cup of satisfaction. Something had led me somehow that morning on a walk through an old-fashioned world that was doomed to disappear eventually. I may have failed to accomplish my original plan but I had succeeded in seeing something more rare and more precious, an image of the past, existing in the present. I soon became confident that the awesome demon had guided me that morning on my walk. I was duly impressed. You need his kind of luck, if you are to see things like that.

The sun had now climbed to its zenith, and shone down on the tallest office building of them all from the right. My 'fix' had been accurate enough. The Bukhoro was standing plain and clear in the space below. I would be back in time for lunch.

* * *

Six awesome demons so far, and seven if you include the one present while I listened to jazz in New Orleans. They all had three characteristics in common. First, not one of them had been anticipated in any clear, pre-defined way. All were in some sense surprises. They were new, and exhilarating for the spirit. I had sometimes heard and seen similar things before, but never with the same result. They altered me. Second, they all had allegiances to the past. Even though playing music and dancing to it took place in the present, and even though everything that happened to me was of course a present happening, I saw and heard what had existed for centuries; even jazz, despite its modern excitements, has been played, I suspect, in its earliest forms from the earliest times. In other words what I perceived as new was in fact old. I merely joined in as a novice. At the time, I asked the question: was what I perceived as new merely a recognition of something I had known subconsciously since the beginning, following a kind of unaware recollection, as Platonists would have it? I felt then, and still feel, it was not. Seeing and hearing what was old for the first time altered me. I was sure it existed before any part of me did, and existed before me by hundreds of years. Its age became my newness. Third, I have an interest in, and some knowledge of, Byzantine and Romanesque architecture. In the nature of things, I have the habit of relating buildings of similar date when seeing them for the first time to that interest and knowledge. If a demon happens to be inside or outside a building, he will join in, and try to make a game of what I am interested in, and think I know. A demon knows he had a sporting chance of altering my perceptions with his playfulness. With music and dance it is different. With music, I am to all intents and purposes illiterate. With dancing, I always feel clumsy and about to fall over. I am also envious of the skills of musicians and dancers. Demons who play with music and dancing can rely on no contribution from me. Neither they nor I know when I am likely to respond to what is happening. For that reason, their magic is a powerful magic, and I am in their thrall. I have no means of applying any kind of critical judgement to what may be tricks and deceptions. In such cases I respond, as mud responds to a jet of water and so is unwittingly cleansed. You could sum up by saying that awesome demons are concerned to teach me aesthetics, if they can. Sometimes, they advance their cause by challenging and adding to the substance of what I already have. At other times, by sleight of hand, they drive mist from my eyes, clear deafness from my ears, and point to things which seem new, and make me listen and see. Half human and half divine, that is what they are.

* * *

A secondary characteristic, following on from the first three, is that I am likely to experience the presence of an awesome demon more often in the old world than I am in the new.

Here I must take account of the complex feelings, mentioned earlier, which I experienced in New Orleans, where I found myself making much of the historical thread which linked local Cajuns, Nova Scotia, the Sun King in Paris, a museum in Lesbos and jazz in New Orleans. It was the kind of joy an awesome demon delights in encouraging. Obviously enough in my case, it is also the kind of joy which is closely linked with personality and preference. The intricacy of the tangled thread, its associations with the historical past and my own personal experiences, and the business of following the intricacy through to an end make a combination which pleases unfailingly. I can find delights of this kind in the new world, but, because of its newness and relative simplicity, less frequently. I found them, however.

Huntington Library, San Marino, California.

Near Los Angeles alone, there were three of them. No visitor to that extraordinary city should neglect to pay them close attention.

First, the Huntington Library, Art Collections and Botanical Gardens at San Marino, twelve miles north-west of downtown LA. Founded in 1919 by Henry E. Huntington, the son of Collis Huntington, one of the founders of the Southern Pacific railroad, the library, the art gallery and the gardens, all on one site, offer just the combined experience, in a closely formal way, which New Orleans offers informally. The library contains among its treasures a Gutenberg Bible, a manuscript of the *Canterbury Tales*, a folio edition of Audubon's *Birds of America*, a collection of early editions of Shakespeare, and, for me, delight of delights, displays of the personal correspondence of Benjamin Franklin. The gallery, once the Huntington residence, concentrates, but not exclusively, on British and French painting of the eighteenth and nineteenth centuries. Some remarkable portraits include Gainsborough's *Blue Boy* and Lawrence's *Pinkie*. The gardens startle, on the side of a hill, looking north-west over the city. Covering 130 acres, they contain displays from the desert, Australia and Japan, and specialist gardens featuring the jungle, palm trees, herbs, roses and camellias. You could not ask for any more concentrated and complicated joy anywhere, so splendid and so typical of the wonders of Southern California. Another product of railway expansion, what is more.

Nearby, in Pasadena, is the Norton Simon Museum, an art gallery combining in one place the best of many worlds. European painting from the early Renaissance to modern times, work from India and South East Asia, and a remarkable specialist collection of Degas paintings, pastels and drawings. All this is housed in a modern building of lofty distinction and elegance. I wonder why it is that some of the best of modern architecture is associated with art galleries. I can think of exceptions, of course.

On the other side of LA, close to the beach at Malibu, on the side of a volcanic hill looking towards the sea, you find the J. Paul Getty Museum. Notorious following scandalously poor attention from the popular media, the museum is in fact a wondrous thing, both as a fantasy made real and as a way of displaying precious things. The building is based on a reputed design for a Roman villa, the Villa dei Papiri near Herculaneum, destroyed by the eruption of Vesuvius in AD 79. Accurate or not in its declared origins, it is nevertheless a distinguished building in its own right. It is now a Roman villa of the mind, built to show off the images of old Campania, an image on rock of volcanic tufa, overlooking a bay of great splendour, at risk itself of earthquake; the Villa dei Papiri of the mind. Inside, round an orthodox peristyle garden, artistic treasures are displayed in abundance on two levels. On the ground floor there are mainly sculptures, vases and mosaics from classical times. On the upper level, you find crowded rooms of paintings from all the major schools of European art. I really did not expect to see a Massacio from Florence in Malibu, but I did. What a story that might make! And you could not forget to mention that it was a portrait of St Andrew. Another tangled thread.

Should you tire of travelling, but would like to go round the world in imagination, nevertheless, take three weeks off in Los Angeles. There you will find a new and modern world, containing, too, many of the valuables of the old. A new kind

The inner courtyard or peristylium, the Paul Getty Museum, Malibu, Los Angeles.

of demon, which I have only met once so far, in Los Angeles. Once I began to think about paintings in any way, strings of magical experiences present themselves. I can not forbear to mention two of them. Demons, it must be made clear first, do not inhabit paintings. Paintings are patently inanimate, and inanimate on purpose. They do however have the power to cause shivers down the spine. Their lifelessness can spring into a new existence, an expanding existence within a carefully defined space. They have the power to tell static stories as nothing else can. Thin surfaces of paint, spread over varying rectangles of material, appear still and lifeless until the moment you look at them, and then become engaged in looking also at what you find in yourself. At that moment your spine begins to shiver. You become excited by seeing and by expanding the limits you both have.

First, take that morning in Vienna when I set out to see the Kunsthistorischer Museum on my own. The Hapsburg grandeur of the building itself I had half expected, and the clatter of feet on marble staircases did not go amiss. I already knew something about the range of pictures there: Raphael, Vermeer, Rembrandt, Rubens, Ruysdael and Velasquez, regal representatives of artistic splendour and of the extent of Hapsburg power in Europe. I knew about that, and I anticipated meeting such representatives with pleasure. What I did not know and could never have anticipated, was what I found round the corner in a side room soon after my arrival at the museum. I had seen it before in surrogate code on television, in magazines; I had even read about it, and I had selected a small print of it to hang in the school hall, long ago. I knew a bit about it, too. Then, springing from its frame on the wall, like a tiger pouncing on its prey, there it was: Bruegel's *Hunters in the Snow*, always in my mind my perfect painting, a painting I had never expected to see in the fullness of its painted flesh; stress and strain on a ground of pure snow, straining for the distant frozen plain down below, men and dogs, aspiring in inanimate paint. But beware the dark bird soaring in the leaden sky. Perfection for me always has its own fragility. I stared and looked for ten minutes. I kept returning to that Bruegel all morning, despite what else there was to see. I could never have expected it to be quite so perfect or quite so white or quite so fragile. I shall return to see it again before next summer is out, in case, being so fragile, it disappears one day. Or I do.

Paintings for me are like that. Friends know that I see them, and at once become unheedingly relentless. They might disappear.

My second choice is a small patch of painting which only Europeans who travel to Australia are likely to see. I refer to the Heidelberg School, which had its roots near Melbourne between 1885 and 1890. When I first came across the work of the school on my own travels — the School's pictures are these days spread evenly about the galleries of capital cities in all states — my spine shivered as I went my way and as I became more and more familiar with its achievement. I had known nothing about it. It did not deserve such ignorance. Everything about it was fresh and good. It helped me to understand Australia, what is more.

In 1888, an exhibition of Australian painting was held to celebrate the centenary of the First Landing. The exhibition was of traditional work, owing much to a line of German and English stylists who were stiff, even rigid, in their interpretation of landscape and portraiture. Tom Roberts, however, a photographer's assistant and an amateur draughtsman originally from Dorchester in Dorset, had returned to England in 1881, at the age of twenty-five. He spent some time studying at the Royal Academy and in Paris. He also met and talked with Whistler, and went on a walking tour of northern Spain. He returned to Melbourne a changed man, for he had decided that Australian art, and Australia itself, needed a radically different approach from that practised by German and English tradition. With a group of friends, Richard Streeton, Charles Conder and Frederick McGubbin, in 1889 he put on a second exhibition to celebrate his change of approach, The Exhibition of 9 × 5 Impressions. The new Heidelberg School, and its new style, had been established.

The Australian continent is a world of clear, bright light, and strong, deep shadows, modified and moderated by the gentle gum tree and a dry, brown land. Buildings in the late nineteenth century in town and country matched the land, pretending to be nothing but themselves, mostly made of wood and corrugated iron, straggling and informal. The paintings of Roberts, Streeton, Conder and McGubbin and company were only revolutionary because they matched the light, shadow and society of Australia where they were painted. In a joint letter, Roberts, Streeton and Conder wrote, 'We will not be led by any forms of composition or light or shade. Any form of nature which moves us strongly . . . is worthy of our best efforts. We will do our best to put only the truth down and only as much as we feel sure of seeing.' Later, Streeton wrote to Roberts, 'I fancy large canvasses, all glowing and moving in the happy light, others bright, decorative and chalky, and expressive of the hot trying winds and the slow immense summer.' All agreed that in Australia no two half-hours were ever alike. So they painted in the open air.

For sure, they owed much to the French tradition of impressionist painting. Indeed, three of them, Roberts, Streeton and Conder, studied in Paris. What they achieved however was separate from their studies; it was Australian. No visitors to Australia who want to have some insight into that country's art and history towards the end of the nineteenth century should neglect to search out in the city where they are staying pictures by Roberts, Streeton, Conder and McGubbin. They shared Australia in common, but, like all Australians, they were determined individualists. I choose four examples of their work, one from each.

As an artist, Tom Roberts was a paragon of his own virtues, adventurousness, independence and ambition. He was socially ambitious; he ended by painting society portraits. I choose one of his earliest pictures, painted soon after his return from Europe, when he began to see afresh the light he wished to represent, *Bourke Street* (1886), to be found in the National Gallery in Canberra. Bourke Street, in the centre of Melbourne, was not in 1886 what it is now, an avenue sky-scraper tall. It was nevertheless a main street in the centre of a large city. For Roberts, looking west along its length up a slight incline, the sun shone in full strength from the north on high. The horse-drawn traffic, ordered into a long line, stood in sharp relief, as shadows move beneath the horses and their carts. A pedestrian crowd was stationary in the deep shade of the north side of the street. Three people, one a child, hurry across from the sunny, southern side; it was hot out there. The buildings, in line but without regulation of any kind, at random offer kinds of shade beneath verandas, attracting few pedestrians in its paucity. Melbourne in 1886 was a bright, brick- and sandy-coloured place, beneath patches of smoke in a cloudless sky of pale blue. Roberts' picture shimmers in the sandy heat. It is alive with heat. One hundred years later Bourke Street is shaded by the sky-scrapers. His more well-known pictures, *Shearing the Lambs* in Melbourne, and *The Breakaway* in Adelaide, are full of working men's action, and were very popular, not like *Bourke Street*, a slow-moving generality in the heat.

Richard Streeton was the romantic one, inclined to go too far and so sentimental sometimes. He used to look back nostalgically to the School's earliest days. The picture chosen is *The Bathers* (1891), in the Queensland Art Gallery in Brisbane. The day was warm but cloudy. Four male bathers in various stages of undress lounge by a broad, slow and sluggish stream. The water reflects the yellow grass and pale gum trees on the further side. One bather is in the shade, the others in half sunlight. Broken logs lie about, like their discarded clothes. There is no sense of order anywhere. Streeton however has ordered his picture and his bathers so that his vision of their peacefulness leads the eye along towards a presiding lowness and flatness. There is not the slightest bit of tension in the mood or the design, nor was there a breath of air to disturb contentment or nostalgia for the wide, pastoral scene at the riverside. Streeton did not care for the tension of the here and now; as 'Banjo' Paterson wrote,

> 'I would fain go back to the old grey river,
> To the old bush days when our hearts were light;
> But, alas! those days have fled forever,
> They are like the swans that have swept from sight.'
> *(Black Swans)*

Charles Conder painted to please. His pictures have a lyrical and decorative air, though always rooted, according to the rules, in reality. *Cove on the Hawkesbury* (1888), for instance, in the National Gallery of Victoria in Melbourne, must have been a pretty spot, following the line of high, wooded hills at a bend in the broad river. Accident had it that a pool of evening sunlight picked out the colour of a red sunshade as a lady beneath it took a stroll in the calm air. The brush strokes created impressions only, and the scene, solid and real enough in colour and shape, was only there for a moment in time before the sun went in.

A decorative fragment was Conder's delight. He loved the seaside for similar reasons, and painted Mentone on Port Phillip Bay like Boudin in Normandy, out to charm with simple elegance. It was strange in his time to show that Australia could be charming, too; it was a new idea.

Frederick McGubbin painted most often in woodland, in the bush. He loved Mount Macedon for that reason. His aim was somehow to catch hold of Australia as a national reality. The land was real enough, but how real were the people, he seemed to ask himself. He painted them in the bush, working, disheartened, mourning a lost one and sometimes lost themselves. This kind of search for reality often ended, naturally enough, in melancholy. It was a lonely business being a pioneer. I choose a picture called *The North Wind* (1891), in the National Gallery of Victoria. Instead of woodland, on this occasion the artist paints the blistering desert as a stage for the miseries of the hot north wind.

A farmer, returning south, leads an ungainly horse, harnessed to a cart; his wife sits on the cart, cowering with the wind at her back. The cart is piled high with their last possessions. A dog, shadowy in the blowing sand, skips alongside the desperate procession. At first sight, the man, the dog, the horse, the cart and the woman dominate the picture, until you realize how much they are suffering. In fact, it is the brown north wind, gusting strongly about, which is all-important; it even attempts to hide the blueness of the sky. Extremely well drawn, the procession, the shafts of the cart in particular, point due south, the direction of failure. The picture's atmospheric effect punishes the viewer as much as the participants. They had been too daring, and giving up was a huge struggle.

Mary Durack, in *Kings in Grass Castles*, wrote of the same period, 'Somehow nothing had gone to plan. Their horses were stolen and in eight months they scratched no more than a meagre living while some men, working alongside, had grown rich. But therein lay the fascination of the golden years that were to leave an indelible mark on the Australian character. Long after the big (gold) rushes the restlessness would remain, the yearning for change, excitement, independence and wider opportunity, a love of wager and hazard — the fall of a coin, the form of a horse.' Some would add impetuosity to this list.

They were simple times, in a sense. A new and growing

nation was evolving its idiosyncratic controversies, about land ownership, money and religion, for instance. Aboriginal rights were not at all an issue. Australian prejudices were beginning to be the prejudices of the Australian white man. In seeking to paint the world as they saw it, members of the Heidelberg School were by no means alone in not seeing their world as it really was (many would now point to the ordering of McGubbin's dismal procession as symbolic of a prejudice which is still possibly typically Australian: man, dog, horse, cart, woman). The eminence of the School was not due in any way to its sensitivity towards social ills, as indeed the eminence of more recent Australian art is, but to its skill in drawing and painting. Its members painted what they saw with open eyes, and with a freshness and a freedom well beyond the stylistic limitations of their contemporaries. They were very Australian in this concentrated, individual kind of achievement. What is more, they painted gum trees, the first to do so, with skill and sensitivity. To my knowledge, not one of their pictures can be seen in London on permanent exhibition. I am ashamed of that.

* * *

The awesome demons I came across lived in places, buildings mostly, where people had once lived or worshipped. A review of these encounters will show that the fame of such places most often had their origin in circumstances of wealth and plenty, and then chanced upon poverty and even penury as time and fortune dictated. Ruins, if they have a demon living among them, have Plenty for a father and Poverty for a mother, as of old did Diotima's Eros. Music and dance, if they are traditional and fundamentally based in the long-ago, often speak too of prosperity first and kinds of suffering next. Their regeneration, like that of ruins, cannot escape the spirit of their origins and history. Feeling the presence of a demon must surely be to do with feelings of spirituality.

Awe, on the other hand, anticipates or follows on from the experience of a demon's presence. The awe I felt in the presence of the terracotta army was not however due to the influence of a demon on the analogy of Diotima's Eros. Quite the contrary. My awe on that occasion was not owed to the offspring of Plenty and Poverty, but to their cousins, tyranny and cruelty. Awe does not discriminate; it is the demon which discriminates. The demon, Eros, you may remember, was a discriminating demon; he concerned himself with beauty, goodness and truth.

To conclude, awesome demons, a self-imposed myth for travelling, offered me solutions only to some of what I saw and felt on my journey. For instance, they offered no solution to the shivering of the spine. Places do not cause spine-shivering. Spine-shivering happened when I saw things, objects like pictures and sculptures. I have not been able to mythologize about spine-shivering. Either spine-shivering happens or it does not. There seems to be no guiding hand. It happened to me, you will know, when I saw the skill of the painters of the Heidelberg School; it happens similarly in Australia with the work of Russell Drysdale, but not with the work of Sidney Nolan. I am unable to explain why. It must be that my eyes are somehow defective. I keep them open, but they fail to see everything, no matter how hard I try.

There was a day, though, at the beginning of January, when everything happened, and when I saw everything. The early part of the day had been sunny, warm certainly. After tea, it became cloudy, and rain threatened. We had seen a performance of sorts, but our enthusiasm for it had been patchy. There had been some jollity, and some entertainment, but I had found myself scarcely part of it, detached from the rest. Quite distinct from listening to jazz in New Orleans. Yet where we were had once been a place of regal entertainment, heroes had played, and where kings and queens had watched. For me, visiting it for the first time, it was hallowed ground, a hall of history where great deeds of old had been enacted. Now the day's events were turning it into a place of desolation. I began to feel as I had done in Armenian Ani. It was a barren, desolate feeling, pauperized by what was happening. From the noise they made, 12,000 people felt as I did.

Suddenly, there was the most splendid sound, bursting upon the consciousness like music from the height of heaven. It happened again. Again and again. Mellow, resonant in the open space, conclusive by design and intent. Accompanying the sound, just in advance of it by half a second, was a kind of dancing, graceful and balanced, and a flickering to and fro, like conjurer's hands, but more magical than mere conjuring. The waiting and the desolation had been worth all the bother. We were watching at last what we had come for. The magic, in its lightness, rested upon two foundations. First, style. Its style had poise, and a measured skill, like the arches and pillars of the cathedral at Mcxeta. The style was monumental, but no monument, because it was in motion. It moved calmly and deliberately, with design and care. Second, clear principles drawn from experience and the past. We had seen it all before, somewhere. It had always been there, ever since we could remember. We had been told about it in our cradles, and some of us had even tried to be like it, ourselves, in our youth. It was a classical matter, a performance purely and completely derived from a classical past.

He could have been holding a violin and playing Mozart, but he wasn't. He was holding a cricket bat, and playing cricket. He was facing bowling as fierce as the hot north wind at both ends. He was standing up against it, using scorn and independence as his weapons. He moved lightly, backwards, forwards and across, attacking the ferocity with a wand, and with easy timing, elegance and charm. Charles Conder, all over again. He had the artistry of a magician who can transform a scene with the magic of his art. Before tea, England had crumbled. Soon they had lost five heroes for next to nothing. We were watching now a romantic legend in the making. At least I was. Imagination soared. He was fighting back against adversity, creating plenty out of poverty.

Between tea and close of play that day, David Gower scored sixty runs, mostly all boundaries. After one early mistake, his bat hit the ball without fail and with an elegant power which was beyond earlier imagining. I am certain that the next time I visit Sydney Cricket Ground I shall meet an awesome demon there. Neither he nor I will ever forget that day, between tea and close of play. Cricket grounds are for both of us places where awesome demons take up residence. England lost, by the way. No romantic legend was established, and no newspaper reported the beauty of it the next day, but I had seen it all. What a wonderful world it has been!

9

Endings

It was indeed a wonderful world. After my return, friends, no doubt anxious to avoid hearing about it all, would ask me which were the best bits. My answer would be unequivocal. There were no best bits; I enjoyed it all. I could pick out nothing which by itself was better than anything else or the whole taken together. For sure, I was often tired, but never bored. If pressed, I would say somewhat unwillingly that there were five places which I have no strong wish to see again. San Francisco was exciting, but I do not believe it would excite me a second time. However, if I were promised the chance of a clear, sunlit morning on which to board again the ferry to Sausalito across the Bay from Fisherman's Wharf, I dare say I would not turn down the invitation. Canberra, with its concentration of civil servants isolated there from the reality of ordinary life and of ordinary people, frightened me. The imminent architectural dominance too of the new Parliament House on Capital Hill I found even more threatening than Canberra's isolation, for the ordinary Australian, that is. But Canberra is not my problem; Westminster and Whitehall are more properly mine; they are in no way isolated from Brixton and Bermondsey, and probably the better for that. I would return to the National Gallery in Canberra, though, any time. The city of Perth is a fine place, but I have no wish to return there, except as a necessity when watching cricket at the WACA, or before and after touring the coast and countryside of Western Australia. Hong Kong is valuable as a place of transit. I shall be compelled to return there on some future journey, I have no doubt, but I shall not do so willingly. Unadulterated capitalism is for me

Golden Gate Bridge, San Francisco.

A street in San Francisco, founded on rock, which survived the earthquake of 1906.

too ugly too often. I hardly gave Bucharest a fair chance, but the memory of its dust and noise discourages any thought of another visit. Were dust and noise the visions of an unadulterated communism, I asked myself. Romania and Romanians however may make a return to Bucharest a necessity too. So it is that I picked up a set of prejudices. I have the uneasy feeling of not being sure that my opinion in regard to San Francisco, Canberra, Perth, Hong Kong and Bucharest was soundly formed. I may have been tired at the time, or I may not have looked closely enough. I should therefore repeat; I enjoyed it all.

I was helped all along by being able to remain fit and well. I had one feverish cold before Christmas while in the Mappin's company, and no fault of theirs. At no stage did I suffer from *mal di stomacho*. I may be fortunate in having a sturdy constitution, but I also took great care about what I ate and drank in uncertain circumstances: no salads, no ice-cream, no iced water, no unpeeled fruit, only well-cooked food, and bottled water or beer. Temptation can be considerable, but always worth resisting, I would say. I used up all the lavatory paper, and lost one of my two plugs for plugless hand-basins.

I can make comments like these, now that the journey is over. I am mindful once more of Herodotus, or rather the words he put into the mouth of Solon the Wise, when advising the wealthy Croesus: 'Look to the end, no matter what it is you are considering. Often enough God gives a man a glimpse of happiness, but then utterly ruins him.'(I.32) It is only now that the journey is over that Solon would allow me any praise for counting my blessings. In the course of a journey, as many know to their cost, things can go sour. Even taking care may not be good enough, as Croesus discovered. I happened upon good fortune, and so I am now in the position to look to the end, no matter what it was I was planning at one time to do.

I have left for myself at the end only one important matter to resolve. I must spend some space resolving it. Prompted by Mr Moore, who reminded me of the relevance of Herodotus for travellers, I carried round the world with me the burden of Herodotus' dictum: 'If anybody at all is given the chance to choose for the rest of human kind the best laws, customs and beliefs from those that exist, after due consideration he would be bound to choose his own. Everybody thinks their own laws, customs and beliefs are the best. He would surely be a madman who would pour scorn on that choice.' I know now that I carried round the world with me my own baggage of personal prejudices, sets of beliefs and native customs. Readers too will be sure of that by now, if they took heed of my early warning to be on guard against parochialism. It was surely no accident that awesome demons usually appeared in places where what was new in appearance was nevertheless consistent with my education and interests. The demon, as we have seen, would appear in the old world, and, what is more, often in the old Greco-Roman world, or at its edges. Russo-Georgian architecture and music after all took up their roots at the edge of the old Greco-Roman world. There were possibly three exceptions to this thesis; in Bukhara, where, by myself, I became for a space conscious of a world apparently different from my own, seeming to exist in its own right and in its own way, and in Xinjiang and New Orleans, where the power of music and dancing was to draw a motley set of separate persons into a kind of temporary mystic society. In fact, Bukhara was no real exception, for it too belonged to the old world, even for a time as part of the European world of Alexander the Great and Marco Polo. In terms of antiquity, the music of the Uighurs in Xinjiang and the jazz musicians in New Orleans were not exceptions either; they too had roots in the long-ago. I had remained loyal to my personal prejudices, sets of beliefs and native customs by seeing awesome demons where I did.

Did then my kind of parochialism preordain the association of awesome demons with the world I visited? Yes, I think it did. I think that, deep down, when an awesome demon appeared, I was in fact saying to myself, 'I like that; it is old; that is something I know about; it is reassuring; it makes me sure.' When they played *It's a long way to Tipperary* in Preservation Hall, the Belgian couple and I exchanged knowing glances. In that way, we shared our past. I think now that it was always like that when a demon appeared. I was not aware of it at the time, but I made up my own demons as I went along; they were really part of me, the subjective at play.

The truth of this is even clearer to me as I think about how I felt when visiting the Huntington Library, the Norton Simon Museum and the Getty Museum in Los Angeles, and also when I saw pictures by members of the Heidelberg School in Australia. I myself was controlling what I enjoyed. Recognizing bits of me in what was on exhibition in far-off lands was reassuring and pleasant. In this way, I became more and more sure of seeing things that I would enjoy. It was indeed pleasant, putting parochialism to work.

Introspection and seeing parochialism at work are however only parts of the whole truth. There are at least two other factors to be taken into account. First, however you score it, anybody from anywhere would have had some appreciation of the places and occasions where awesome demons appeared. They were all remarkable in a global sense, and there were many others too, similarly remarkable, in other places and on other occasions, which happened not to interest and excite me quite as much. In other words, the standard of things to be viewed and to be experienced in the world at large is extremely high. My selection from this list of such high standard was really the only thing which represented me in the matter. The total number of items on display was huge. I too was smitten by the sight of the Yellow River in Gansu Province, and that small troop of Tibetan travellers crossing its metal bridge. Its significance was that I just could not think about it in the same expansive way as I did the entrance to the Bosphorus. It was just as remarkable, nevertheless. My selection was a small thing in face of all there was to take account of. Second, as you travel, you travel continually in a state of tension. There is always a string stretched between you as the person you are and the place which is foreign to you. Whenever your jaw drops in amazement, you provide the amazement, and the place is the cause of it. Tension of this kind, as I have remarked elsewhere, can cause feelings of schizophrenia in the traveller concerned. It is difficult at such times to know for certain whether the reality is you or the place, when in fact it is both. This uncertainty is, to my mind, a valuable part of the experience of travel. Disentangling uncertainty, as I found after seeing Matisse's account of jazz in the New Orleans Museum of Art, if successful, can be a supreme experience, leading to feelings of pleasure, joy and satisfaction. Parochialism, moments of high quality outside the parish, and schizophrenia disentangled make enjoyable travelling companions if you care to take them with you.

As an illustration of the pleasure of being in their company. I remember now my last evening on the island of Malolo Lailai in Fiji. After dinner, I went for a walk on the beach by the lagoon. There was no moon, and it was dark but cloudless. Slowly, as my eyes became used to the darkness, I began to find my way by starlight among the coconut palms, as the sand shelved towards the sea. It was still and warm, and I was alone with myself and the beach. I looked upwards, expecting to see once more the stars of the southern hemisphere, to which during some three months I had become accustomed. Suddenly, to my surprise, halfway up the sky to the north I suppose, I saw Orion, albeit upside down. I had not seen Orion since I had left Hong Kong. Following surprise, I felt delight, as though meeting up with an old friend. I remember laughing aloud. The occasion demanded even more from me than that, in the way of emotional release. I picked up a coconut, a smallish one lying in the sand, and bowled an off-break with it, aiming at a palm tree some fifteen yards away. I hit it. The world and I became transformed in a moment. Parochialism, a moment of high quality outside the parish and schizophrenia disentangled walked beside me on the beach that evening. All four enjoyed it.

In extending the experience of parochialism beyond the parish, and then back again into the psychological domain, I am guilty of misusing Herodotus' dictum. He wrote about beliefs as though they were immutable. While travelling he relied upon his beliefs for security and for sanity. He could never change from being Greek, and become a barbarian. For him that was impossible, even though he might reflect upon the possibility from time to time. As for me, I found my parochialism expanding the further I travelled. First, I found it expanding out of narrow Englishness into Europeanism. Despite the difficulties of the concept, Europe, in practice an uneasy, restless, contradictory, discontented, divided giant, I found Europe secure enough as an idea. It rested after all on Greco-Roman conquests, and Christianity for a religion. Even while crossing the difficult political frontiers of Hungary, Romania and Bulgaria, I felt I was in Europe throughout, and I was part of it as a European. The blemishes were obvious, but the basic idea was a good one. Each country, seeing itself as a nation, was in fact a parish as England was, and a member, each with its neighbours, of the same international club. Europe had a wider kind of parochialism. I felt myself part of it, and recognized it as part of me.

I did not lose this feeling, even while travelling through Turkey. Much of the Greco-Roman world was still on the surface of things, and the Turks themselves did not look upon us strangely; they either smiled and said, 'Hello', or disregarded us completely. Travelling east as we were, I did not feel a stranger in Turkey, as a Westerner and a European.

Crossing over into Soviet Armenia and then Georgia was like turning westwards again. We were in Europe once more, and feeling European was like feeling at home. There was nothing English about Armenia and Georgia, but there was much that was European. The demons made sure of telling me that.

A quality of strangeness, of non-European sameness, first appeared in Azerbaijan, in Baku. In Baku at last, I knew I had advanced beyond the limits of my cultural tether. In Baku I met up with 'barbarians' for the first time. No Christianity and no Greco-Roman world there of any kind.

As the reader already knows, I liked those 'barbarians'. They seemed to me relaxed, friendly people, quietly going about a daily routine, which, though not exciting, offered security and peace. I grew to believe that no-one where I travelled in the

Soviet Union wanted war again. The word for peace, MNP, alongside a dove in flight, appeared in many public posters, and the attitude of the population at large always seemed to nod symbolic assent in the direction of those posters. Individuals have too much to lose. Life, still simple and rather drab, even rough at the edges, used to be so much worse. Much has been achieved for small people by small people since the Great Patriotic War. And now small people are asserting themselves more and more.

I suppose, too, sentiment played a part in my liking them. Their courage in the Great Patriotic War had been crucial to its final result. At the time, we admired that courage from a distance. We soon came to realize however that, but for them, we ourselves would not have survived. The fact that their war only began in 1941 became obscured in the deep darkness of the time. Now they never forget their struggles, and we older people retain a memory of them as valiant and invaluable allies.

A less obvious reason for liking them was the apparent seriousness of their young people. They were no doubt envious of their contemporaries in the West, of their noise, of their colour and of their uninhibited variety. Certainly, alongside their contemporaries they would appear placid and possibly lacking in spirit. But they did not lack a social conscience. Komsomol, the official communist youth organization, no doubt played a heavy-handed part in achieving a kind of compliance in this way. No busy street crossing however lacked for a pair of young people to see the elderly and the very young safely across to the other side, and no public car park went unattended by a group of young persons, thus enabling older people to enjoy themselves at some occasion or other. Those who officiated in this way wore appropriately designed badges as evidence of their public service, without embarrassment of any kind. It all seemed to me rather sensible, and I did like them for it.

Others in our party could never believe that communism in any guise would be sensible. Their kind of parochialism was of the adamant sort. Like Herodotus, they believed that once a 'barbarian' always a 'barbarian'. Tension between that kind of belief and what they saw in Eastern Europe, the Soviet Union and China became so crippling that they would no longer give any credence to the evidence of their senses, and see something else instead. I came to think that those of us who were intent on seeing as much as we could and believing what we saw were fortunate in the end in the flexibility of our parochialism. 'Barbarians' for us were just another kind of people, in essence the same as we were. It was as though strangeness relaxed the tension for us between what we were and what we saw. Among 'barbarians', some travellers base their judgements on their beliefs, and others on what they believe they see. You can never be sure, but you try to be as sure as you can.

I loved what I saw of the Soviet Union; I greatly look forward to travelling there again. If travel restrictions become more relaxed in the course of time, so much the better. In any event, I shall return most willingly, and must meanwhile learn to speak more Russian more correctly. I must at least be able to ask the way, and to understand the reply.

I feel differently about China. I know that I ought to return to China, because I know I learnt so little from my first visit. It is as though I wish to make ignorance an excuse for not going again. Ignorance, though, is the most severe form of parochialism there is, and I would not be proud of being as parochial as that. I feel I have a personal duty to return, and that, too, is a forbidding thing to feel. I have not felt like that since I studied for my last exam. Travelling in China is rather like being in an examination room. I had not thought of taking any more exams.

White Australia is quite another matter. Would that I could return there and watch cricket every English winter! In the context of parochialism, however, Australia and white Australians were to teach me a great deal, not only about my own kind but, more importantly, about the Australian, which is different and so valuable as a learning device.

Like all our parochialisms, the Australian sort consisted of an extricable mixture of fact, myth and legend, of past, present and future. Let a quotation from the Australian Prime Minister on television serve as an introduction to its complexity. 'My vision is for an Australia which is gradually being brought to a confidence in its own capacity. We here in Australia, going towards the end of the twentieth century, have a constitutional arrangement which reflects a system draw up in a little island off the coast of Europe, hundreds and hundreds of years ago, which was really set there to make arrangements for the bishops and the barons, and the burghers to put their points of view to the king. Now, what I have been doing and this government has been doing is to reshape our relations with the region, to gradually reshape our education system, to gradually reshape our industry, and it is all with a view to trying to ensure that this Australia is not going to be any longer just in reality an outpost of Europe or a station of America.' In reply to a question about change, he said, 'The most obvious change is that Australia has become a multi-cultural, a multi-racial society. Forty percent of the population were born overseas, or have one parent born overseas. It has affected just everything we do, the way we eat, drink, dance, think, to some extent.'

The main substance of Australian parochialism is to be found in that quotation: fact, myth, legend, mingled in a pool of past, present and future. One is forced to sympathize with Prime Ministers and Presidents the world over. Their trade insists that they purvey parochialism as a species of patriotism, instead of vice versa, which would be nearer the truth of the matter.

Never mind the accuracy of the Prime Minister's statement, what it establishes in political terms is clear enough: Australia has been dominated by Britain, Europe and the United States for too long; the country needs to grow closer to the part of the world in which it is situated; meanwhile the government is changing its institutions so as to make this closer growth more possible; in addition, the country's population is changing its established characteristics, and so the characteristics of Australia itself are changing too; there is a great deal of change on hand.

I could see good sense lying behind what the Prime Minster said. What surprised me was that he thought Britain and Europe still dominated Australia in any political way. If he had meant culturally, as part of the parish of Australia, I would have understood him, but would have gone on to think that Britain and Europe would continue to influence Australian cultural life for a long time yet. As would the English language, spoken too by both the British and the Americans. Some things you cannot change quickly; Australia's cultural ties will not loosen, not until forty percent of the population, at least, have their origins in the continent of Asia and close by, and the language is changed accordingly.

For sure, Australia was held back by Britain in the nineteenth century, as a result of the distance involved rather than deliberate intention, I would guess. Much of the white Australian's determined individualism grew up in the fight against the unreasonable land and the unreasoning British. The philosophy of 'fair go', despite the vagaries of violently changing economic climates, gave birth to three additional ideas: Australia was a free agent with its own destiny; Australia was the 'lucky country', and 'Life on the Hill' would be a dazzling success. These three ideas were based on the notion of proper reward for a past fiercely won, often in sentimental ballad terms, where

> 'There's a track winding back
> To an old-fashioned shack
> Along the road to Gundagai.'

Englishness, however, was never to be exorcised completely. Indeed, I have never seen anything quite so English as the members' enclosure at the Melbourne Cricket Ground. Or the independent school system, albeit subsidized from public funds. Or the number of Australians who support England at Test Matches because they came from England in the first place. English, yet not English. The Poms are bastards, and you are always left guessing whether they mean it or not. John Ponder was educated in England, emigrated to Australia before the war, fought behind the lines in Greece during the war, and returned to Australia when the fighting was over. In retirement, he looks after a garden in the shadow of Mount Macedon, and prints lovely books by hand in the old Melbourne market. He is Australian in his views, through and through. Having returned to visit England and Greece, he found that they had changed out of all recognition, and he will not visit them again. He speaks old-fashioned English with a cultured English accent. John Ponder's place in the Prime Minister's plans leaves me puzzled. Might there be two parishes, where there should be one?

I have two stories, which illustrate my puzzlement further.

I went by myself to the third day of the Fourth Test at the Melbourne Cricket Ground. I took the train from Macedon to Spencer Street station, and went to the ground from there by taxi. Only a few trams were running that day, as it was still part of the Christmas holiday period. My taxi driver was Greek. He quickly started a conversation once he knew that I had been to his home town of Olympia in the Peloponese. He had a sad tale to tell. He had emigrated after the war. He had married, and brought up a family in Melbourne. Things then began to go awry. He was now divorced from his wife, and saw little of his children, and lived alone. He said he had earned a living in Melbourne, such as he could never have earned in his native land, but he had had no kind of life there. He had often been desperately unhappy. Australia was a selfish place. Everyone was out for themselves in Australia. You just had to take care of no-one else but yourself. It was not like that in Greece, in Olympia. People looked after each other in Olympia. They were happy there. I asked about the poverty. He said he would sooner be happy and poor than unhappy and reasonably well-off, as he was in Melbourne. He would be able to retire in a year's time. He would go back to Olympia. He too went to the cricket sometimes. He would not miss it, though. He would not miss anything about Australia. I realize that a single whinging Greek does not make a winter. He did not seem to be a whinger. He was just very sad. I know he would not have agreed with the Prime Minister about Australia being a multi-cultural, multi-racial society. Greeks could only be Greeks in Greece, he now firmly believed.

Earlier, in December, the reader will remember that, while in Adelaide, I took a bus tour to the wineries of the Barossa Valley, guided during the day by that splendid chap who had married Queen Victoria off to King William IV. During the tour, we passed through a number of small villages, which had been settled by German Lutherans from Silesia about the turn of the century. Each village had a pretty little wooden church as evidence of the fact. At one point, our driver said, 'The village we are passing through now used to be called Garten Frei, a German name meaning 'Free Garden'. During the First World War, we changed the name, because German names were very unpopular at that time. We changed it to a good old English name, Marrananga.' I do not know what Marrananga means, but I do know that it is certainly not a good old English name. And I wonder about Garten Frei, too. Does Marrananga mean 'Free Garden' in an aboriginal language? What would be the political consequences of that? Might there not really be two parishes in Australia? One for the English, and another for the rest?

I am personally unable to answer such questions, nor would it be proper for me to attempt to do so. I am not qualified. The questions themselves however have, by their existence, had an effect on me, and how I think about Australia and its people. I have concluded that my Englishness intrudes upon how I think about Australia; even my Europeanism intrudes. If I am to have a clear idea about Australia, then I should study it without any reference back to where I come from, to my own kind of narrowness. It was the Englishness of Australia which taught me this. If I were to attempt to join it, I would only be a fraud; if I were not to join it, then, at least I would have a chance of being sure about what I saw and heard.

Conclusions based on arguments like this one have two consequences. First, you have to be quiet. You have to listen and observe with as much attention as you can muster, with detachment and without comment. You have to be as neutral as you can possibly be. If you are asked an opinion you cannot give it, because you do not have one. You have to talk about what interests you. If anyone wants to know about England, tell them what you know. They do not usually want to know anything about England, though, which is interesting in itself. Second, it means setting aside Herodotus's dictum while you are in Australia. You no longer have to believe that your own native customs and the religion you were brought up to are the best. For the time being, they are not. If there are any good native customs, and if there is a good religion, then, they are Australian native customs, and Australian religion. After all, you came to Australia to discover what Australia meant, not what was English about it. Most important of all, observe and listen to the land, all the way from Bunbury and Toodjay in Western Australia, via Alice Springs, Mount Macedon, Marrananga, and Gundagai, to Kangaroo Point across the Brisbane River. The land and its history will tell most of what you first need to know about Australia. It is far older than England.

A wider consequence of this argument also now affects the rest of travelling for me. England is a parish, Scotland is a parish, Wales and Ireland are parishes. Europe is made up of parishes. Each parish has its own parochialism. Each parochialism is appropriate where each parish is.

As I travel, I do not find the world is a global village, as Marshall McLuhan once forecast it soon would be. Far from it. I discover something different, and really rather obvious. Each place I visit is a small place, bounded always by the men and

Olvera Street, in old Los Angeles.

women who live in it. The word parish means a place where people live, a small place where horizons are limited. I think of England like that; England is a small place where horizons are limited. The United Kingdom consists of four such small places, Europe consists of twenty-four or so, and so on round the world. All round the world I came across these small places, where horizons were limited and parochial. If you travel, that is what I think you too will discover. Be careful; do not take your own parish with you. It is best left behind. You see more if you leave it behind. If in addition you look carefully and attentively, as Tom Roberts and company did, you will be sure of seeing what you are looking at, and not something else.

I had a useful example of this mode of travelling in California, and most useful of all in Los Angeles, or LA, as I have now become used to calling it. Detached at last from my English and European parochialisms, I uncovered some of the truth about LA. I like to think that parochialism played no part in the process. I discovered that LA really lived its legend, and that the myth and romance learnt in boyhood at the local cinema had a basis in fact. It was a lovely discovery. Don and Sally Too met me at its symbolic Union Station. I was fortunate indeed in having them as my guides. I arrived blinded only by my imagination.

First, I learned of its shapeless vastness, seventy miles square, spread out along the beach to the north-west and to the south-east, occupying a hilly, volcanic plain as far as a ring of distant mountains. This huge amphitheatre has no centre; there is no focus downtown; it is a collection of alluvial villages, each set in its own nucleus of tall buildings. They are linked by a formal, rectangular network of boulevards and streets. Above ride freeways, which join everything with everywhere like a nervous system. By night it was magical and totally unintelligible; by day it was real, vibrant and alive. The first lesson I learnt then was about its vigorous, untidy hugeness. From now on, the mystery of celluloid and this sprawling reality would be able to live in unity.

Second, change, variety, freedom and money combined long ago to make the modern personality of LA. In 1868, a man called Robert M. Widney, with $100 in his pocket, fell in love with Southern California, riding the hills, valleys and fields on horseback. He printed maps, circulars and the *Real Estate*

Advertiser to attract purchasers. He had a furious energy. The price of land rose by five times in a month.

Co-operatives and mutual groups bought it up, and started the villages. Thirty Methodists from Stockton, near San Francisco, built Compton at five dollars an acre. In 1867, Danish immigrants had already bought 5,000 acres. An English agent went on to buy 100,000 acres for British settlers. The French, Swiss and Germans joined in. There was no end to it. Widney made Southern California world news, nor was he the last. The miseries, resulting from the end of the Civil War further east, had no effect on Southern California. There all was alive and well. By the end of 1868, he had turned seventy-five cents an acre into ten dollars an acre. It was easy to see a motivation for turning the village conglomerates into something larger. Presently, they were to find oil below the land. And, then, some forty years later, on the land above the oil, they discovered a village called Hollywood, and 'motion pictures'. Shake the box, and anyone can change the basis of LA's prosperity. Change, variety, freedom and money were the main substances in use. No wonder it grew to be larger than life. You do not have to like what happened either. When they dropped *Star Trek* from the television schedules, all the students from Cal Tech went out on a protest march. Don called it, with some conviction, a crazy town. A hole-in-the-head society.

Third, somehow it works, but at a cost. They say that there are always losers in such a society. The Southern Pacific Railroad, building its way from San Francisco, was not to be left out of Widney's land bonanza. It advertised land, on the written assurance that it would be sold to its occupiers at a later date. The price was between two-and-a-half dollars and five dollars an acre; any improvements made to any allotment would be taken into account at the time of sale. Those who took advantage of the offer discovered that the land was parched and infertile. Collaborating, the settlers brought water down from the mountains. Their land soon became wonderfully rich. They flourished for a time. In 1877, the Southern Pacific offered the settlers' land on the open market, at between twenty-five dollars and forty dollars an acre. In law, the land and the improvements still belonged to the railroad. Indeed, cases in front of a federal court upheld the railroad's rights. Evictions began to take place. Soon shooting started. The railroad, in control of all means of communication, called for immediate action against insurrection. The settlers were dispossessed by force, and their land sold at great profit to others. There are always winners and losers in Southern California. That way, the film moguls ran assembly lines with scenery, and Hollywood became the most glamorous slave market in the world. One day, Don and I had lunch at Musso and Frank's on Hollywood Boulevard; pretending to be Humphrey Bogart, I ordered 'Today's Special'. I enjoyed the pretence, but remembered all the losers.

Fourth, everyone loses in a way. Part of the price LA pays for its zany brilliance is paid in pollution. Only in recent years did the city finally abandon the trams which provided the background for the comedies of Buster Keaton, trams provided by courtesy of the Pacific Electric Railroad. The city chose instead the internal combustion engine and an expanded freeway system. Even now, it would not be beyond the skill of the city's engineers to design a transport system which would be less dangerous than the automobile is, personally and environmentally. But I doubt that present day Angelenos would put up with it. To be ensnared in traffic is part of their inheritance. The lumbering wagon trains of the gold rush days queued up along the trail no less efficiently than rush-hour traffic does today. You could even say that the freeway, giving just enough space for each individual to do as he wants to do, albeit slowly, is the Angeleno's psychological substitute for the wagon train. The freeway is merely an extension of the frontier mentality. They even pop off guns there still, when the weather gets hot and tempers become fraught. For the time being, the city and its inhabitants choose pollution as a way of extending their mythology, and the resulting sunsets amid the palm trees are weirdly and magnificently wonderful. I would willingly wager, though, that in ten years' time they will be choosing something else to perform a similar function. That is the force of the myth. Meanwhile, they design in twenty-four hours and construct gas stations, drive-in restaurants, mobile vans for promoting private lifestyles and car parks for new marinas. 'No change' is the choice which is chosen for now, but never for long.

Fifth, the people I met in LA were all so agreeable. It was not just my good fortune in knowing the Braytons and being introduced to their friends. Waiters and waitresses everywhere, those who sell books, those who frame pictures, those who go to concerts, those who stroll down Rodeo Drive or by a sausage stall at Venice Beach, all possess a similar attitude; a briskly articulated, old-world courtesy that London forgot long ago. I was quite unable to inspire anything but courtesy. I found discontent, churlishness and even plain ill-manners nowhere. It made me regret once more my unspeakable rudeness towards Ruby that evening over dinner in the hotel in the Soviet Union. She behaved perfectly throughout. Symptomatic of good manners in LA was the behaviour of traffic towards pedestrians. The rules are simple. Pedestrians have undisputed right of way when their light is green. At junctions where there is no light, pedestrians can be sure of having right of way, even when traffic is turning left or right. No such automatic luck in any English city. Nor do motorists who flash indicator lights have an automatic right to go as they please; such motorists, if without forethought, have to seek the courtesy of others, not demand it. There was yet one more symptom of old-world courtesy in a new world context: a promise made on the telephone is invariably kept, I found, even a promise to call back. In England, I normally find I have to write a note to confirm the existence of any such informal contract. In LA there was no need for such a rigid interpretation of informality. It was indeed true; everyone I met was so agreeable, and so were many of their customs; 'good morneeing', 'have a nice day', 'you're welcome', and, even, 'hi! I'll wrap it up', economical and curt though it is. Democratic universalism, some call it. Whatever they call it, I enjoyed it and I liked it. What is more, I really saw the myth and the romance working as a living legend.

Looking to the end of it all, I believe now the truth is that you can only enjoy what you see and hear on a journey in any fundamental sense if you train yourself to leave your parochialisms behind. My misleading thumbs-up sign as a gesture of farewell to the saddened ex-soldier in far-off Jinte was a mistake due to parochialism. I would have done better to use the universal language of a smile instead. The problem is to be yourself, without being parochial about it. It is no more difficult, I find, than remembering your passport.

* * *

I handed my passport over for inspection for the last time at

A piece of the Atlantic Ocean at the end of the Elysian Fields, my last frontier.

six thirty am on 23rd February, 1987, at the newish terminal at Gatwick Airport. Tired though I was — the overnight flight from Atlanta had seemed interminable — I took in at once what greeted me. No matter how hard they try, the English always exhibit no taste at all in their use of plastic and bright coloured paint. Gatwick lacked the dignified neo-classicism of Victoria Station, but I saw at once that both partook of a similar tawdry modernism when it came to plastic and paint. In a flash, too, I was reminded of our inveterate slovenly grubbiness, litter belonging to food and drink everywhere and feet resting where other people might wish to sit. It was unpleasant, facing up to this kind of English reality once more. I had not seen feet on other people's chairs for five and a half months. I hoped that this was not to be the lasting symbol of my parish homecoming.

Fortunately it was not. The customs officer who beckoned me to show him what I had purchased abroad — I always choose the red section on principle — was friendly and efficient. I had my list of purchases and the price I paid for them all ready. He took a quick look, smiled at its quaintness, and charged me £3.50. I was about £40 over the limit. He gave me a receipt, and I was away. A straightforward procedure, straightforwardly administered.

Early though it was, Ralph Cox, the friend who had stayed in my house, met me, his car nearby. It was good to see him standing there. I had already reached a decision, however. I knew what I had to tell him. Would he mind? Would he take my baggage back home for me, and would he feel offended if I took the train from Gatwick to Victoria? Of course he would, and of course he would not. He smiled in an amused way. He saw that I was feeling a little fragile.

Sentiment alone made me ask for this odd favour. I knew that I was feeling emotional about my journey and its completion. I did not want to complete it by car. I had just crossed my last frontier. A train, my last train, would have to come next. I had left Victoria by train, and I wanted to return there by train. Trains had been my main means of transport over land. Completion by train might be therapeutic, and ease the tension I was experiencing. I bought the ticket, a single from Gatwick to Victoria.

You do not have to wait long for the Gatwick-London intercity express. It was quite empty when I boarded it. I could choose to sit where I liked. You would not believe it. In that empty train, of all things, someone came and sat down beside me. I turned disapprovingly, and looked to see who it was. It was the ghost of a sympathetic and friendly awesome demon. He clearly was firmly in favour of my having chosen to travel my last journey by train. He told me at once that he knew that I would be pleased to be home. I had indeed already looked forward to seeing my family and my friends again, and to being in my own home once more. What I had not fully realized was the importance to me of my awesome demons. I was back again, you see, in the old world. This demon, like his fellows, was at one with this old world of ours. As in the past, he would drive mist from my eyes, clear deafness from my ears, point to things which seemed new, and make me listen and see. Here I was back where emotionally I was at home. Indeed, it did seem all new again, as though I had forgotten how refreshing a cup of tea could be. I looked forward to my first cup of tea. And marmalade, made at home from oranges from Seville. Tea and marmalade, two emblems on my parish coat of arms. The pale sunlight clothed the houses and the land in a mist of

Englishness. It was all so new. I could not believe it. It made me very happy. The demon smiled, nodded and disappeared. He had been only the ghost of a demon. I was back in my own parish, in my own part of my own continent, where demons of all sorts have their being. This one had no need to stay long. He made me very happy. He knew he would.

I would do it all again, of course. Certainly I would travel like that again one day, by some other route, perhaps. If return and completion were always like this, travelling again would always be worth it. Poor Herodotus! His work unfinished, he died aged fifty-four. We are so lucky these days. If I can save money, I will surely have the chance to travel round the world a second time. Southwards and northwards, perhaps. They say it is round that way, too. I must check up on what they say. I swore to myself not to neglect a second chance, if it came. Especially if return and completion were always like this.

I descended light from the train at Victoria, without my baggage for once. Free of all baggage at last. Victoria had not changed a bit. And do you know? I had a sudden urge to tell the ticket collector at the barrier, at my last barrier, that I had just been round the world. Mindful of the parish I was in, and fearful of an uninhibited rejoinder, I decided not to.

LIST OF ILLUSTRATIONS

Maps of the journey	8
The first dinner party aboard the train with Sally Also and Sally Too	21
Don and Sally Brayton on Danube river trip near Budapest	21
About to depart from the Gare de l'Est for Salzburg and Vienna	31
Picnic spot, mid-morning, near the Chinese border with the USSR	44
Han Chinese, by a new settlement, near the Soviet border, in Xinjiang	52
The city of Perth, Western Australia, from the river front	57
Parsee fire temple outside Baku — fire from oil discovered long ago	69
Caravanserai in Baku, like that used as a restaurant by us	72
Our new Chinese train, waiting for us at Daheyon	74
My compartment on our Chinese train	75
The *Indian-Pacific*, stopping at Cook, half-way across the Nullabor plain	83
The *Indian-Pacific* reaches Parkes in New South Wales	85
Narrow and standard gauge tracks in Western Australia	87
The Glenelg tram	89
A corner of old Adelaide	89
The Australind, the small gauge train for Bunbury from Perth	90
The Rose Hotel, Bunbury	91
The Freemason's at Toodjay	92
Tranby House, up river from Perth, built in 1839, remaining as furnished by the original family, the Hardeys from England	93
About to depart from Haydarpasa station (sketch by author)	98
The *Sunset Limited* arriving in Tucson for New Orleans, my baggage in the foreground	100
Mission Church, Carmel, California on the El Camino Real	102
The author's hotel in the French quarter of New Orleans	108
The centre of modern Kayseri still boasts the ruins of a Roman aqueduct	113
Rock formations in Cappadocia	114
In middle distance, Bob Williams, the former engine-driver on the *Indian-Pacific*, astride Heroes Square, Budapest	122
Bicycles in Turfan, near the post office	130

A street artist in Lanzhou cuts out a paper image of the author	141
Lunch-time photographers in Bucharest	150
Bran Castle in Transylvania, near Sinaia, by repute the home of Dracula	151
Our welcoming band outside Timisoara, avoiding the hubbub on the station platform	152
The vegetable market at Bukhara, with Uzbekh salesmen	155
Sydney, an unusual view of the Opera House and Bridge from the Botanical Gardens near Mrs Macquarie's Point	161
Manly from Mosman	162
Tea-time at the 'Gabba' (sketch by author)	171
The Adelaide Oval and St Peter's Cathedral (sketch by author)	173
St Louis Cathedral, New Orleans, looking toward the old quarter, a musician in the left foreground	177
St Louis Cathedral, seen from the old quarter with the modern city beyond	178
Modern Tucson	186
Tucson as it used to be	187
The Olgas	191
Red River gums at Ellery Creek	195
Wild donkeys near Alice Springs	197
Selling carpets in Turfan	202
The monastery and the caves of the thousand Buddhas and their valley	202
The Flaming Mountains and an intrepid photographer	203
Jiaohe, the ancient rival of Kaochang	207
The only photograph we were allowed to take at the Magao Caves	211
Camels in the sand near Dunhang, the author riding last (by kind permission of Nan Warren)	214
Madrasah of the Twin Minarets, Erzurum. The second minaret rises to the left (sketch by author)	218
Gum trees in the Mappin's garden	222
Main street, Maldon	226
Apollo Bay harbour	234
Five of the Twelve Apostles (sketch by author)	238
London Bridge near Loch Ard Gorge, destroyed by bad weather in the winter of 1990	239
Melbourne across the River Yarra, showing Flinders Street Station at ground level	241
Melbourne, iron-work and a train, looking toward Flinders Street Station	242
Jack's Place, Malolo Lailai, Fiji	243
Our welcome to Xi'an	255
A tourist market near the Terracotta Warrior Exhibition	256
A tea room in a Buddhist Temple in Lanzhou	259

Ground plan of St Saviour in Chora	263
Church of Metexi, Tbilisi (sketch by author)	272
Church of Metexi, Tbilisi	273
The sixth century church of Ančisxati in Tbilisi	275
Porch of the church of Ančisxati, facing Turkish-style domestic wooden balconies	276
Church of Dzvari, near Mcxeta (sketch by author)	278
Cathedral church at Mcxeta, the former Georgian capital, the church of Dzvari on the hill beyond	281
Two fortified sixteenth century churches in the lower Caucasus	283
Seventeenth century *madrasah* in Bukhara	285
A corner of old Bukhara, which I failed to find on my solitary walk	289
Huntington Library, San Marino, California	293
The inner courtyard, or peristylium, the Paul Getty Museum, Malibu, Los Angeles	295
Golden Gate Bridge, San Francisco	305
A street in San Francisco, founded on rock, which survived the earthquake of 1906	306
Olvera Street, in old Los Angeles	317
A piece of the Atlantic Ocean at the end of the Elysian Fields, my last frontier	322

INDEX

Abbreviations not used in the text

USA
Al Alabama
Az Arizona
Ca California
Ga Georgia
La Louisiana
Tx Texas

AUSTRALIA
ACT Australian Capital Territory
NSW New South Wales
NT Northern Territory
Qld Queensland
SA South Australia
Tas Tasmania
Vic Victoria
WA Western Australia

All cities and towns, other than those in the UK, are identified by province, state or country.

A

aboriginal Australians, 61,143-4, 197
accommodation, 23, 24, 28
Adelaide, SA, 15, 24, 84, 87-8, 90, 94, 96, 97, 142-3, 172-4, 190, 193, 196, 299, 315
Aegean sea, 70, 229
Afghan camel drivers, 94
Afghanistan, 51, 73, 280, 283
Afrasiab, 250-3
Alabama, Al, 42, 106
Alamo, Tx, 104
Alexander the Great, 112, 206, 250, 284, 308
Alice Springs, NT, 29, 94, 143-4, 193-4, 196, 197, 244, 316
Alma Ata, Kazakhstan, 18, 43, 51-2, 157, 159
Amtrak, 19, 100, 104, 106-8
Anadolu Kavak, Turkey, 230
Ančisxati, church of, Tbilisi, 275-7
Ani, Turkey, 267-273, 274, 302
Ankara, Turkey, 17, 41, 129, 153, 260
Apollo Bay, Vic, 233-6, 238, 240
apricots, 55
Arabs, 113, 252, 267
Aragvi river, 277
architecture, 28, 261-291
the 'Argo', 227-8
Arizona, Az, 50, 59-60, 180, 185-6
Ark fortress, Bukhara, 284-5

Armenia, 40-1, 43, 46, 55-6, 160, 267-73, 274, 302, 310
Arpa river, 55, 269, 271
art galleries, 106, 293-301, 304, 309
Asia, 25, 77, 205, 217, 229, 280, 294
'Asiatic Vespers', 229
Assisi, Italy, 249
Atlanta, Ga, 23, 100, 104, 106-8, 158, 322
Atlantic Ocean, 19, 109, 322
Athens, Greece, 249
Attila, 230
aul, 159
Austrailpass, 18, 81, 88, 90, 108
Australia, 16, 18-20, 22-4, 29, 30, 50, 61, 81-2, 94-5, 102, 106, 116-7, 129, 134, 135, 140, 142-3, 148, 160-1, 164, 165-76, 180, 189, 190-3, 196, 205, 219, 223-6, 233, 235, 240-2, 294, 297-303, 304, 312-6
Austria, 32-3, 50
Ayers Rock, NT, 112, 191, 193, 196, 247
Azerbaijan, USSR, 43, 70, 73, 156, 160, 272, 310

B

Babylon, 11-2
Baku, Azerbaijan, 18, 69, 70-3, 135, 233, 310
baggage, 25-6, 28, 36-8, 45-6, 58-9, 70-1, 85, 95, 100, 110, 119, 120, 134, 307, 323-4

328

barbarians, 12, 310-2
Barossa valley, SA, 16, 205, 315
Bass strait, 29, 233, 235, 239
Bathurst, NSW, 84, 189
Beijing university, 47
Belgium, 308
Beshiktash, Turkey, 231
Bezeklik, Xinjiang, 209-10
Bibi-Khanim, 156, 251-2
Bidwell, John, 181-2, 188, 190
Big Sur, Ca, 236
Birmingham, Al, 42, 106
Black Sea, 11, 38, 55, 227-9, 231
Blue Mountains, NSW, 85, 99
Bonaventura Hotel, LA, Ca, 216-7
Bosphorus, 38, 227-232, 250, 309
Boulogne, France, 30-1, 38
Brest Litovsk, treaty of, 55, 267
Brier, Rev Mr and Mrs, 183-4, 188
Brighton, 60
Brisbane, Qld, 18-9, 24, 82-8, 96, 99, 143, 164, 170-2, 196, 240, 242, 299, 316
British Museum, 210, 213
Broken Hill, NSW, 84, 88
bronze charioteer, Delphi, 258
Brueghel, Pieter, 296-7
Bucharest, Romania, 17, 34, 148-9, 150, 153, 306
Budapest, Hungary, 17, 21, 33-4, 122
Buddhism, 202, 205-6, 209-10, 212-3
Bukhara, Uzbekhistan, 18, 129, 135, 154-6, 159, 283-291, 307
Bulgaria, 35-7, 148, 227, 310
Bunbury, WA, 90-1, 233, 316
Byzantine architecture, 261-266, 275-7, 281-3
Byzantium, 113, 115, 228-9, 231, 233, 261-7, 270, 291

C

Cable and French, missionaries, 77-79, 188-9, 201
Calais, France, 30
California, Ca, 20, 134, 180-5, 189, 219, 236, 294, 318-321
camels, 94, 196, 214
el Camino Real, 101-2

Canberra, ACT, 24, 143, 242, 298, 304, 306
Cape Otway, Vic, 233
Capone, Al, 107-8
Cappadocia, Turkey, 112-5, 223, 229, 270, 282
Caspian Sea, 55, 70, 72-3
Caucasus mountains, 67, 277, 283
caves of the thousand buddhas, 202, 209
Central Pacific railroad, 184
Chagall, Marc, 106, 179
Chalcedon, 228-9
Channel, English, 29-31, 38, 62, 108-9, 216-7, 235
Char-Minar madrasah, 184
Chicago, Illinois, 247
China, 11, 13, 17, 22, 41, 43-54, 62, 73, 75, 79-81, 95, 99, 112, 117, 121, 123-4, 128, 131, 133, 135, 138-40, 184-5, 190, 197, 200, 204, 206, 210, 212, 213, 253-5, 260, 280, 283, 311, 312
Chinese language, 123, 135
Chorsu, 251
Christians, 56, 115, 267-280, 282, 310, 319
Cilento, Italy, 236
the *Coast Starlight*, 101
cockatoos, 221
Colchis, 227
Colorado, 99, 180, 188
Colosseum, 166-7, 169, 176
communism, 57
Conder, Charles, 92, 297-301, 303
confirming flights, 24-5
Constantinople, see Istanbul
Cook, SA, 83
von le Coq, Albert, 209-10
costs, 11, 14, 18-20, 22-4
Crayfish Bay, Vic, 237
Crete, 228
cricket, 12, 16, 18, 22, 30, 164, 165-76
Crimea, 229
Crocker, Charles, 184, 189
Croesus, 307
crowds, 27, 145-79
Cuidad Juarez, Mexico, 104
Curtici, Romania, 34, 150
customs and excise, 31,39, 45-7, 322
Cyaneae, the Blue Rocks, 228
Czechoslovakia, 223

329

D

Daheyon, Xinjiang, 73-6, 125
Danube, River, 152, 230
Darlinghurst, NSW, 164
Darling river, 190, 240
Darwin, NT, 18, 81, 196
Death Valley, Ca, 183-4
deserts, 27, 76-9, 157, 180-215, 294
Dilley, Graham, 174
Diotima of Martinea, 249, 301
Dolmabahce palace, Istanbul, 231, 232
donkeys, 196-7
Donner family, 182-3, 188, 190
Dover, 29
Dunhuang, Xinjiang, 75, 80, 199, 210, 213-4
Durak, Mary, 300
Dzvari, church near Mcxeta, Georgia, 277-280

E

El Paso, Tx, 103-7
Elysian Fields, New Orleans, 109-10, 322
England, 29, 43, 56, 82, 154, 159, 167-9, 179, 192, 219, 231, 251, 310, 313, 316, 318-22
Eros, 249, 301
Erzurum, Turkey, 17, 217-9, 270
the Euxine, see Black Sea
exploration of the American West, 180-5
exploration of Australia, 189-90

F

fatigue, 110, 120, 144, 306
Fiji, 19, 22, 24, 50, 244, 246-7, 309
finances, 11, 14, 18-24, 39, 58
Flaming Mountains, 203, 205
Flecker, James Elroy, 250
Folkestone, 28-9, 38
Franklin mountains, Tx, 104
Fremantle, WA, 29, 233
frontiers, 18, 26, 29-63, 88, 148

G

the 'Gabba' the Brisbane Cricket Ground, 24, 82, 170-2, 241
Gadsden Purchase, 185

Galatia, 229
Gatwick, 23, 29, 322-3
Geelong, Vic, 236
Genghis Khan, 250
Georgia, USA, 106
Georgia, USSR, 43, 55, 67, 227, 268, 270, 272, 274, 277-83, 307, 310
Gilroy, Ca, 101
the 'Ghan', 94-5
ghost gum, 196
glamour, 105
Glenelg, SA, 88-9
Gobi desert, 11, 76, 78-9, 180, 185, 197, 280
gold, 184, 189-90, 227, 320
Golden Fleece, 227
Golden Horn, Istanbul, 261, 266
Gower, David, 303
grammar, see glamour
Great Australian Bight, 233, 237
Great Ocean Road, Vic, 236, 240
Great Patriotic War, 157, 311
Greek Language, 119-21
gum trees, 84, 194-6, 221-3, 245, 302
Guri-Emiv, 151
Gundagai, NSW, 314

H

Halicarnassus, Turkey, 11
les Halles, 216
Han Chinese, 52, 75, 118, 127, 131, 205, hand-basin plugs, 26, 307
Han dynasty, 53, 137, 180, 205
Hanging Rock, Vic, 225
Hapsburg, 33, 296
Hawthorn, Vic, 233
Haydarpasa station, Turkey, 97, 98, 232
health, 15, 19, 34, 110, 121, 128, 143-4, 306-7
Heathrow, 29
Hegyeshalom, Hungary, 33
Heidelberg, school of artists, 297-302, 308
Herodotus, 11-3, 20, 25-8, 307, 310-1, 316, 324
Hong Kong, 17-9, 22-5, 41, 50, 56, 58, 62, 112, 143, 145, 233, 304, 306, 309
Honolulu, 19, 50, 56, 60, 100, 247
Houston, Tx, 105
Hsuan-tsang, pilgrim, 213
Hungary, 26, 33-4, 50, 99, 148, 310
Huntington, Collis, 184, 293
Huntington Library, San Marino, Ca, 293, 308

330

I

the *Indian-Pacific*, 18, 81-5, 88, 94-6, 131-2
Inning, Xinjiang, 53, 125, 135-7
insurance, 19-20
Intourist, 73, 130, 155, 159
Ismail Samani mausoleum, 284
Islam, 45, 53, 71, 125, 156-7, 204-6, 260, 262, 286-7
Istanbul, 17, 38, 97, 120, 129, 152, 229-31, 260
Ivanhoe, NSW, 84

J

Jackson, Andrew, 105
Jason and the Argonauts, 227-8
jazz, 106, 176-7, 292
Jiaohe, Xinjiang, 206-8, 269
Jinte, Xinjiang, 117-8, 125, 321
J Paul Getty Museum, Malibu, Ca, 294-5, 308
Judah, Theodore, 184
Justinian, Emperor, 264, 266

K

Kalgoolie, WA, 87-8
Kangaroo Point, Qld, 164, 316
Kaniye Museum, Istanbul, 261-6
Kaochang, Xinjiang, 205-8
karez, 201
Kars, Turkey, 18, 41, 64, 120, 267
Katoomba, NSW, 85
Kaymakli, Turkey, 115, 117
Kayseri, Turkey, 17, 41, 112-3, 115
Kazakhstan, 43-4, 52, 154, 159
Kiev, Ukraine, 160
King Island, Tas, 233, 235
koala bears, 221
Komsomol, 157-8, 311
kookaburras, 221
Korgas, Xinjiang, 50-4, 124-5, 210
Kunsthistorischer Museum, Vienna, 296
Kura river, 274, 277, 282
Kusam iba-Abbas, 252
kymiss, 159

L

Lafayette, La, 105

Lafitte, La, 105
Lanceville, Vic, 225
language, 68, 79, 119, 128, 134, 170, 261, 277
Lanzhou, Gansu, 18, 75-6, 141, 259-60
laundry, 25, 124, 134
lavatories, 45, 50, 106, 128-9, 134, 307
Lenin, 150, 253, 275, 282
Leninakan, Armenia, 41-6, 51, 56, 64
Lithgow, NSW, 84-5
Loch Ard Gorge, Vic, 238-9
Loire river, 249
Loköshava, Hungary, 34
London, 17, 19, 23, 27, 145, 158, 166, 201, 204, 216, 217, 254, 323-4
Lorne, Vic, 236
Los Angeles, Ca, 20, 23, 100-1, 103-4, 107, 142, 144, 181, 216-24, 294, 317-321
Louisiana, 104-6
Lucullus, 55

M

MacDonnell Ranges, NT, 193-6
Magao caves, 210-3
magpies, 221
Maldon, Vic, 225-6
Malolo Lailai, Fiji, 243-7, 309
Manly, NSW, 60, 162-4, 240
Marco Polo, 72, 76-77, 79-80, 180, 188, 213, 308
Maritime Terminal, Istanbul, 38, 231,
Marmara, Sea of, 232
Marrananga, SA, 315-6
Marsh, Dr John, 181-2
McGubbin, Frederick, 92, 297-301
McLuan, Marshall, 316
Mcxeta, Georgia, 277-283, 303
Megara, Greece, 228
Melbourne, Vic, 20, 22, 88, 96, 120, 142-4, 165-6, 172, 196, 221, 233, 239, 241-2, 244, 298, 314-5
MCG, Melbourne Cricket Ground, 165-71, 175-6, 314
Menindee lake, NSW, 240
Mersey river, 29
Metexi, church, Tbilisi, 272-4
Mexico, 50, 59, 60, 104, 106, 109, 143, 180, 183
Mirian, king of Georgia, 277
Mississipi river, 105-6
Mithridates VI, 229-30
Mojave desert, Ca, 183

Monemvasia, Greece, 265
Mongolia, 127
Montmartre, 217
Montparnasse, 217
moon, 180-215
Moreton Bay, Qld, 102
mosaics, 265-6, 294
Moscow, Russia, 43, 160
Mount Li, Shaanxi, 253-8
Mount Macedon, Vic, 165, 189, 221, 223-5
Munich, Germany, 32
music, 106, 176-7, 279-81, 292, 301
Mycenae, Greece, 228, 249, 269

N

Nagorny Karabakh, Azerbaijan, 69
Nandi, Fiji, 19, 25, 246-7
Nesehir valley, Turkey, 113
Nevada, 180
Newhaven, 29
New Orleans, La, 23, 25, 100, 104-6, 108, 130, 142, 176-8, 185, 279, 291-3, 302, 307-9
New South Wales, NSW, 29, 43, 85-8, 189, 240
Nogales, Mexico, 50, 59-60
Norfolk, 240
Norman architecture, 281-3
Northern Territory, NT, 18, 23, 191, 193
Norton Simon Museum, Pasadena, Ca, 294, 308
Nullabor plain, WA and SA, 82, 99, 121, 193

O

Oakland, Ca, 101
obesity, 143
Olgas, NT, 191-3, 219
Olympia, Greece, 315
Orange, NSW, 84
Orange, Tx, 104-5
Oregon, 180-1
Osicka vineyard, Vic, 223
Otway cape, 233, 236, 238, 240
Oval, Adelaide, 173-4
the *Overlander*, 96

P

Pacific Palisades, Ca, 200
painting, 293-301, 304, 309
Palm Beach, NSW, 240
Pamphilov, Kazakhstan, 45, 47, 52
Panathenaeic Procession, 258
parakeets, 221
Paris, France, 17, 31, 33, 152, 216-7
Parkes, NSW, 84-5
parochialism, 12-3, 28, 308-16, 321,324
parrots, 221
passport, 18, 31-35, 39-40, 45-7, 58, 60, 321
Persia, 155, 201, 229, 280
Perth, WA, 18-9, 24, 50, 56, 81, 86-90, 92, 142, 193, 196, 304, 306
pharmacopoeia, 144
Planctae, the Wandering Rocks, 228
Plato's 'Symposium', 249
Playa del Rey, Ca, 219
Pliny the Younger, 230
Pompey the Great, 55, 229
Pompidou Centre, 216-7
Pontchartrain Lake, 109
Pontus, 229-30
Port Augusta, SA, 87-8, 94, 96
Port Campbell, Vic, 238-9
Port Phillip Bay, Vic, 233, 235
Port Pirie, SA, 84, 88
post offices, 129-34
poverty, 35, 41, 140
Prater, Vienna, 111-2
Preservation Hall, New Orleans, 176-9, 279-80, 308
Princes, Islands, Sea of Marmara, 233
Propontis, 232

Q

Qin Shi Huangdi, emperor, 253-4, 258
Queensland, Qld, 24, 87-8, 164, 172, 299

R

railways, 16-20, 23, 27, 38-43, 51, 62-109, 319, 320
railway stations, 96-8, 103-4
Rawlinna, WA, 84
Redondo Beach, Ca, 219
Registan Square, Samarkand, 251
Rhine river, 32
Rhodes, 229

Roberts, Tom, 92, 297-301, 318
Romanesque architecture, 45, 185, 269-70, 282-3, 291
Romania, 34-6, 50, 65, 95, 99, 129, 134, 148-53, 227, 306, 310
Roi Soleil, 106, 292
Rome, Italy, 229-30, 249, 270, 307, 310
Romsey, Vic, 225
Rosenheim, Germany, 32
Rumeli Kavak, Turkey, 230
Ruse, Bulgaria, 35-7, 51, 227
Russian language, 39, 65, 121, 158, 277

S

Salzburg, Austria, 31, 33, 227
Samarkand, Uzbekhistan, 18, 73, 129, 156-7, 250-3, 284
Saint Gregory of Abugamrents, 270-1
Saint Gregory of Cappadocia, 270
Saint Gregory of Gagik, 271
Saint Louis Cathedral, New Orleans, 177-8
Saint Saviour in Chora, Istanbul, 261-6
San Antonio, Tx, 104
San Francisco, Ca, 19, 23, 58-9, 100-1, 107-8, 142, 144, 181, 304, 306, 319
San Vitale, Ravenna, 277
Santa Barbara, Ca, 102
Santa Costanza, Rome, 270
Santa Cruz, Az, river, 186-7, 194
Santa Monica, Ca, 220
Sant'Apollinare in Classe, Ravenna, 45
Santa Sophia, Istanbul, 260-1
Sappho, 215, 232
Sarikamis, Turkey, 38, 41, 119, 217, 267-8
Sausalito, Ca, 304
Scotland, 29, 43, 198, 316
Scythia, 229
seagulls, 174
Seljuk Turks, 113, 268, 270
Serra, Junipero, 101
Shaanxi province, 137
Shakhi-Zinda, 252
Sherdor, 251
Shihezi, Xinjiang, 43, 52, 123, 125
Sierra Nevada, 182-4, 228
Silk Road, 17-8, 53, 180, 210
Sinaia, Romania, 149, 151
Skene's Creek, Vic, 233, 235, 240
skullcaps, 145, 251, 287-8
Small, Gladstone, 168
Socrates, 249
Sophia, Bulgaria, 37

Solent, 29
Solon, 307
South Australia, SA, 82, 87-8, 190
Southend, 60
Southern Pacific railroad, 108, 185, 319
Spanish trail, 181, 183
Stanford, Ca, 20, 101
Stanford, Leland, 184
Stein, Sir Aurel, 209, 213
Strathfield, NSW, 85
Streeton, Sir Richard, 92, 297-310
Stuttgart, Germany, 32
Suleïman the Great, 262
the *Sunset Limited*, 100, 103-4 107
Sveti-Cxoveli, cathedral, Georgia, 281-3, 303
Sydney, NSW, 22-5, 29, 53, 81-6, 88, 96, 99, 142-4, 161, 175, 196, 221, 240, 244, 246-7, 303
Symplegades, the Clashing rocks, 228
Syracuse, Sicily, 258
Szechwan province, 139

T

Tamacàcori, Az, 185
Tamerlane, 156, 159, 250-3, 272, 284
Tarcoola, SA, 84, 94
Tashkent, Uzbekhistan, 18, 73, 157-9
Tasmania, Tas, 87, 233, 235
Tbilisi, Georgia, 18, 64-8, 105, 120, 135, 272, 274-7, 283
terracotta warriors, 253-8, 301
Texas, Tx, 103-5
Thames river, 249
Tibetans, 140, 308-9
Tienshan mountains, 43, 185, 200, 208-9, 250
Tillya-Kari, 251
Timisoara, Romania, 150-2
Tiryns, Greece, 249
Todd river, NT, 193-4, 248
Toodjay, WA, 92, 316
Torcello, Italy, 249
Tucson, Az, 23-4, 59-60, 100, 104, 142, 185-9
Tungan, 53
Turfan, Xinjiang, 18, 43, 73, 124-5, 129-33, 198, 200-6, 210, 232
Turkey, 17, 38-9, 41-2, 51, 55, 64, 99, 112, 119-21, 143, 153-6, 227, 229-30, 231, 261, 264, 267, 270, 287, 310
Twelve Apostles, Vic, 238

U

Uighur, 52-4, 118, 125, 127, 135, 201, 204-5, 280-1, 308
Ulughbek, 251-2
Urumchi, Xinjiang, 18, 43, 51-3, 126-8, 135
USA, 17, 19, 22, 24, 50, 58, 60-1, 88, 100, 108, 116-7, 129-30, 135, 140, 142, 180, 197, 313
Uskadar, Turkey, 97-8, 229, 232
USSR, 17, 22, 38-9, 42-8, 51-6, 62, 64-8, 95, 99, 121, 123-4, 130, 135, 140, 154, 156-61, 267, 269, 311-2, 321
Uzbekhistan, 43, 52, 112, 145, 154-5, 159, 179, 253, 286

V

Varna, Bulgaria, 35-7
Vauxhall, 158-9
Versailles, France, 217
Victoria, Vic, Australia, 29, 43, 86-8, 143, 189, 221, 224, 233, 299, 300
Victoria, queen, 16, 75, 91, 96, 315
Victoria, station, 28-9, 147-8, 322-4
Vienna, Austria, 17, 31, 33, 99, 111-2, 143, 268, 296

W

Wang, abbot, 212-3
war, 15, 67, 157, 267, 311, 315
water, 216-248
weather, 25, 27, 216-248
Western Australia, WA, 18, 56, 81, 86-7, 233, 304, 316
WACA, Western Australian Cricket Association, 56, 82, 175, 304
Whale Beach, NSW, 240
Wiener Riesenrad, 111-2
William IV, 16, 315
wombats, 221

X

Xi'an, Shaanxi, 18, 75, 81-2, 129, 137-40, 155, 253-6, 260
Xinjiang, 43, 51-4, 75, 117, 124, 198, 201, 204-5, 269, 280, 307-8

Y

Yellow river, 140, 308
Yuega lake, 215
Yuma, Az, 99
yurt, 44, 159

Z

Zarafshan river, 250, 284
Zwarthnotz, Armenia, 271-2